$ 35.00

D0082723

Music, Education, and
Multiculturalism

Music, Education, and Multiculturalism
Foundations and Principles

Terese M. Volk

New York   Oxford
OXFORD UNIVERSITY PRESS
1998

Oxford University Press

Oxford   New York
Athens   Auckland   Bangkok   Bogota   Bombay   Buenos Aires
Calcutta   Cape Town   Dar es Salaam   Delhi   Florence   Hong Kong   Istanbul
Karachi   Kuala Lumpur   Madras   Madrid   Melbourne
Mexico City   Nairobi   Paris   Singapore   Taipei   Tokyo   Toronto   Warsaw

and associated companies in
Berlin   Ibadan

Published by Oxford University Press, Inc.
198 Madison Avenue, New York, New York 10016

Oxford is a registered trademark of Oxford University Press

Cover photograph courtesy of Jerry Gay

Library of Congress Cataloging-in-Publication Data
Volk, Terese M., 1948–
Music, education, and multiculturalism : foundations and
principles / Terese M. Volk.
p.   cm.
Includes index.
ISBN 0-19-510609-1
1. Music—Instruction and study—United States.   2. Multicultural
education.
MT4.V65   1997
780'.71'073—dc21   96-53476
                                                          CIP
                                                          MN

1 3 5 7 9 8 6 4 2

Printed in the United States of America
on acid-free paper

There already exist considerable attempts to deal with foreign music cultures in . . . music education. . . . It would be appropriate to recognize . . . the pathfinding values of the experience gained by such experiments . . . [and] make this information available and practical for music education in all countries.

—ISME recommendation, 1966

Contents

Preface

The issue of multiculturalism is not one to be ignored in education today. It has been the topic of discussion in venues as separate as academic forums and political debates, faculty lunch rooms and popular magazines. What it is, how it developed, and what it means for teachers, education, and especially for music education is the essence of this book. Though primarily designed to assist music educators at all levels in understanding and implementing multicultural music education, the information contained herein may prove useful to general educators as well.

This book is intended to provide a picture of multicultural music education today, specifically in America and, more generally, around the world. It is divided roughly into thirds: the philosophical underpinnings of multicultural music education; its historical development; and implications for music education. Each chapter ends with conclusions, implications, and questions for further research or class discussion. Many of these questions have no answers, but they are questions that need to be asked. I hope that they will be answered in the future.

Part I addresses the philosophical ideas behind multiculturalism, and the problems and possibilities it raises for both education and music education. A succinct discussion of the various rationales for, and concepts of, multiculturalism follows. This section concludes with current applications of these concepts for music education.

To begin to understand multicultural music education, we need to step back and see whence it developed. Set in both the historical and educational contexts of the times, each chapter in Part II (chapters 2–8) follows multicultural music education in the United States as it paralleled changes in general education influenced by immigration, desegregation, the civil rights movement, federal foreign policy, and educational legislation. These changes resulted in a gradual inclusion of musics from a variety of cultures in the school music curriculum, and the shift from a Western music perspective to a multicultural perspective in music education.

We are not alone in dealing with this issue. Many other countries in the world are finding their own ways to incorporate world musics in their curricula. Chapter 9 describes the state of multicultural music education internationally. This chapter offers a comparison of four countries in some depth (Great Britain, Australia, Canada, and Germany) and a snapshot of the current situation of multicultural music education in eight other countries around the world.

Part III (chapters 10–12) is concerned specifically with the implications of multiculturalism for music education, both in teacher training and in the classroom. All the philosophical and historical information about multiculturalism will be for naught if it is not incorporated in teaching. If we are to engage our students in critical thinking in and about music, then we must make music in its various forms accessible and understandable to our students as best we can. It is up to the colleges and universities to provide teachers adequately prepared with a multicultural perspective, and for in-service teachers to employ methods and materials in their classroom that present their students with a world view of music.

This book presents a segment of music education long undocumented, but beyond history, philosophy, comparative music education, or even implications for the profession is the issue that lies at the heart of multiculturalism: unity versus diversity. The discussions continue. How that discussion is resolved is of utmost importance for us as music educators. The answer will change the way we teach. The material in this book can show us where we have been, and where we are now, but it is up to us to formulate the future.

Acknowledgments

I am grateful for permission to reprint parts or all of the following articles in this book:

WILLIAM M. ANDERSON, "Symposium Resolutions for Further Directions and Actions," in *Teaching Music with a Multicultural Approach*, ed. William M. Anderson (Reston, VA: MENC, 1991), 89–91. Copyright 1991 by Music Educators National Conference.

ALLEN BRITTON, Charles Gary, and Arnold Broido, "The Tanglewood Declaration," in *Documentary Report of the Tanglewood Symposium*, ed. Robert Choate (Washington, D.C.: MENC, 1968), 139. Copyright 1968 by Music Educators National Conference.

EGON KRAUS, "Recommendations of the Seventh International Conference," *International Music Educator*, #14 (October 1966), 452–53. Copyright 1966 by International Society for Music Education.

EDWIN SCHUPMAN, "Lessons on Native American Music," *Music Educators Journal* 78, no. 9 (1992): 33. Copyright 1992 by Music Educators National Conference.

TERESE M. VOLK, "Satis N. Coleman's 'Creative Music': Precursor for World Music Education?" *Music Educators Journal* 82, no. 6 (1996): 31–33+. Copyright 1996 by Music Educators National Conference.

TERESE M. VOLK AND JEFFREY SPECTOR, "Achieving Standard #9 with Your Performing Groups: Diverse Music Cultures and the Question of Authenticity," *NYS School Music News* 59, no. 2 (1995): 29–30. Copyright 1995 by New York State School Music Association.

TERESE M. VOLK, "Chinese Folk Music for Violin Ensemble" and "Chinese *luogu* for Percussion Ensemble," in *Strategies for Teaching Specialized Ensembles*, ed. Robert Cutietta (Reston, VA: MENC, forthcoming).

TERESE M. VOLK, "Folk Musics and Increasing Diversity in American Music Education: 1900–1916," *Journal of Research in Music Education* 42, no. 4 (1994): 285–305. Copyright 1994 by Music Educators National Conference.

TERESE M. VOLK, "The History and Development of Multicultural Music Education as Evidenced in the *Music Educators Journal*: 1967–1992," *Journal of Research in Music Education* 41, no. 2 (1993): 137–67. Copyright 1993 by Music Educators National Conference.

Without the help of the following persons, this book would have many unanswered questions. They have my deepest gratitude for their time and gracious assistance through personal interviews for this research:

WILLIAM M. ANDERSON, Associate Dean for Academic Affairs, College and Graduate School of Education, Kent State University

ALLEN P. BRITTON, Dean Emeritus, School of Music, University of Michigan, Ann Arbor

PATRICIA S. CAMPBELL, Professor of Music, University of Washington, Seattle

CHARLES L. GARY, Professor of Music Education, The Catholic University of America, Washington, D.C.

O. M. HARTSELL, Professor Emeritus of Music Education, University of Arizona, Tucson

PAUL LEHMAN, Professor Emeritus of Music, School of Music, University of Michigan, Ann Arbor

WILLIAM P. MALM, Professor Emeritus of Ethnomusicology, University of Michigan, Ann Arbor

DAVID MCALLESTER, Professor Emeritus of Anthropology and Music, Wesleyan University, Middletown, Connecticut

ANTHONY PALMER, Associate Professor of Music Education, University of Hawaii, Manoa

ALLEN SAPP, Professor of Composition, College Conservatory of Music, University of Cincinnati

BARBARA SMITH, Professor Emeritus of Ethnomusicology, University of Hawaii, Manoa

JAMES STANDIFER, Professor of Music Education, School of Music, University of Michigan, Ann Arbor

RICARDO TRIMILLOS, Professor of Ethnomusicology, University of Hawaii, Manoa

I am also indebted to the following persons for their insights and patience reading sections of the manuscript:

FRIEDHELM BRUSNIAK, University of Erlanger-Nürnberg, Germany

ROBERT A. CUTIETTA, School of Music, University of Arizona

PETER DUNBAR-HALL, Sydney Conservatorium of Music, University of Sydney, Australia

DONALD FARR, Department of Education, Canisius College, Buffalo, New York

LUCY GREEN, Institute of Education, University of London, England

MARY HOOKEY, Faculty of Education, Nipissing University, North Bay, Ontario, Canada

My thanks go to Peter Dunbar-Hall and Kathyrn Marsh, University of Western Sydney, Australia, for their unflagging interest and generous sharing of information for the Australian segment of this project. Thanks also to Ana Lucia Frega, president of the International Society for Music Education; Ramon Santos, University of the Philippines; Kathy Primos, University of the Witwatersrand, Johannesburg; Elizabeth Oehrle, University of Natal; Jimmy van Tonder, University of Cape Town; Friedhelm Brusniak, University of Erlangen-Nürnberg; Wilfried Gruhn, Hochschule für Musik, Freiberg; and Siegmund Helms, Hochschule für Musik, Köln, for their assistance with information on music education in their respective countries.

Finally, and not least, my thanks go to my parents, Angelo and Christine Battaglia, for their constant love and support.

Music, Education, and Multiculturalism

PART
I
The Philosophical Debate

1

The Difficult Question of Multiculturalism

In short, unless our education . . . recognizes that the peculiarity of our nationalism is its internationalism, we shall breed enmity and division in our frantic efforts to secure unity.

—JOHN DEWEY, 1916[1]

Multiculturalism is among the most discussed topics in American education in the twentieth century. Historically, the concept of multiculturalism has had many names.[2] Nonetheless, no matter what the terminology, multiculturalism in education has always been based on two premises: the acknowledgment of the diverse population of the United States, and the intent to help students understand the world and the American society in which they live.[3]

One of the earliest efforts in multicultural education in the public schools began in the late 1920s. "Intercultural education," as it was then called, was intended to develop an understanding of the ethnic backgrounds and cultural contributions of the large immigrant populations within the United States. International understanding was also emphasized during this period.

Several decades later, in the early 1960s, the term "ethnic studies" appeared in educational literature. Ethnic studies were intended to enhance the self-esteem of selected minority groups and were often region-specific.[4] By the late 1960s, educators realized that all students, not just specific groups, should learn about the various cultures in the United States. The term "multiethnic education" accommodated this new viewpoint. All these terms represented educational concepts that dealt primarily with issues of race, ethnicity, and occasionally religion. Today the term "multiethnic" is used only when speaking specifically of multiple ethnic backgrounds.[5]

The currently accepted phrase, "multicultural education," developed in the 1970s when educators no longer considered knowledge of ethnicity alone to be educationally acceptable. In order to understand people from any culture, students needed to encounter the beliefs, values, and environments of that culture. This concept of multiculturalism expanded throughout the 1980s to include differences of religion, age, gender, socioeconomic status, and exceptionality.[6] "Multicultural education" now carries all the implications of this extended definition.

Multicultural music education has likewise had many titles, most of them similar to, or derived from, whatever term was in use in general education: "international relations in music," "multiethnic music," and the like. Today "multicultural music education" is accepted in the profession. It refers to the teaching of a broad spectrum of music cultures in the music curriculum, primarily focusing on ethnocultural characteristics rather than the larger definition of multiculturalism accepted in education today.[7] This is the definition upon which this book is based.

These are not the only definitions of multicultural education or multicultural music education, however, nor is "multicultural" the only term in use today. Many others, all with their own definitions and connotations, are often employed, sometimes simultaneously or even synonymously (and not always accurately), in discussions of multiculturalism. Added to the mix are issues such as environmentalism, antiracism, and world citizenship. For clarity's sake, the definitions found in the glossary (see Appendix A) may prove helpful.

MULTICULTURALISM IN EDUCATION AND MUSIC EDUCATION

The literature on multiculturalism in both general education and music education is so extensive as to be beyond the scope of this chapter. As early as 1976, there were already over two-hundred documents in the Educational Resources Information Center (ERIC) dealing with multicultural education,[8] and resources burgeoned throughout the 1980s and into the 1990s.[9] In addition, major journals for professional teachers' organizations have devoted entire issues to the topic.[10] Nearly all of these resources cite the need for multicultural education both in the classroom and in teacher training.

Reflecting the emphasis in general education, many journal publications in music education have focused on teaching music from a multicultural perspective. These have ranged from the implementation of music from various cultures in the classroom to considerations of the importance of a world viewpoint in music classes, and the need for studying a variety of music cultures.[11] In addition, much music education research relating to world musics has dealt with curriculum development, unit lessons, teacher's sourcebooks, and the like.[12] In 1972, 1983, and again in 1992, the *Music Educators Journal* (MEJ) published "special focus" issues on multiculturalism in music education.[13]

Rationales for Multicultural Education

There are several rationales for incorporating multiculturalism in general education. The first is a social rationale based on the changing demographics within the United States, and it acknowledges the diverse student populations in the American classroom.[14] According to the 1990 Census, the United States population is composed of African-Americans (12 percent), Hispanics (nearly 9 percent), Asians (3 percent), Native Americans (just under 1 percent), and persons of European extraction (76 percent). Predictions of population growth based on these figures indicate that by the year 2020, the minority population will have doubled while the population of those from a European background will hardly have grown at all. In some cities the reversal of the population ratio from majority to minority is already a statistical fact, and several schools in the country boast a student body that speaks twenty or more native languages. Through the study of various cultures, students can develop a better understanding of the peoples that make up American society, gain self-esteem, and learn tolerance for others.

A second rationale focuses on world-mindedness. By studying the various cultures around the world, students can develop a better understanding of international relationships. In addition, knowledge of world cultures can facilitate working within a worldwide economy, and help lead to world peace.[15] These two rationales have been most clearly articulated since the 1970s; however, they have been the basis for all the multicultural educational changes in the curriculum since the formalization of intercultural education in the 1920s.[16]

Most recently, a third rationale has developed. This is a global rationale that emphasizes ecological interrelationships between people and the earth on which they live. The study of people and how they live, in combination with ecological issues, can foster concern for balance, tolerance, the wise use of resources, and respect for the other inhabitants of the earth. Students can learn from other peoples how to live within their own world spaces.[17] This rationale is also linked to the development of studies in critical thinking. Critical thinking allows for decision making based on information gained through seeing all sides of an issue. William Dorman, an advocate of critical theory in education, believes that students "cannot acquire a global perspective without developing critical thinking skills . . . and cannot be considered critical thinkers without a global perspective."[18]

Rationales for Multicultural Music Education

All the rationales mentioned above also apply in some measure to music education. For example, the demographic changes identified in the social rationale above also have their impact on music education. The multiplicity of cultures within the United States is paralleled by the multiplicity of their musics—so much so that Bennett Reimer has called America a country with a "multimusical culture." As such, students are not only entitled to learn

about America's Western music heritage, but also to learn to respect the musics of its various cultural subgroups, and to learn enough about at least
some of these musics to access them if they choose.[19] The global rationale
also relates to music education. Music is a world phenomenon, and critical
thinking about the various musics around the world and the people who
make it can help students form this worldwide perspective.[20]

Additionally, other rationales specifically support the inclusion of a multicultural perspective in music education.[21] One rationale is based on the
role of music in society. Students study a particular music culture as a way
to understand the people who make the music.[22] Music functions in society
as a mode of nonverbal expression in the context of rites and rituals, as affirmation of governmental or political beliefs, or as emotional release.[23] By
learning how the people in another culture express themselves musically,
students not only gain insights into others but also learn about themselves.[24]
By learning to perform the music of other cultures, bi- or even multimusi-
cality (the ability to function effectively in two or more music cultures) can
be developed.[25]

Another rationale is based in the elements of the musics themselves.
Studying the musics of other cultures can broaden the students' sound base,
enabling them to be more open and tolerant of new musical sounds. Learning the concepts of music as they are applied worldwide also gives students
a wider palette of compositional and improvisational devices. It can also
help them place the Western classical (art) music tradition in perspective as
part of the world of musics.[26]

Along with this "musical concepts" rationale, and in some ways comple-
menting it, there is also an aesthetic rationale. Listening to, performing, or
composing music from any culture can lead to aesthetic experiences for the
students. The intrinsic value of music from any culture may be appreciated
to some extent by anyone, regardless of background.[27] Bennett Reimer and
Abraham Schwadron say these aesthetic responses derive primarily and inherently from the music itself, while for Lucy Green, a British music education researcher, both the intrinsic and delineational (cultural-contextual) elements of music contribute to this response.[28] Since many cultures have music
that is intended primarily for aesthetic contemplation (for example, Chinese
and Japanese musics), these musics can be used to enhance aesthetic development in the music program. Though this appears to imply a universality
to music, the fact that music is *not* a universal "language" has often been
pointed out. There is agreement, however, that the greater the knowledge one
has about the culture, and the expectations or rules of its music, the greater
the understanding, or perception of meaning, of that music will be.[29]

The Problems and Potentials of Multicultural Education

Although multiculturalism appears to be well accepted in educational circles, this issue has also proven controversial, a fact documented in feature
articles, newspapers, and opinion essays across the country.[30] Some of the

controversy is centered on the definition of culture and the concept of culturalism. Anthropologists have been arguing this issue since the 1970s with no resultant consensus. The definition of culture as "learned patterns of behavior" remains viable. However, critics of culturalism say a homogeneous culture is rare for any group, hence the idea of subgroups must be introduced to explain differences, and still further differences must be accounted for through human actions and choices for change.[31] Others point to the dynamic nature of culture, and question the "museum mentality" of preserving outmoded cultural practices in the classroom.[32] All these criticisms indicate that education cannot simply be an agency that passes on traditions, but must also challenge and clarify cultural values to promote self-actualization through critical thinking.[33]

Some researchers have been concerned that too much emphasis on multiculturalism will result in a splintering of what it means to be an American. They fear a division in the educational system because they see multiculturalism giving emphasis to individual segments of the society over the common whole.[34] Others see multiculturalism as an agenda for specific subgroups seeking affirmation, to which the proponents reply that if a multicultural curriculum is properly taught, no one group would be promoted over any other.

Other critics have commented on what they see as the lack of intellectual rigor in multicultural education. They also feel that multiculturalism provides an easy solution to minority student underachievement, and in some cases even see it as a "politically correct" expedient without much substance. On the other hand, proponents say that these critics really fear multiculturalism because it poses a threat to the "American way of life," or at least the current status quo.[35]

Some researchers feel that ethnic diversity is a strength and that education employing a multicultural approach can develop students who are "mindful of the value of . . . cultural diversity."[36] In response, critics such as Brian Bullivant have warned that "teaching *all* children about cultural differences in their societies may reinforce and not reduce their sense of distinctiveness."[37]

A more radical charge against multicultural education declares that it simply doesn't go far enough to break the systems of oppression in this country. These critics tend to support multicultural education that is reconstructionist or antiracist, that is, restructuring education to provide equity for all, teaching against racism and discrimination, and discussing issues of equality, justice, and, ultimately, social empowerment. There are advocates of the current multicultural education programs in the schools who would agree that racism, social class, and sexism are not well addressed. Others say that well-taught classes already include issues of racism and inequality, and that students cannot learn to be critical thinkers on these issues without a multicultural perspective.[38]

The issue of multiculturalism in education has its proponents and critics abroad as well. In Great Britain, those in favor of multiculturalism as a

policy for education see it as a way to acknowledge social diversity with political unity. Critics see this stance as merely another manifestation of assimilation and think it needs to be extended into antiracism as a major policy and basis for radical change in current education practice. For them, this
includes changes in curricula, materials, teacher education, and job opportunities in education as part of the fight to end injustice and powerlessness
in society for minority groups. In the middle ground, some British researchers feel that both multiculturalism and antiracism have value and seek
a compromise that includes both: "anti-racist multiculturalism."[39]

In Australia, critics complain that their current policy of multicultural
education is superficial, often with tokenistic implementation, and comment
on the unsystematic method for curriculum implementation countrywide.
They note that it does not provide for teacher training (or retraining), and
does not deal with the racism inherent in Australian society. They frequently
argue for adopting antiracist education. On the other hand, proponents say
that a good multicultural education program will include teaching for antiracism, though they agree that teacher training and countrywide implementation are issues yet to be solved.[40]

Although multiculturalism is national law in Canada, some Canadian
researchers feel that antiracist education holds more potential for change
than multicultural education. They feel that multiculturalism does not do
enough to promote institutional transformation and sociopolitical changes.
Liberal multiculturalists, on the other hand, see antiracism as inherent within
well-taught multiculturalism.[41]

Controversial it may be, but even its detractors tend to agree that there
is a need for multicultural education, especially given today's social environment.[42] However, to what extent school curricula can promote cultural
diversity and not be the source of cultural divisions remains a potent question for education, both here and abroad.[43] These strong and often differing
opinions have brought about discussions in both music and art education
as these areas try to understand the issues involved in multicultural education as they apply to their respective fields in arts education.[44]

The Problems and Potentials of Multicultural Music Education

Just as multicultural education has its proponents and detractors, so does
multicultural music education. Some people see multiculturalism in music
as a "politically correct" fad that has become a part of the curriculum. Many
also feel that the whole movement is merely the latest justification for the
inclusion of music education in the curriculum. Those in favor of multicultural music education point out that the primary purpose of music education is to teach music, and music is inherently multicultural. Using multicultural music education for other than musical purposes is self-defeating.

The place of Western art music in the music curriculum is another concern as music educators try to balance existing curricular requirements with
a broader world perspective.[45] They often say there is not enough time to

teach the required Western music curriculum, let alone world musics. Proponents once more point to the multicultural nature of music itself and question how a rounded music education curriculum could leave out musics from around the world.

There are those who say that although it is well and good to teach about other musics, music educators cannot forget that they are teaching music to Americans and, for them, that means teaching American (Western) music.[46] Responding to this, proponents point out that the American music culture "has always had the benefit of ideas of many different ethnic groups."[47]

Although many agree that teaching from a multicultural perspective can enable students to more clearly understand other people through their music, there is the concern that an inauthentic presentation of that music could confirm stereotypical ideas about these people. Indeed the entire issue of authenticity comes into question when considering that the very act of transferring music out of its cultural context and into the classroom destroys its authenticity.[48] Proponents acknowledge this problem and say the simplest ways around it are to use recordings of authentic musics and to invite community culture bearers into the classroom to present their music firsthand.

CONCEPTS OF MULTICULTURALISM IN EDUCATION

With so much discussion of the topic, researchers have tried to clear the picture by outlining concepts of multicultural education as implemented, or as it should be implemented, in the schools. Margaret Gibson, James A. Banks, Richard Pratte, Carl A. Grant, and Christine E. Sleeter are among the most prominent researchers in general education who have discussed approaches to multiculturalism, and the purposes and educational implications of each. The following is a brief outline of their ideas.[49]

Margaret Gibson: Five Approaches to Multicultural Education[50]

1. *Education for the culturally different* (benevolent multiculturalism): educational opportunities for the culturally different so they can "fit in" to the regular school program
2. *Education about cultural differences*: education for all students to achieve cross- and intercultural understanding
3. *Education for cultural pluralism*: education to preserve cultural integrity of ethnic groups
4. *Bicultural education*: produces competency in two different cultures, usually the dominant culture and one other
5. *Multicultural education*: produces competency in multiple cultures, leading away from a dichotomy between cultures toward a fuller range of human interactions

James A. Banks: Multiethnic Perspectives[51]

1. *Anglo-American–centric model*: presents only the white Anglo-Saxon Protestant viewpoint, with no changes to the existing educational system
2. *Ethnic additive model*: information is added to the existing educational program, with no other changes; sometimes called a "tagged-on" approach
3. *Multiethnic model*: offers many views, no one perspective superior or inferior to another; sometimes called a "national" approach
4. *Ethnonational model*: events are studied from multiethnic and multinational perspectives resulting in a global perspective

✳ Richard Pratte: Ideologies of Cultural Diversity[52]

1. *Assimilation*: students learn Anglo-Saxon values and attitudes
2. *Amalgamation*: students learn about intercultural interaction
3. *Insular cultural pluralism*: ethnic studies focus on learning about individual cultures
4. *Modified cultural pluralism*: multiethnic studies focus on learning about multiple cultures
5. *Open society*: students learn to form their own identity and are indifferent to racial, religious, ethnic, or other distinctions
6. *Dynamic pluralism*: goes beyond special interest groups to form a society based on mutual concern; subgroups work together to solve the problems of the larger society

✳   Carl A. Grant and Christine E. Sleeter: Approaches to Multicultural Education[53]

1. *Teaching the exceptional and culturally different*: prepares students to enter mainstream society
2. *Human relations approach*: prepares students to live and work together
3. *Single-group studies*: in-depth study of a single culture group
4. *Multicultural education*: attempts to redesign the educational program so it reflects the concerns of all diverse groups and thereby produces an affirmation of that diversity
5. *Multicultural and social reconstructionist education*: extends the definition of multicultural education to include education toward a reformed society with greater equity for all its members

The first concepts each of these researchers identified are those that result in assimilation and amalgamation.[54] Historically, assimilation was epitomized shortly after the turn of the century when the European-based educational system in the United States was challenged by the influx of immigration. Public education provided the primary means for new immigrants to enter the mainstream of American life. Amalgamation was best described by the metaphor of the "melting pot." The schools, particularly through the intercultural education movement of the 1920s to 1940s, taught how various ethnic groups contributed to the "oneness" of American society.[55] These researchers rejected both concepts as not useful toward producing a truly multicultural education because the aim of these models is to produce a unified culture through the absorption of diversity. Assimilation forces the different culture to accept the mainstream culture; amalgamation tries to blend the different culture and the mainstream culture to create a new third culture.

Gibson, Banks, Pratte, and Grant and Sleeter also identified ethnic studies and multiethnic models in education. Found in the curricula of the 1960s and 1970s, these models often targeted only selected populations. While useful to some extent, the researchers felt these models were too limiting in scope. Taking multiculturalism to its fullest extension, their final models all recommend a reformation of the current educational system which would enable students to function in multicultural contexts.[56]

CONCEPTS OF MULTICULTURALISM IN MUSIC EDUCATION

While there is no definitive concept of multicultural music education, since the 1970s there has been some development in this area.[57] Because scientific and technological advances following World War II brought countries of the world into closer contact with each other, it was inevitable that music educators would be "musically and educationally drawn to develop the potential for the inclusion of world musics in formal, public education."[58] In what was perhaps the first real application of philosophy to multicultural music education, Abraham Schwadron advocated basing music instruction on comparative aesthetics.

In Schwadron's view, comparative aesthetics and ethnomusicology would be closely aligned, the latter providing the research upon which to base the former. He sought a philosophy that would honor the universality of music as a human phenomenon, yet acknowledge that all musics occur within and are inseparable from their sociocultural contexts. Schwadron saw comparative aesthetics encompassing both the feelingful responses anyone may experience with any music, and the specific responses of the trained musician (performer or listener) to the interactions of the musical sounds themselves (balance, climax, repetition, density, etc.). The study of comparative aesthetics would eventually lead to a consideration of (1) those ethnocentric tendencies and attitudes that inhibited the development of a pluralistic aesthetic; (2) the possible revision of Western aesthetic theory; and (3) its implications for education, bimusicality, and world communication.[59]

Following Schwadron, David B. Williams and, more recently, David J. Elliott have paralleled general education investigations in attempts to identify concepts and approaches in multicultural music education. The concepts of these two researchers are outlined below.

David B. Williams: Four Approaches to the Selection of Ethnic Folk Music for Use in Elementary Music Programs[60]

1. *Traditional approach*: students learn Western European music with a relatively small representation of songs from various ethnic groups
2. *Non-Western approach* (either uni- or multidirectional): students learn one non-Western music culture in depth (unidirectional approach); or they learn a wide selection of non-Western musics (multidirectional)
3. *Ethnic-American, unidirectional approach*: students learn one ethnic American culture selected for in-depth study
4. *Ethnic-American, multidirectional approach*: students first learn many of the diverse musics of America and then study the musics in the rest of the world

Williams identified problems with each of the first three approaches: the traditional approach frequently neglected ethnic musics; a lack of teacher training as well as the questions of whose culture(s) should be chosen for study negated the non-Western approach; and a narrowness of focus made the uni-directional ethnic-American approach less acceptable. Williams thought the fourth approach conceptualized "the relationship of a child to his society,"[61] and so, for the most relevance in the music classroom, he recommended the ethnic-American, multidirectional approach.

✳ David J. Elliott: Concepts of Multicultural Music Education (based on Pratte's model)[62]

1. *Assimilation*: the exclusive study of the Western European classical tradition in its various historical periods. This model is concerned with the cultivation of "good taste," the aesthetics of "fine art," and the implied elevation of this classical tradition over all other musics
2. *Amalgamation*: a limited amount of ethnic music, but primarily as it has been incorporated by Western classical composers
3. *Open society*: music is seen as a personal expression, but only in the context of the development of the larger social group. Cultural heritage and musical traditions are irrelevant
4. *Insular multiculturalism*: the musics from one or two cultures, usually those of the local community, added to the Western tradition; does not change the original curriculum in any other way
5. *Modified multiculturalism*: several musics included in the curriculum, often selected on the basis of geographical boundaries, ethnicity, or religion. The musics are frequently compared and contrasted in their ap-

proaches to musical elements, or roles in society, and are taught through the accepted teaching methodology of that culture

6. *Dynamic multiculturalism*: a world perspective applied to a wide variety of musics. In this model, much of the modified multicultural approach is retained, but musical concepts original to the culture replace a strictly Western aesthetic perspective

Elliott rejected the first four approaches as either ethnocentric or not truly multicultural. He felt the fifth approach came closer to his multicultural ideal than any of those preceding, but rejected it because it still retained Western perspectives in its approach. For example, the idea of "teaching from musical concepts" is a Western approach that is not necessarily found in other cultures. Elliott recommended the sixth approach. Dynamic multiculturalism lends an objectivity to the study of music and fosters a two-way interaction between various music cultures and topics such as tuning systems, the role of teachers and listeners, or music and other art forms.[63] (See Figure 1.1.)

Elliott has also developed a praxial philosophy of music education based on the fact that music, as a human expression, is quintessentially the action of making music. As Elliott defined it, "The term *praxial* emphasizes that music ought to be understood in relation to the meanings and values evidenced in actual music making and music listening in specific cultural contexts."[64] Since music is found worldwide, "MUSIC is a diverse human practice."[65] (Elliott uses the term "practice" to encompass all musical genres, for example, the practice of jazz, the practice of Chinese music, the practice of Baroque music.) Following this line of thought, he continued, "If MUSIC consists in a diversity of music cultures, then MUSIC is inherently multicultural. And if MUSIC is inherently multicultural, then music education ought to be multicultural in essence."[66] Elliott saw multicultural music education as humanistic education, enhancing both self-concept and self-understanding through "other-understanding." He explained it as a connection between the individual and "the personhood of other musicers and audiences in other times and places."[67]

Elliott suggested that students can be taught to function within a variety of musical practices. This could be accomplished within the constraints of the school curriculum by taking into consideration the students' interests, teachers' abilities, availablity of authentic materials, and employing the various regional musics of the area before moving on to more unfamiliar ones.

The Guiding Principles of Multicultural Music Education

From all of the divergent thinking on the topic, several principles guiding any viable multicultural music education program stand out. They have been enunciated by ethnomusicologists and music education researchers over the past twenty-five years, and most recently by the International Society for

MULTICULTURAL MUSIC EDUCATION: CURRICULUM MODELS

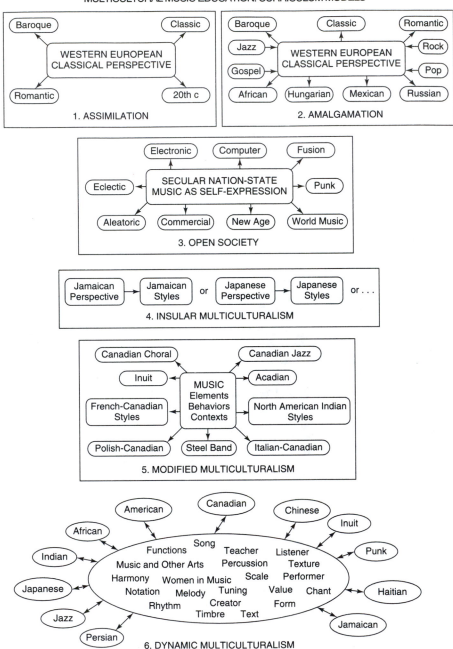

Figure 1.1 From David Elliott, "Key Concepts in Multicultural Music Education," *International Journal of Music Education* 13 (1989), 15. Used by permission.

Music Education (ISME) through its Panel on World Musics. These principles are:

1. There are many different and equally valid music systems in the world.
2. All music exists within its cultural context.
3. Music education should reflect the inherently multicultural nature of music.
4. Given that the American population is made up of many diverse cultures, music education should also reflect the diverse musics of the American population.
5. Authenticity is determined by the people within the music culture.

The remainder of this book will examine multicultural music education—its history, current methods and materials, and future possibilities—in the light of these principles.

SUMMARY

Multiculturalism has been a recurrent theme in both general education and music education in the United States for most of the twentieth century. However, the "concepts" or "perspectives" of multiculturalism have changed greatly since 1900. Researchers studying these concepts have identified five basic viewpoints: assimilation, amalgamation, ethnic studies, multiethnic models, and multicultural curricular reform. These concepts developed in sequential order, although each did not totally displace its predecessor. As a result of these concurrent and conflicting viewpoints, the issue of multiculturalism in education is a controversial one today.

Nonetheless, in recent years, researchers have discussed various rationales for multiculturalism in education and music education. They also have provided many suggestions for teaching methodologies and materials for implementing multicultural perspectives in the classroom. As a result, even with its detractors, multiculturalism has become a part of contemporary general education and a regular component of music education.

Conclusions, Implications, and Questions

With so many definitions, rationales, and approaches to multiculturalism in education, it is important for music education to find a workable philosophy of multicultural music education. Elliott recommended that such a philosophy "be conservative in its concern for preserving the artistic integrity of musical traditions, yet liberal insofar as it goes beyond particular cultural preferences to confront larger musical ideas, processes, and problems."[68] That is a tall order, and easier said than done.

Issues of aesthetics and praxis need to be resolved. Questions still loom unanswered: What is the place of the Western classical tradition in a multicultural classroom? If we add other musics to the curriculum, whose music(s) do we choose? Why? What about curricular implementation? Both pre- and in-service teachers need training to be able to present these musics accurately to their students. What does this mean both for teacher training institutions and school districts? For the teachers themselves?

Multicultural music education implies a critical approach to music teaching and learning. Conversely, it is not possible to teach critical thinking about music without a multicultural perspective. Could music education, by virtue of its subject matter, be in a unique position to lead the education profession in incorporating a multicultural approach in the classroom?

PART

II

The Historical Perspective

CHAPTER 2

Prelude to the Twentieth Century

Not things but men; Not matter but mind.
—Motto, Chicago World's Fair, 1893

Multiculturalism in one form or another has been a part of American music education for nearly one hundred years. However, before delving into multicultural music education in the twentieth century, it is important to establish the nineteenth-century conditions from which it evolved. Throughout the latter half of the nineteenth century, both general education and music education subscribed to European philosophies and educational methodologies. In addition, music education looked to Europe, especially to the classical music tradition of Germany, for its classroom material.

HISTORICAL CONTEXT

Industrialization and Urbanization

Throughout the last quarter of the nineteenth century in the United States, inventions such as electricity, improved mining and steel-making processes, refrigerated freight cars, sewing machines, and mass production assembly lines brought about incredible industrial growth. Because these new industries, particularly steel, textiles, and meat packing, provided jobs for countless numbers of people, urban areas expanded rapidly around the factories as people crowded into the central city in order to be within walking distance of work.

Modern city life began with the advent of streetcar lines and skyscrap-
ers. With cities now overcrowded and housing at a premium, the wealthy
and upper middle classes, who could afford the streetcar fares, moved out
to the suburban fringe of the city. The large, newly vacated houses of the
wealthy were soon divided to accommodate several families. In addition,
land developers began to build apartments and tenement houses, often designed to house as many people in as little space as possible. The lower middle classes, the newly arrived immigrant populations, and the poor took
over these spaces in the central city, which, between overcrowding and de-
terioration, soon became slum neighborhoods. It is in these urban districts
that the first settlement houses were established, among them Hull House
in Chicago in 1889 and the Henry Street Settlement in New York in 1893.

Social Darwinism, Immigration, and Segregation

Toward the end of the nineteenth century, Darwin's theories of evolution
and natural selection (that through competition, the strong would endure,
and the unfit would be eliminated) formed the basis of a "social theory"
made popular by the writings of the English philosopher Herbert Spencer
and William Graham Sumner of Yale University. This philosophy of the
"survival of the fittest" soon became known as Social Darwinism, although
Darwin never intended some of the applications given his theory. Social Darwinism appealed to many people in the United States and was used to explain, among other things, imperialism (strong nations dominate over
weaker ones), the accumulation of wealth (business tycoons were smarter
than their competitors), and social and intellectual levels (Northern European Caucasians were at the top of human development while Africans and
other "colored" peoples were at or near the bottom).[1] In the late nineteenth
century, this last application was used as justification for the restrictions
placed on the immigrants and persons of color in the United States.[2]

From 1870 to 1900, over ten million immigrants came to America, with
particularly large numbers arriving from Southern and Eastern Europe. A
movement soon arose in reaction to these increasing numbers of immigrants
who were so different from the white, Protestant, Northern European background of the Americans already in the United States. While life in America was confusing and strange to the immigrants, the native white Americans found their new neighbors equally so. Samuel P. Hays's description of
their reaction left no doubt that one could hardly sleep well at night with
these "hordes of newcomers" around. They

maintained strange customs, spoke peculiar languages, dressed oddly, and
practiced alien Catholic and Jewish religions; they had not the proper rev-
erence for American values, symbols, and heroes. Moreover, they were intimately involved with the most vulgar and unpleasant features of industrial society. They worked at the most menial jobs, lived in the most
repulsive sections of town, frequented the most distasteful dives and bawdy
houses, [and] had the most revolting personal habits.[3]

Lest the American "racial stock" be contaminated, nativists began efforts to limit immigration. In 1882, Congress passed a law establishing a fifty cent duty for each person seeking to enter the United States, and denying admission to "any convict, lunatic, or any person unable to take care of himself or herself without becoming a public charge."[4] Further restrictions in 1885 excluded contract laborers, and in 1891 Congress added people with contagious diseases, polygamists, and anyone convicted of a "crime or misdemeanor involving moral turpitude" to this list.[5] Also in 1882, Congress passed the Chinese Exclusion Act which not only forbade further immigration to the United States from China, but also forbade citizenship to those Chinese already in the country.[6]

In addition, the Immigrant Restriction League, founded in 1887, began to advocate screening immigrants for literacy before admission to the United States. With Senator Henry Cabot Lodge as the League's leading spokesperson, Congress passed a bill requiring a literacy test for entry into the United States in 1897. Although this bill was vetoed by President Grover Cleveland, it would not be the last of the efforts to place a literacy test restriction on immigration.[7]

In an effort to bring the Native Americans into "civilized" American life, Congress passed the Dawes Severalty Act in 1887.[8] There were also laws to officially curtail the rights of African Americans. These Jim Crow laws, intended to keep the African American population "in its place," had been passed for many years following the Civil War. However, their constitutionality had not been challenged before 1895 when the case of *Plessy v. Ferguson* came before the Supreme Court. At that time, public transportation was segregated in Louisiana, and Plessy, an African-American, had been physically removed from a "white only" railroad coach. Plessy charged that this was a violation of his civil rights guaranteed by the Constitution. The Supreme Court not only upheld the railway company's right to maintain racially separate coaches, but in effect sanctioned all other forms of segregation by law in the United States, including schools, with the stricture that the facilities provided were "separate but equal."[9]

Between the Jim Crow laws and immigration restrictions, the United States was effectively segregated into white and colored populations at the end of the nineteenth century.[10] In addition, within the white population, differences were discouraged and the newly arrived immigrants from Europe were expected to Americanize and assimilate into the mainstream society as quickly as possible. However, a few voices were beginning to speak out advocating equality of all people before the law.

Early Voices of Cultural Pluralism

At the same time Social Darwinism was emphasizing the development of the "fittest," which would eventually result in a kind of sameness at the top of the evolutionary ladder, William James was developing a philosophy to encompass the diversity he saw in the world. James embraced a multifac-

eted world filled with endless variety.[11] His philosophy accounted for
uniqueness in the world by seeing all things in relationship to everything
else.[12] James celebrated diversity. Given this viewpoint, it is not surprising
to see that James advocated the coexistence of all countries and nationalities, feeling each to be so special that comparisons between them were use-
less.[13] In an age of segregation and assimilation, James's ideas of equality
and coexistence, diversity and individuality, were singular. At the turn of
the century, his pluralistic philosophy had already begun to influence progressive reformers.

   One of the first African-Americans to speak for racial equality was
Booker T. Washington. Arguing for vocational education, economic gains,
and the adoption of middle-class standards as the only ways to show American society that African-Americans were prepared for the rights and priv-
ileges due them through citizenship, Washington became the first African-
American to gain a national audience. In his famous speech in Atlanta in
1895, he urged hard work and cooperation between the races as the road to
eventual equality, though tacitly implying an acceptance of the segregated
system.[14]

   W. E. B. Du Bois was another African-American leader emerging at the
end of the nineteenth century. The first African-American to graduate from
Harvard University and a student of William James, Du Bois was deeply affected by James's philosophy, which became the foundation of his own work.
He opposed both the idea of working within the segregated system and
Washington's advocacy of vocational training, arguing that equality could
not be obtained unless all people had equal chances for all types of education and advancement. His leadership in the advancement of African-
Americans, like that of Booker T. Washington, continued well into the twentieth century.

   In addition, the settlement houses in the large urban areas were concerned for the immigrant populations. Urging urban reform and education,
they sought to better the life of the immigrants and help bring them into
American life as accepted, equal citizens. Jane Addams of Chicago's Hull
House in particular spoke in favor of these reforms. She first voiced her concerns at the International Congress on Social Settlements held in conjunction with the Chicago World's Fair of 1893.[15]

The Chicago World's Fair of 1893

It is probably accurate to say the Chicago World's Fair of 1893 was the grand-
est international event of the 1890s. Featuring one of the most elaborate series of displays proclaiming the advancements in industry, the World's Fair
was a celebration of the accomplishments of Western, particularly American, civilization. Built along Chicago's lakefront, the World's Fair attracted
thousands of visitors from around the world.

   Often called the "White City," the Exhibition's spectacular displays included lavish buildings dedicated to mining, manufacturing, transportation,

agriculture, and the arts, as well as huge sculptures and water fountains. European, Asian, Central and South American, and Caribbean countries all sent delegations and contributed buildings that housed their national exhibits.[16] Both the architecture of the buildings themselves and the exhibits within were stunning. The Electricity Building was lit with thousands of light bulbs, the Music Hall housed an ornate concert stage, and the Japanese Building was an accurate reproduction of a historic Japanese temple.[17]

Along with the architecture and art exhibits, the Midway Plaisance proved very popular. As one of several displays of the Ethnology Department of the Fair, the Chicago Midway Plaisance was originally intended as a scientific, ethnographic exhibit showing human development from the "primitive" to the "civilized."[18] For this display at the Exhibition, entire families from all over the world were transplanted into villages representing their way of life. With almost three thousand people from forty-eight nations, including Algeria, China, Dahomey, France, Germany, Hungary, India, Indonesia, Japan, Lapland, Persia, Samoa, the Sudan, and Russia, to mention only a few, the Midway literally provided a trip around the world within a few city blocks. At the re-created Javanese village, German beer garden, Irish castle, Japanese bazaar, or the "Street in Cairo," visitors could see the dances and hear the songs of the people, try local refreshments, witness native theatrical productions, or buy handicrafts. In short, it was a way for thousands of people to see how other thousands lived. With such "exotic" people as the Algerians, Dahomians, Laplanders, and Samoans to be seen, undoubtedly there was a lot of staring on the part of the Fair visitors. This was probably the first time that many people paid any attention to other cultures in the world.

In addition, and in some ways more important, many congresses convened in conjunction with the Fair, bringing together intellectuals and scholars from around the world to discuss everything from religion, commerce and finance, medicine, and education, to the role of women, literature, public health, and social reform. These congresses were truly international, with participants from many countries and all the states of the United States.[19] Of particular significance were the World's Parliament on Religions, the Congress on Women, the Congress on Medicine and Surgery, and the Congress on Education. The World's Fair motto, "Not things but men; Not matter but mind," was no better exemplified than at these congresses, which set a precedent for cooperation and scholarly exchange between nations.

The Rise of Professionalism

During the latter part of the nineteenth century, many professional organizations were founded in an effort to advance their respective professions and to maintain the expertise of their members. Local medical associations were established throughout the 1890s, though the American Medical Association was not officially organized until 1901. Legal bar associations were common in many states throughout these years as well, and in 1895, industry joined the trend for professional associations with the National Association of Manufacturers. Even professional sports organized; the National League of Baseball was founded in 1876, the American League following in 1901.

The establishment of settlement houses also gave rise to the professional social worker, and social work joined teaching and nursing as one of the acceptable professions for women. In addition, the nonprofessional women's clubs, which were often involved with cultural activities and social reform, organized the General Federation of Women's Clubs in 1892, giving more power to their individual clubs through a national organization.

EDUCATIONAL CONTEXT

Industrialization and Americanization

Like society in general, the educational system was also affected by industrialization. Structural steel allowed for larger school buildings, and schools were designed with high ceilings and plenty of windows to let in light and air because of the generally polluted atmosphere of the industrial city. Even the title of School Superintendent was derived from the organizational system of the factory, and in classes, punctuality and attendance were stressed since those were virtues in the new industrial workplaces.[20] For more efficient governance, the burgeoning urban schools were structured into a district plan, and the general curriculum, including music, became standardized—often to the extent that, in a given grade, the same subject was to be taught at the same time during the week across all the schools in the city.[21]

There was very little talk of accommodating education to the thousands of new immigrant children in any way; in fact, the opposite was more often true. Though some high schools began to include foreign language study late in the nineteenth century, it was mainly the modern foreign languages (French, German, and Spanish). For the immigrants who spoke Czech, Yiddish, Italian, or Polish, these classes did little to help them learn English.[22] The immigrant population was to adapt to America, in school as in everything else. The task set for public education was "to break up these groups or settlements [of immigrants]," and encourage Americanization.[23] English was the language to be learned and American behaviors were expected.

At the same time that the schools were attempting to assimilate the new white populations, the school system itself was segregated. This "separate but equal" system included Native American reservation schools, Chinese schools, particularly on the West Coast, and African-American schools (then called Negro schools) throughout the country. There were also government-run, nonreservation boarding schools for Native American children.[24] District school systems often governed these segregated schools, and the curriculum remained essentially the same as in the white schools. The exception may have been the emphasis on Americanization and vocational training which was deemed appropriate for these populations. There was no official attempt to address cultural differences in any of the schools, segregated or not, although this may have occurred on an individual basis.

European Influences on American Education

Throughout most of the nineteenth century, Europe was the home of new ideas in education, and American schools readily adopted them. Educators who had visited Europe, such as Horace Mann, Charles McMurray, and Frank McMurray, brought back the philosophies and methodologies of Johann Heinrich Pestalozzi, Friedrich Wilhelm Froebel, Johann Friedrich Herbart, and Herbert Spencer. Their ideas soon became part of the teachers' repertoire in the United States from the middle of the nineteenth century onward. Edwin A. Sheldon was the first to incorporate the Pestalozzian method of sense experience before symbol (for example, pictures before written words) in the teacher training program of the normal school in Oswego, New York, in 1860, and Superintendent W. T. Harris established the first public kindergarten based on Froebel's design in St. Louis, Missouri, in 1873. Herbart's ideas on the science of education, and education as investigation rather than the rote parroting of information back to the teacher were adopted by many educators in the latter nineteenth century, especially through the teaching of Frank and Charles McMurray at Teachers College, Columbia University, and Peabody College for Teachers, Nashville, Tennessee, respectively.[25] The goals of "character building" and "right living" so often seen in the educational writings of the late nineteenth century derive from the Spencerian belief that the purpose of education is to learn "to live morally and completely through rational foresight of consequences."[26]

In the midst of all the changes of the late nineteenth century, the schools remained a stabilizing factor in American society. The subjects which were taught in the last quarter of the nineteenth century remained essentially the same: reading, writing, arithmetic, English, spelling, American history, geography, nature study (science), drawing (art), music (vocal music), and lastly physical education.[27] The primary function of this curriculum was to mold the character of the students, impart morality, ensure literacy, and assist in vocational guidance.[28] In short, at the turn of the century, though American education had incorporated some of the advances of industrial methodology, it was basically operating as it had for most of the century, with a practical curriculum founded on European philosophies and methodologies.

Professionalism in Education

Professionalism came early to education with the founding of the National Teachers Association in 1857. This organization became the National Education Association (NEA) in 1879, and along with this organization, several regional accrediting agencies were formed between 1886 and 1895 (the New

England, Middle States, North Central, and Southern Associations of Colleges and Secondary Schools) to ensure quality standards in teacher education. At the annual meetings of the NEA, teachers heard lectures and participated in discussions on such topics as the latest educational methodology, the need for additional subject areas in the curriculum, teacher training, and the results of early research efforts.[29] They also heard reports from members who attended other conferences or congresses of education.[30] The proceedings of these meetings often contained transcriptions of the discussions that followed the featured speakers. Like many of the topics presented, these discussions frequently referred to "the need and value of the new subjects, and the desired changes in the nature of the school itself."[31]

For education, one of the landmarks of the late nineteenth century was the international Congress on Education held in conjunction with the Chicago World's Fair in 1893. To take part in this congress, the NEA invited representative educators from the United States and around the world. More than one hundred and fifty papers were presented on topics that ranged from discussions of educational psychology and business education, to kindergarten education, art instruction, and vocal music, to journalism in education and professional training of teachers. An impressive array of educators, especially from higher education, attended this congress. It was the largest and most well-attended education congress of any known at the time. Though the discussions were strictly within the realm of academia, international contacts were established, many probably for the first time.

MUSIC EDUCATION

European Influences on Music Education

Like much of American education in the latter half of the nineteenth century, music education was based in Pestalozzian theory.[32] This methodology had been employed since public school music education began in Boston in 1838 under the leadership of Lowell Mason.[33] In addition, just as the choice of the Pestalozzian method reflected educational standards, the song material chosen for the schools reflected the cultural standards of American society, which also looked to Europe, particularly Germany, for "quality" music.[34] In this light, it is not unusual that Mason chose to anchor his school music materials in the Euro-Germanic classical music tradition, or that the almost exclusive use of this tradition continued to be accepted in music teaching until well after the turn of the century.

Later in the century, another music educator, Luther Whiting Mason, also adopted European teaching methods. L. W. Mason borrowed the idea of visual charts and the use of folksongs from the German singing teacher Christian Heinrich Hohmann. Mason incorporated these in his lessons and, following Pestalozzian methodology, taught many rote songs before he introduced music reading.

The music classes in the new kindergartens, like the classes themselves, reflected Froebel's philosophy. Eleanor Smith's *Songs for Little Children* and Alice Riley and Jessie Gaynor's *Songs of the Child World* were collections of composed songs designed specifically for kindergarten.[35]

The Herbartian method of scientific, organized lessons with measurable results was adopted in music education, especially in the note-reading methodology advocated by Hosea Holt. In addition, some American music educators in the latter decades of the nineteenth century adopted the tonic sol-fa system of notation, which had developed in Great Britain around 1840.[36] Both these methodologies were in conflict with the more Pestalozzian "rote-first" approach and the controversy continued until the turn of the century, though both "rote" and "note" methods were accepted in music education.

Music Curriculum and School Music Texts

As the first public school music educator in Boston, Lowell Mason had to design his own curriculum, train the teachers under him, and write his own materials. His publications were numerous, and he is generally credited with having written the first music text series, *The Song Garden*, used in the schools. In his choice of music for the classroom, Mason made no pretense that he considered the German tradition to be of the highest quality. His *Song Garden*, Books I and II, included songs with melodies by Wolfgang Amadeus Mozart, Ludwig van Beethoven, and Hans Georg Nägeli, as well as a few German and Swiss "airs" (folksongs); the rest of the songs were Mason's compositions, often in this same classical style.[37] Mason freely admitted that he took much of the poetry and music for the *Song Garden* from German sources.[38] The songs in some of Mason's other songbooks are drawn from the works of Handel, Bellini, Rossini, German hymns, and occasionally a Scottish folk song.[39] The words for these songs often have no relationship to the original text of the folk song. For example, in *The Song Book of the School Room*, one song, entitled "The Sailor Boy" is set to the tune of "Boonie Doon," and "Auld Lang Syne" is used as a melody for two different songs.[40]

This lack of authenticity between the folk song text and music apparently did not concern Mason. More important was the fact that the melody was beautiful and useful for teaching the elements of music (for example, rhythm or intervals), and that the words were uplifting, "tending not to abase or degrade, but rather to exalt, ennoble, and purify the thoughts, feelings, and associations of the young."[41] The choice of songs was of great concern to Mason, and he often emphasized the need for "good" music, even if it meant the exclusion of some styles of music in favor of others. As early as 1822, he stated, "We should see that the songs of your families are pure in sentiment and truthful in musical taste. Avoid Negro melodies and comic songs for most of their tendencies is to corrupt both musically and morally."[42]

Until the 1870s, Lowell Mason remained a primary provider of school music, though many other songbooks were used in the schools.[43] In 1870, L. W. Mason published his graded music text series, the *National Music Course*.[44] While teaching in Cincinnati, he had become acquainted with the work of Christian Heinrich Hohmann, and the folk song tradition within Cincinnati's large German population. Noting that Hohmann incorporated German folk songs in his music teaching method, L. W. Mason adopted this, and not only began to use German folk songs in his teaching, but also included them in his *National Music Course*.[45] Of the sixty-four songs in the *First Music Reader* of the *National Music Course*, fifty-eight of them can be traced to German sources.[46] One song is identified as an English folk tune. Although Mason's addition of these folk musics extended the school music repertoire, the music curriculum remained based in the Germanic tradition.

Even though Lowell Mason had included a few folk songs in his songbooks, it was not until after L. W. Mason's adoption of folk songs in his graded music series that other school songbooks and music texts also included folksong material. The authors did not often acknowledge the sources of the songs in most school music texts, although they did sometimes credit the melody to a classical composer or call it an "air" from a given country.[47] By the late nineteenth century, a few English, Irish, and Scottish folk songs were starting to appear. However, songs based on German airs were by far the majority, and even greater numbers of songs were derived from the works of such European composers as Beethoven, Mendelssohn, Mozart, Handel, Haydn, and von Weber.[48]

During the latter part of the nineteenth century, the texts of these songs continued to be whatever the authors deemed appropriate.[49] Folk songs often had completely new texts, as for example, the German song "Muss i' denn" ("Must I then"), which became "My Pigeon House" in Walker and Jenks's songbook, and the song "Du, Du liebst mir im Herzen" (roughly, "You love me in your heart"), which became "Soft Music is Stealing" in McCasky's *Favorite Songs and Hymns for School and Home*.[50] The reason for the change in lyrics was always the same: character development. As Lowell Mason so emphatically stated in 1856,

> It is a matter of the first importance that the songs introduced should ever be of an elevated character. If this point be not carefully guarded, or if, in school-singing, such words or melodies be permitted, as tend to vulgarity, coarseness, rudeness, or to mere trifling and frivolity, we may, ere long, regret the day when music was added to the list of school studies.[51]

Mason's injunction was taken to heart by the music educators of the nineteenth century, and this commitment to quality music and carefully chosen texts, even to changing the text entirely for the sake of teaching a good melody, remained well into the twentieth century.

The emphasis on character building was not the only factor influencing the use of folk musics in the schools. During this period, the theory of Social Darwinism was also applied to the development of music. "Primitive" music was considered to be at the lower end of musical evolution, folk music slightly higher, and fine art music at the top of the evolutionary ladder. As McCarthy pointed out, this hierarchy "had the effect of legitimizing Western art music in the public school curriculum."[52] It is not surprising then to find only limited use of folk musics in the schools, and no "primitive" music at all, in spite of Anton Dvořák's advocacy of African-American and Native American musics as worthy musical styles from which American composers could take inspiration.[53]

While the school music texts contained primarily German-based songs or songs composed in the German classical style, some songbooks contained a much wider range of folk songs. In 1894, the Ginn Company published *The National School Library of Song*, edited by Leo R. Lewis. This series was intended for use in normal schools, and included a complete section of folk songs from thirty nations.[54] Two pages of notes provided some contextual information about these songs, source acknowledgments, and pronunciation guides. Unfortunately, the editor acknowledged that he provided few translations of the original texts, but that he had tried to replace them with English poems that would convey a similar idea as the original.[55]

McCasky's songbook, *Favorite Songs and Hymns for School and Home*, included "slave hymns" (African-American spirituals) among his selections of folk songs. The authenticity of these songs is unusual for the time, as the editor asserted that these African-American songs were correctly transcribed and that they met with the approval of the original singers.[56] However, for all the care given to these particular transcriptions, even McCasky could not refrain from changing the lyrics of some of the other folk songs in his book to suit propriety.

Professionalism in Music Education

The Music Teachers National Association (MTNA, founded in 1876) took its place along with the other professional organizations in the latter part of the nineteenth century. The organization was, and still is, intended as a venue for the exchange of ideas about teaching music and the dissemination of these ideas through publication. This organization was founded by private music teachers, but as the organization grew, many school music educators joined and for many years there was a close association between the private and public music teachers within the MTNA.[57]

The bulk of the proceedings of the MTNA dealt with vocal production, finger technique for various instruments, and music literature. However, the MTNA was also one of the first forums to acquaint music educators with the musics of other cultures. In 1883, L. W. Mason presented a talk titled "Music in the Schools of Japan," based on his two years spent teaching in Japan at the invitation of the Japanese government.[58] Mason introduced the Western music system to the Japanese schools, including what he knew how to teach best, German folk songs. He also learned a little about the Japanese music system, and his talk before the MTNA describing his work in Japan included information about Japanese music. Some of the difficulties he encountered in teaching in Japan were the result of the "clash" between Japanese and Western music cultures. As Mason described it:

> One of these difficulties was the difference of scales; and the difference was even greater than I had expected, in some respects. I expected at first that their scales would be like ours, our fourth and seventh being left out. But the leaving out of those gaps made the third variable, and made it sharper than a major third. There was the great difficulty. The seventh being left out, the sixth was variable—very much the same as it is in our minor scale, of course; and this was the tendency—more so in Japan than in China.[59]

Mason brought along a Japanese flute to illustrate his point. He also described Japanese customs and clothing, as well as the way he managed the protocol of his position when teaching in the Japanese imperial schools. Today Japanese school music texts still reflect the Western music Mason taught in that country.

In 1884, the NEA approved the formulation of a Department of Music Education. Once established, the department became very active within the NEA. Music selections were common at these meetings. In 1891, Sims Richards of Toronto, Canada, presented a recital of Canadian and American national songs. ("National" songs conveyed the national characteristics of a country; they did not necessarily have to be patriotic.) Following the performance, a resolution was passed: "That a committee be appointed to request publishers of school music books and readers to adopt a universal arrangement of national melodies, also a number of songs strictly American in character of words and music to be inserted in same."[60] This was one of the first indications of a need for national (or folk) melodies in the school texts, and also for music that would be specifically American.

By the end of the nineteenth century, the need to assimilate the growing immigrant population was beginning to be felt in the schools. At the 1892 NEA meeting, music educators discussed the topic of music as a means to assist with Americanization.[61]

Within the Congress on Education sponsored through the NEA at the Chicago World's Fair of 1893 was a week set aside for a Department Congress of Instruction in Vocal Music.[62] Music educators from the United States and Canada presented papers at this congress. Honorary vice presidents for this event included the composer Max Bruch, director of music of the Berlin Academy, and Eduard Hanslick from the University of Vienna. There was also a separate Musical Congress, under the direction of the American College of Musicians, which involved the MTNA and was also international in scope. These two congresses were probably the first international meetings of music educators, setting precedent for future contacts.[63]

Perhaps the greatest value of the MTNA and the NEA Department of Music Education was that they provided forums where music educators could meet and discuss new ideas in a day when telephones and mass transportation were still new inventions. These meetings not only provided for the personal exchange of ideas and information, but also reached a much wider audience because their *Proceedings* were published and disseminated to the entire membership.

SUMMARY

At the end of the nineteenth century, music education, like education in general, reflected a European viewpoint, heavily influenced by advances in German educational methodology, especially that of Pestalozzi, Froebel, and Herbart. Music educators were primarily concerned with teaching notation for efficient sight reading, promoting good vocal tone, and designing the best methods for cooperating with the general classroom teachers.[64] The examinations of the period emphasized sight singing and the elements of music theory, while classroom music lessons focused on melody, rhythm, and harmony through the medium of the European masters and some German and British folk songs.

These folk songs had beautiful, singable melodies that lent themselves to the didactic purposes of the music class, such as scalar passages or rhythms. There was often no acknowledgment of song context in the school music texts beyond identifying the melodies as German, Swiss, or Scottish "airs." No emphasis was given to the place these songs held within their culture, or even to the fact that they were musical exemplars for their cultures. At the turn of the century, although music educators were willing to hear about the music of other cultures, music education essentially taught only one music culture, the Euro-Germanic art music tradition.

Conclusions, Implications, and Questions

As the nineteenth century closed, dramatic changes were beginning to occur that would sweep American education and music education into the twentieth century. However, changes are more easily measured from a stable reference point. The methodologies and materials of the music curriculum of the late 1890s are the foundation of music education as we know it today. They also form the backdrop against which multiculturalism in music education can be highlighted. How does knowing this reference point help the music teacher today?

The differences between music education now and a hundred years ago are easily identified: technology in the classroom, Orff and Kodály methodologies, and instrumental music education, among others. What about similarities? How much of a music educator's daily plan today would sound familiar to a music teacher in 1890? How much of the classroom repertoire?

CHAPTER **3**

The First Steps: 1900–1928

It is the function of teachers to help their pupils realize that the world is a unity, . . . and that true nationalism is not inconsistent with true internationalism.

—RESOLUTIONS OF THE WORLD FEDERATION OF
EDUCATION ASSOCIATIONS, 1925

From 1900 to 1928, the demographic makeup of the United States changed radically owing to the heavy influx of immigration from Southern and Eastern Europe, and the schools, in particular, felt its impact. Many music educators, like their colleagues in general education, found themselves facing a multicultural classroom for the first time. As a result, music educators gradually came to know and accept the folk songs and dances from many European countries.

HISTORICAL CONTEXT

In the first quarter of the twentieth century Americans experienced changes that affected nearly every part of their lives. Inventions and rapid mechanization took them from horse-drawn buggies to automobiles and airplanes, from iceboxes to refrigerators, and from Edison cylinders to Victrolas and sound motion pictures. Novelists and a "muckraking" press exposed abuses in politics, industry, and urban slum living conditions, high school education became more readily available, and Prohibition and women's suffrage became constitutional amendments.

These first decades were also a time of contradictions as Americans fought in a world war to preserve democracy, yet used the "separate but

32

equal" ruling of the Supreme Court in *Plessy v. Ferguson* (1895) to validate both the segregation of African-Americans and restrictions placed on Asian-Americans. For the most part, the general population ignored the Native Americans, who were confined to reservations, while missionaries and government agencies tried to "civilize" and Americanize them.[1] Adding to the complexity of an American society already dealing with the effects of industrialization, urbanization, and internationalization, increasingly large numbers of Southern and Eastern European immigrants came to America in the early part of the century.

Americanization: Assimilation and the Melting Pot

The prevailing philosophy of the period from 1900 to 1928 continued to be Social Darwinism. Nativists often applied this philosophy as a way to "keep America for the Americans," and to keep the "American stock" pure, preferably by the exclusion of immigrants who were considered to be nonassimilable. Having already restricted Chinese immigration before the turn of the century, in 1906 Congress succeeded in limiting the number of Japanese entering this country. With the huge numbers of immigrants entering the United States after 1900, Americans began to fear "racial dilution" even more. The rhetoric of the time speaks of "mongrelization," and even refers to these immigrants as "indigestible aliens."[2] In an effort to keep these "undesirables" from coming to America, the nativists put their efforts into lobbying for new immigration restrictions. With Henry Cabot Lodge still their chief voice in Congress, the nativists tried in 1913 and 1915 to require a literacy test for admission to the United States, but it was vetoed by Presidents William Howard Taft and Woodrow Wilson. However, with nativism growing in intensity because of World War I, a bill with this restriction passed over Wilson's veto in 1917.[3] Further restrictive measures were added in the Immigration Act of 1921, which limited the total number of immigrants allowed in the country each year, and set a quota on the number of immigrants to be admitted from any given country.[4] The Immigration Act of 1924 further reduced the total number of immigrants, and included a formula for setting future quotas based on "national origins" effective in 1927, a formula that was not actually implemented until 1929.[5] The nativists insisted that those immigrants already in this country adopt the mainstream culture, or "Americanize," as soon as possible.[6] In particular, the public schools were to assist this process by educating the immigrant population for American citizenship and the American way of life.

In 1909, Israel Zangwill's play *The Melting Pot* lent its name to another view of Americanization. Zangwill called America "a Crucible" into which all persons would be welcomed, and out of which would emerge "the American," a "fusion of all races, perhaps the coming superman."[7] The concept of the melting pot was very attractive both to those who were trying to assimilate the new immigrant population into mainstream American life, and to those who saw the American people as an amalgamation of its many constituents.

Early Cultural Pluralists

There were other persons during this period who saw a type of cultural pluralism as the acceptable alternative to both nativism's assimilation process and the amalgamation of the melting pot. Progressive reformers who embraced this view derived their basic convictions from the philosophy of William James. In particular, James's views of equality and coexistence formed the basis of W. E. B. Du Bois's efforts to fight discrimination against African-Americans early in the twentieth century. In order to effect change, Du Bois urged the most talented African-Americans to get as much education as they could, encouraging them to study law, medicine, and public administration. In 1910, he helped found the National Association for the Advancement of Colored People (NAACP).[8]

Marcus Garvey was another African-American who protested discrimination in America. Working for equality through economic power, he helped to lay the foundation for many African-American businesses, and urged his followers to be proud of their color and their African heritage.[9]

Horace Kallen, another student of William James, first voiced his ideas of cultural pluralism in 1916, although it was not until after the publication of his book *Culture and Democracy in the United States* in 1924 that he became generally well known. Kallen's idea of cultural pluralism can best be described as unity from diversity. While multiculturalists today often speak of a "stained glass window," "salad bowl," or "mosaic," Kallen's favorite metaphor was that of the symphony orchestra. He saw the orchestra's many instruments each playing individually yet contributing to the final harmony of the music as representative of the many different cultures that make up a democratic country.[10]

The Settlement Houses and the Promotion of Immigrant Cultures

American social worker Jane Addams's belief that new immigrants should not forsake their distinctive heritages in the process of learning to be Americans came from her years working at Hull House in Chicago. She deplored the loss of the immigrants' native cultures, especially for their children, believing that America was richer for what she called the "gifts of the immigrants." She encouraged the continuation of the immigrants' arts, crafts, songs, dances, and festivals,[11] and she suggested that it was in sharing these aspects of immigrant culture with the community at large that democracy, respect, and tolerance were fostered.[12] Although Hull House did not sponsor such festivals directly, it commended their potential as presenting "an infinite variety of suggestions and possibilities for public recreation."[13] The Henry Street Settlement in New York City did encourage such celebrations and, under its auspices, Garibaldi Day (named for the nineteenth-century

Italian patriot), Jewish festival days, and the Fourth of July soon became times for sharing music and dancing in a festival or pageant.[14] These festivals, with their attendant crafts, songs, and dances from many cultures became the model for folk festivals in other urban areas (see Figure 3.1). A typical finale for these festivals gathered together all the participants to sing "America" with the audience.

Hull House also encouraged the development of urban recreation space, and advocated folk songs and dancing among the activities to be shared in these playgrounds and parks.[15] Other urban settlement houses followed this practice. The Henry Street Settlement in New York City was among the first agencies to organize folk dancing and games as recreation.[16]

In addition, Addams and her friend John Dewey believed the public schools were not doing a creditable job in educating the immigrants. They both felt the schools should adopt a form of ethnic studies, at least in the schools servicing the first- and second-generation immigrant populations.[17] Addams suggested that foreign languages be taught and that teachers learn something about the cultures of their students,[18] while Dewey advocated history, geography, and literature classes as the academic areas in which to incorporate ethnic studies.[19] It is their suggestions for how schools could

Figure 3.1 Performance of Russian folk dance given during the exhbition Arts and Crafts of the Homelands at the Albright Art Gallery, Buffalo, New York, November 1919. *Academy Notes* 15, No. 1 (1920), 20. Photograph courtesy of the Albright-Knox Art Gallery Archives, Buffalo, New York.

best educate the immigrants that paved the way for the early intercultural education movement.

EDUCATIONAL CONTEXT

Americanization: Educating the Immigrants

There is no doubt that at the beginning of the twentieth century educators "believed that one of the important tasks of the public schools was to help the children of immigrants to assimilate, as quickly and as painlessly as possible, into the common American culture."[20] Indeed, the role of education as expressed by Ellwood Cubberley in 1909—"to assimilate or amalgamate these people as part of the American race, and to implant in their children the Anglo-Saxon conception of righteousness, law, order, and popular government"—was the generally accepted view.[21] This Anglo-conformity required that only English be taught in the schools. It is not unusual then to find that, when possible, the immigrants preferred sending their children to ethnic parochial schools where their native language was spoken and their culture preserved.

Observing that immigrants at these bilingual parochial schools had better attendance and made better academic progress than they did in the public schools, Jane Addams felt this progress was due, not just to the language spoken, but to the parochial school teachers' attitude of respect for the students' cultures.[22] As a result, she suggested that teachers in the public schools learn something about the heritages of their students. In a speech before the National Education Association (NEA) in 1908, she proposed "ethnic-cultural elements" in the curriculum. She insisted that the students be taught respect for their parents and their cultural heritage by the incorporation of their arts, folklore, and language in their classes.[23]

Since John Dewey believed that history, literature, and geography classes were the place to incorporate mutual respect and cultural appreciation, he established a curriculum at the Laboratory Schools of the University of Chicago that correlated foreign languages, handcrafts, music, and art with academic studies.[24] Other laboratory schools and private schools espousing the progressive educational methods soon followed suit.[25] It is to the credit of these progressive reformers that some of their suggestions for "ethnic culture" in the public schools (for example, foreign language classes and the use of correlated units of study) eventually did become a regular part of the school curriculum.[26]

Folk Dancing for Recreation and Physical Education

Following directly out of the settlements' advocacy of folk dancing as a community recreation, the Playground and Recreation Association of America established a Folk Dance Committee under the chairmanship of Elizabeth

Burchenal in 1905.[27] Through the cooperative efforts of Burchenal and the Folk Dance Committee, the popularity of folk dancing grew and soon became an accepted part of the physical education curriculum.[28] In some systems, teachers of dance acted as supervisors to teach the dances to the physical education instructors, while in others the instructors relied on Burchenal's publications, which included instructions for the dance steps. Because nearly every facility had access to either a piano or a Victrola for accompaniment,[29] Burchenal herself transcribed and arranged the dance music for the piano, and worked with the new Victor Talking Machine Company to ensure that the dance musics recorded by that company for use in the schools were authentic.[30] The dances were nearly all from Northern and Central European countries or were American dances that had been developed by settlers from these countries. This is not unusual since these are the countries where Burchenal studied the folk dances, transcribing the music and dance steps in detail.

Educators in the early physical education programs saw the great benefit of the inclusion of folk dancing in their curriculum. It was an activity that provided exercise, that afforded "educational gymnastics," and that could be performed indoors or outside, even in the smallest of school playgrounds. Folk dancing was especially recommended for girls because educators considered its graceful exertions more appropriate than some of the athletic events.[31] Luther Gulick, one of the first advocates for physical education in the public schools, attested to the healthful exercise folk dancing provided. He also saw the dances as the personal expressions of the people who created them, calling them "aesthetic folk-movement."[32]

Physical educators also were aware that these dances would help give the children an appreciation of their parents' home country and "would do much to overcome the common tendency amongst Americanized foreign children to feel a certain contempt for their parents."[33] Since these folk dances were the most popular part of the schools' end-of-the-year festivals of play (wherein the students demonstrated the games, dances, and gymnastic exercises they had learned), they also helped to educate the general public "whose knowledge of the newer American is woefully meager and whose horizon would be broadened by the cultural advantages acquired through contact with people of other countries."[34]

The Beginning of International and Intercultural Education

In the years following World War I, there was a great deal of hope that such a catastrophe would never happen again. The genuine desire for world peace and cooperation held out by the League of Nations fostered many school lessons on international friendship. Educators began to teach for world understanding, particularly in the wake of the negative feelings toward Germans and "foreigners" in general that overran America during the war years and into the 1920s.[35] Phrases such as a "new world" or "new democracy," and "good citizenship" occur frequently in the educational literature of the

time.[36] One of the first resolutions of the World Federation of Education
Associations (established in 1925) dealt with "international relations":

> It is the function of teachers to help their pupils realize that the world is a
> unity, that nations and peoples are interdependent economically and oth-
> erwise, and that true nationalism is not inconsistent with true internation-
> alism.[37]

In creating lessons for world friendship, educators began to employ the
idea of correlated lesson units long modeled at the laboratory schools, especially in history and geography lessons. These often included the folklore
and music of the individual countries studied. While fostering world-mindedness and understanding between nations, teachers found they could also
develop understanding among the various cultures in their own classrooms.
The ethnic studies which Addams and Dewey had suggested found a dual
purpose: Americanization and international understanding.

Rachel DuBois (no relation to W. E. B. Du Bois) was among the first educators to develop "ethnic curriculum materials" for use in the public
schools. DuBois was a social studies teacher in charge of school assemblies
at Woodbury High School in New Jersey in 1924. She devised a series of assembly programs in an attempt to familiarize students with the contributions of immigrants to America, and to accentuate the cultures of their countries of origin. Each assembly featured dramas, speakers, and artistic
performances focused on a particular cultural group. DuBois took great care
not to reinforce ethnic stereotypes. Unfortunately, her work in the schools
was too far ahead of her time. People criticized her for "spotlighting" ethnicity, accused her of Bolshevik tendencies, and pressured her to resign.
Though she had the support of the local school superintendent, after several years of countering these criticisms, she left her teaching position. Following her resignation, DuBois began to work for the Service Bureau for Intercultural Education under the Works Progress Administration (WPA)
developing what she called "world-mindedness materials" for the classroom.[38]

MUSIC EDUCATION

At the turn of the century, music educators were intent on teaching music
reading, proper vocal tone production, and an appreciation of European classical music. The materials they used to implement these goals were vocal
exercises, composed songs, German folk melodies, and sometimes songs
transcribed from operas or symphonies.

This was so much the standard repertoire in the schools that even in the
records from the first Music Supervisors National Conference (MSNC) meeting (Keokuk, Iowa, 1907), there is no reference to folk music of any kind.
Yet, as Allen Britton pointed out, these music educators "knew that their
country contained blacks, Indians, and Mexicans, and that the cities were

full of immigrants from Europe and Asia."[39] The musical heterogeneity of this population, and especially its diverse folk music, was simply not a consideration in the music curriculum at that time. Following the Darwinian thinking of the time, folk music was generally conceded to be somewhere above "primitive" music and below "fine art" music. Its value was in the fact that classical composers frequently took their inspiration from folk melodies.[40]

In one of the first statements citing the need to expand the range of music taught in the public schools, Louis Elson, cofounder of the Music Teachers National Association (MTNA), complained that children were not being taught "the different scales used by the nations of the earth, [and] the meaning of the folk-songs of various countries."[41] His own *Folk Songs of Many Nations* contained descriptions of a Chinese pentatonic scale, a Byzantine scale, an old church scale used in Scottish folk songs, and a scale used in Hungarian Gypsy music.[42]

Folk Songs of Many Nations was not the only folk song collection available to music educators. Like Elson's, many of the collections, such as Bantock's *One Hundred Folksongs of All Nations*,[43] and Brown and Moffat's *Characteristic Songs and Dances of All Nations*,[44] harmonized the songs and arranged them for the piano, though not in deliberate disregard for the original accompaniment, or lack of it.[45] The chief aim of these collections was to increase the popularity of songs from a wide range of cultures, and to allow the average amateur musician to play them at home. Though primarily European song collections, these books often included a few songs from the Americas, Africa, Asia, Europe, the Middle East, and Oceania, and presented them with accurate melodic transcriptions.[46]

While it is doubtful music educators ever used these songs in class, it is possible they may have owned these volumes. If so, they were, however slowly, being made aware of a musical world beyond the classical European tradition.

MTNA, MSNC, and NEA Conferences

The most prominent music education organizations during this period were the Music Teachers National Association (MTNA), the Music Supervisors National Conference (MSNC), and the Music Department of the National Education Association (NEA). It was not uncommon for music educators to hold dual memberships, and the most active music educators in the public schools attended all three meetings regularly.[47] As a result of these overlapping memberships, music educators received a broad exposure to what was being said about the musics of various cultures, especially as they began to perceive these musics as relating to the school music curriculum. At MTNA meetings they had the opportunity to hear lecture/demonstrations of Creole, Swedish, and Jewish folk music, as well as Percy Scholes's address describing British music education in which he first broached the idea of an international conference for music educators.[48] At MSNC conventions there were folk dance exhibitions given by school children, concerts of African-American spirituals, and lecture/performances on Philippine and Native American musics.[49] Those attending the NEA meetings heard lectures on the value of folk song in education, and the need for a standardized collection of national (American) songs.[50]

In addition, music educators also became aware of a wider world of music through the reports of the North American Section of the Internationale Musikgesellschaft (International Music Society or IMS), which was founded at the 1906 MTNA meeting in Oberlin. Although there was only a small number of original members, those who could participate in the European conferences sponsored by the IMS made regular reports to the MTNA membership, since at that time the North American Section (after 1914 called the United States Section) met in conjunction with the MTNA.[51]

During these early years, most of the interest focused on the folk songs of European countries. However, the topics presented at these meetings began to give music educators an awareness of other musics in the world around them and, though limited in number, set a precedent for future sessions and lecture/demonstrations highlighting a variety of musics.[52]

Folk Songs in the School Music Texts

At the turn of the century, music texts still relied heavily on the German folk and classical traditions. There were only a few folk songs from the British Isles and still fewer from other European countries. English and French folk songs began to be included in the music series texts around 1916. Both the *Progressive Music Series* (New York: Silver Burdett and Co., 1916) and the *Hollis Dann Music Course* (New York: American Book Co., 1916–1917) had high percentages of songs from the British Isles and France. From 1916 to 1924, English, French, and German folk songs were widely represented in the music texts, to the near exclusion of any other culture.[53] Possibly the publishers included the English and French songs partly as a result of the rising anti-German feeling that developed during and shortly after World War I.[54] Robert Foresman's collection, *Book of Songs* (New York: American Book Co., 1925–1928), was the first music textbook to acknowledge all Western European folk musics for classroom use.[55] Over two hundred songs throughout the series represented more than twenty Northern and Central European cultures. This series also contained a small percentage of songs from Eastern and Southern European cultures, America, Japan, Hawaii, and the Caribbean Islands.[56] There is a similar increase in the number of European folk songs in *The Music Hour* (New York: Silver Burdett and Co., 1927–1930).[57]

Patriotic and Folk Musics for Americanization

Like the general educators who saw ethnic studies as a means of teaching both Americanization and the subject material of their disciplines, music educators saw the same dual purposes in teaching folk songs: Americanization and music instruction. The belief was that "We, the melting-pot nation, can amalgamate all these diverse peoples more quickly through music than in any other way,"[58] and folk songs became the means of "melting the nationalities."[59] Immigrant children would feel "at home" when they recognized their own folk melodies, and singing the songs in English translation, or with substituted English texts, would help them learn the language.[60] Although some people believed that the translations needed to be done carefully, others were concerned that the texts might prove improper for children to sing in school.[61] For the most part, however, the text remained of secondary importance. Music educators still selected songs because they considered the tune a beautiful melody.[62]

School folk festivals and pageants were especially good for presenting lessons in Americanization. Many such festivals carried a patriotic theme that often allowed for the inclusion of several folk songs and dances, and always featured the entire cast singing a patriotic song for the finale (see Figure 3.2).

In addition to acknowledging the Americanization work done in the public school music classes, much literature of the time also praised the contributions of municipal performing groups to the Americanization of the European immigrants.[63] This fact, in addition to the patriotic fervor generated by World War I, led music educators to incorporate the teaching of a body of American songs (national, patriotic, and folk) in all the schools for eventual community use. Music educators, and especially Peter Dykema, editor of the *Music Supervisors Journal*, worked to develop a list of such songs. The original publication presented to music educators in 1914 was a pamphlet containing eighteen songs; *55 Songs* was introduced for school and community singing just as the United States entered the war.[64] In keeping with its purpose as a basic repertoire for all Americans, the songs which were selected for both the original pamphlet and *55 Songs* were all considered American songs, though many of them were actually European folk songs which had already been assimilated into American musical life.[65] It is these songs that became the backbone of the community singing movement.

Folk Songs and Dances in Curriculum Correlation

Music educators had long been advocates of intersubject correlation, though the practice was slow to develop in general education. As early as 1905, Elizabeth Casterton proposed that the Music Department of the NEA form a committee to formulate a course of study in which music and all subject areas were correlated as closely as possible for every grade level,[66] but it was not until the 1920s that folk musics began to be correlated with other subject areas across the school curriculum.[67] Geography was a favorite subject to correlate with music because, as Anne Faulkner said,

> The folk music of every land reflects so decidedly the characteristics of the people, their customs and habit, that it would seem to be a natural sequence that this music should be sung and danced and studied during the period when one is learning of the natural boundaries and national characteristics of certain peoples.[68]

"Music Unites the People"

American Patriotism

THE NEED OF THE HOUR

"The question of Americanization has been made acute on account of the war in Europe. Americanization is the problem of education. Natives are as sadly in need of Americanization as foreigners . . . . The task before us, as great and as inspiring as that which confronted a Washington or a Hamilton, is to unite into one people the multitude of divergent races that have made their homes here."

—(*From Extension Bulletin, Columbia University.*)

Contest of the Nations

Operetta with dances, Text by Frederick H. Martens, Music by N. Clifford Page, brings 18 different nations together in friendly rivalry of song and dance, in striking contrast to what is going on abroad.

Each nation is shown at its best, to the pride of all.

The history of America is traced through song and dance, and America is triumphant, as the land of Justice, Fellowship and Opportunity.

The work arouses American Patriotism to the highest pitch of enthusiasm—"our souls, our lives we dedicate to Thee, America."

It unites all aliens in the bond and spirit of true Americanism.

In bringing practically the entire world into view, at its spiritual best, it creates enthusiasm for what President Wilson meant when he said that a person to be a good American must be a citizen of the world.

It is a work of far-reaching social and community significance.

THE "CONTEST" is an ENORMOUS POPULAR SUCCESS.

"8,000 people enthusiastically applauded, tramped and shouted through the colorful performance."—The Chautauqua (N. Y.) Daily.

IT IS A WORK OF ART, AND AN HONOR TO AMERICAN COMPOSITION.

"done with mastery, in a way that few men writing music in America today can hope to rival."—A Walter Kramer, Composer and Critic.

List price, $1.00; time an hour and half.

Copy sent on approval

C. C. BIRCHARD & COMPANY, BOSTON, MASS.
Leading Publishers of School and Community Music

Figure 3.2 Advertisement for "Contest of the Nations," C. C. Birchard Co., *Music Supervisors Journal* 2, No.3 (1916), 9. Copyright by Summy.Birchard Music, A Division of Summy.Birchard Inc. Used by permission.

Even more than Faulkner, Frances Elliott Clark stressed the fact that folk musics were a reflection of their contexts, which is perhaps why she advocated correlation so strongly.[69] Unfortunately, the contextual information provided in the music series books was often limited, sometimes only indicating the country of origin, and the most that could be offered was whatever independent research the music teacher did in preparation for the lesson. While folk musics were acknowledged as musical expressions of the people, national characteristics were often stereotyped, for example, the happy, sunny music of Italy, or the melancholy music of Russia.

Music educators frequently correlated music with other subject areas within the music class, and classroom teachers sometimes reinforced these lessons, especially in the laboratory schools.[70] In the public schools, this intersubject cooperation was most noticeable in the production of pageants, festivals, or operettas, which provided opportunities for lessons in history, literature, dramatization, homemaking, and manual and fine arts. In preparation for the production, students often sewed their own costumes, learned about different foods, wrote the dialogue, and sometimes composed songs. Because of the new interest in other parts of the world following World War I, these school productions often had settings in China, Arabia, or other countries equally "exotic" in the eyes of Americans.[71]

Folk Dancing in the Music Program

As stated earlier, the Victrola frequently accompanied folk dancing in the schools. In 1910, Luther Gulick, a leader in the physical education movement, asked Frances Elliott Clark to assist in gathering the music for folk dancing.[72] It was this encounter that led Clark to Elizabeth Burchenal, and eventually to extol the RCA Victrola recordings of folk songs and dances for use in the schools. Until these recordings had been produced, music supervisors were

> rather slow to endorse the Folk Dance Movement or to lend material assistance to the physical culture teachers in preparing dances for entertainment and festivals on the ground that the music commonly found for such dances and drills [were] largely of absolutely worthless character.[73]

In recommending the Victor recordings, Clark attested, "The music used is in every case the genuine old folk-music, belonging to the dances brought over by Miss Burchenal." These recordings would help ensure that the music used at festivals and pageants was "genuine, authentic, and cultural."[74] In an age where there was concern that children learn beautiful songs and dances (music educators of the time considered the currently popular modes of each as "bad music" and "unspeakable modern dance"), the folk song and folk dance were considered "a simple original joyous expression" that was "safe, sane, and beautiful" for children.[75]

Folk dancing was not confined to the school stage for pageants or theatricals or to the gymnasium for the physical education program. There was a "dual need of music for folk dancing and folk dancing for the rhythmic work in music," and it soon became a mainstay of the music classroom. Folk dancing provided movement exercise and rhythmic experiences as well as ethnic representation. Clark called folk dancing the expression of a people through movement, as the folk song was its expression through melody. Through the folk dance, the history, occupations, and traditions of each culture could be traced. Clark frequently discussed these aspects of both folk dance and song and recommended them for use in music classes.[76] She could see "no reason why our children should not know the music of the world just as well as its history and its literature. . . . They must know the songs [of various countries] . . . to properly understand these people."[77]

In 1911, the National Summer School promoted by Ginn and Company offered an extra week preceding the general session for teaching folk songs, dances, and games,[78] and included these folk dancing classes yearly through 1916.[79] The American Book Company also featured folk dancing in its "New School of Methods in Public School Music."[80] Along with Burchenal's books, many other publications that included folk dances and games became available.[81] The popularity of folk dancing is evident from student dance exhibitions at public folk festivals and music supervisors' annual conference meetings.[82] Many of the dances performed by the children can be found in Burchenal's publications.

Cooperation with the new physical education programs and the entry of folk dancing into the music curriculum must have been exciting for the music educators of that time. Forty years later, Clark recalled "the teaching and dancing of the folk music of all nations" along with "the discovery of recorded music in education" as a high point of the first decade (1907–1917) of the MSNC.[83]

Folk Musics: A New Subject in Music Appreciation Classes

Along with folk dances, Victor recordings also carried the songs and instrumental compositions of a variety of cultures. The most often used text to accompany these educational recordings, especially in the music appreciation class, was Anne Faulkner's *What We Hear in Music*, which contained an entire series of chapters on national characteristics in music.[84] Each edition progressed through many countries individually, describing the history, music, and musical instruments of each. The first and second editions listed only Western European countries and America. These editions included many European folk songs and dances as illustrative examples. Native American and African-American musics were mentioned primarily as sources for composed songs. For example, Faulkner suggested Charles Cadman's "From the Land of Sky-Blue Water" sung by Alma Gluck as an example of Native American music. In the fifth edition (1924), Faulkner added a chapter on Oriental musics (China, Japan, India, Arabia/Egypt), and in the sixth edition (1928), she included short chapters on the influences of geography and political conditions on folk music, national characteristics found in folk music, and the music of the Balkan states. (No mention was made in any of these editions of the musics of Africa or Latin America.) Faulkner included the titles of the RCA Victor recordings that exemplified the music discussed with each chapter and an index of descriptive annotations for all these recordings.

As more recordings became available, each edition carried a greater variety of musical examples, and what appears to be more authentic examples. The 1928 edition included recordings of African-American spirituals, an Arabic *oud* (lute) solo, a Chinese orchestra, a Hungarian gypsy orchestra, a Japanese song with samisen (lute) accompaniment, Native American chants (Hopi and Penobscot), a Serbian *tamburitza* (string) orchestra, and Swedish folk songs.[85] However, the later editions still contained arrangements of folk songs, or compositions based on folk materials, probably not unusual given the state of research into the musics of various cultures at the time.

The Introduction of Native American Songs and African-American Spirituals

During this period, music educators viewed Native American and African-American musics, like folk musics in general, as stages in the development of classical or art music. The literature often cited Native American songs as examples of the "primitive musics" at the lower end of musical development, with African-American spirituals seen as a more intermediate step on the way to becoming art songs.[86]

Early ethnomusicologists, especially Alice Fletcher, Francis La Flesche, and Frances Densmore, had been recording the musics of Native Americans since the turn of the century.[87] As a result of their research, a limited number of Native American songs, and songs composed in the Native American style, found their way into music classes where they were taught originally for their historical value. School pageants portraying the chronological development of music in America typically began with the "primitive" songs of the Native Americans, and progressed through Revolutionary and Civil War songs to the songs of the Western settlers and newly landed European immigrants.[88]

Though authentic, those few Native American songs which were selected for use in the schools were not usually representative of the most characteristic songs of the culture.[89] This is probably because the compilers of school music texts would have chosen music whose melody was appealing to the European, Western-trained ear, and therefore seemed more like folk songs to them. Those Native American songs that exhibited unfamiliar characteristics, (for example, wide vocal range, descending terraced melodic line, and vocal ornamentation) would have been omitted entirely.

Like Native American musics, African-American musics received slight attention in the schools. Before 1906 there were no African-American musics included in the school music texts, and those few songs that were published often carried the label "slave" or "old Southern" songs,[90] and represented only a small proportion of the total number of songs in the music texts. There is evidence, however, that African-American musics were being taught in the "colored" schools within the segregated public school system,[91] and eventually this provided the impetus to include African-American folk songs in the overall music curriculum.

The MENC first introduced African-American spirituals at its annual meeting in 1918 (Evansville, Indiana). Bringing this music to the attention of music educators was one of the purposes of this national meeting.[92] The convention's opening concert featured performances of spirituals given by

African-American school children and community groups and received so many ovations that they were forced into encores.[93]

Four years later, music educators had the opportunity to hear a performance of spirituals by the Fisk Jubilee Singers, the long-established African-American chorus from Fisk University, at the MSNC meeting in Nashville, Tennessee. These two concerts must have been impressive. Twenty years later, Frances Elliott Clark still vividly recalled "the presentation of real spirituals" at those conferences.[94]

Following these concerts, greater numbers of African-American folk songs, predominantly spirituals, were included in the school texts beginning with Foresman's *Book of Songs* (1925) and *The Music Hour* (1928).[95] However, many inaccuracies abound in the published versions of these songs. Publishers frequently reduced syncopation to simpler rhythms, added a four-part harmonic accompaniment for the piano, and changed the African-American dialect of the text to standard English.[96] While an affront to the authenticity of the music, this practice was in keeping with the policy of the time that no foreign languages or dialects be spoken in the public schools.

Though African-American spirituals found acceptance in the school music curriculum, another form of African-American music was not so easily welcomed either in the schools or in polite society. From 1900 to 1928, African-American popular music styles developed from ragtime to jazz. Variously considered vulgar, cheap, immoral, or evil,[97] it is not surprising that jazz was forbidden in the music curriculum. Nonetheless, there were some who believed jazz had musical value. Carl Engel, chief of the Music Division of the Library of Congress, told music educators attending the 1922 MSNC convention in Nashville, "Good jazz is a composite, the happy union of seemingly incompatible elements. Good jazz is the latest phase of American popular music."[98] The fact that he classified jazz as "good" for any reason probably astounded the music educators present. Engel went on to praise the skillful improvisation exhibited by good jazz performers, and he concluded with a plea that jazz be studied and appreciated because of its ability to combine melody, rhythm, harmony, and counterpoint. In effect, he asked music educators to give jazz a chance. It would take fifty years, however, before jazz would be officially admitted to the music curriculum.

"Creative Music," a Multicultural Methodology

In the laboratory schools, model curricula and experimental methodologies were not limited to the traditional academic areas. Art, music, and industrial arts teachers worked cooperatively with the classroom teachers but were also encouraged to develop new programs of their own.[99] In New York City, Satis Coleman developed what became known as "creative music" at the Lincoln School of Teachers College, Columbia University.[100]

Coleman had begun to implement her ideas of how children could creatively make music in 1916 in her private piano studio in Washington, D.C. She often augmented her piano lessons with singing, dancing, and making simple musical instruments.[101] In 1918, she began teaching at the Lincoln School where she was given the opportunity to freely experiment with her ideas.

"Coleman saw spontaneous, creative, improvisatory musical experiences as part of the core of her music programme."[102] Based in developmental psychology and a child-centered curriculum, Coleman's work also reflected the currently accepted idea of musical evolution. In *Creative Music for Children*, Coleman spoke of how she came to develop her methods. "The natural evolution of music shall be my guide in leading the child from the simple to the complex."[103]

Coleman felt it was important for children to perform on instruments they made themselves, beginning with simple drums and then moving progressively from xylophones to keyboards, and from lyres to fiddles. In teaching children through instruments, her premise was the younger the child, the simpler the instrument, and she took patterns for these instruments from both historical sources and various cultures.[104]

When investigating a new instrument, Coleman told her students not only the history of the instrument in its European development, but related folklore and performance practices from around the world. In addition, she took them on field trips to museums to see collections of instruments from many countries. The influence of their research can be seen, for example, in the Native American styles with which they decorated the drums they made for a class assembly about Native Americans (see Figure 3.3).

In their explorations of sound production, Coleman's students studied about, and created homemade versions of, the Chinese *kin* (zither) and *tche* (horizontal flute), the Egyptian *ney* (vertical flute), panpipes, marimbas, and many types of drums. In so doing they had discussions on such diverse topics as the Chinese scale, a Native American rain dance, and the Greek lyre

Figure 3.3 "Creative Music: The fourth-grade pupils made drums and rattles and accompanied the fifth-grade and sixth-grade pupils, who sang an Indian song at an assembly." From James S. Tippett and the Staff of the Elementary Division of the Lincoln School, Teachers College, Columbia University, *Curriculum Making in an Elementary School* (Boston and New York: Ginn and Company, 1927), 327. Copyright 1927 by Silver Burdett Ginn, Inc. Used by permission.

and pipes of Pan.[105] However, the children did not play on the actual native instruments, and all the melodies they created and played on their homemade instruments in Coleman's classes were very much Western.

Bells, The Drum Book, and *The Marimba Book* are all the result of Coleman's work with her students and are illustrative of her techniques.[106] Along with directions for making these instruments, and employing them both in creative and guided lesson situations, all these books have chapters with historical references to the instruments. There are photographs, sketches, and art reproductions of instruments from the Metropolitan Museum's Crosby-Brown collection of musical instruments, the Bureau of Ethnology, and the research of ethnomusicologist Frances Densmore. Myths and legends that accompany the instruments from various cultures are included, as is information about how these instruments were used in their respective societies, for example, African "talking" drums.[107]

Although there is no indication in any of Coleman's books that listening to the sounds of these original instruments was part of this program, it is hard to imagine that this teacher who was so interested in instrumental sounds would not have availed her classes of the popular RCA Victrola recordings of these musics. Coleman was, after all, the full-time music teacher in the Lincoln School, and her duties, like other music teachers of her day, included teaching musical notation, voice placement and control, music appreciation, music composition, and correlation with the classroom teachers' lessons.[108] Seen from the perspective of these more regular music teaching duties, her contribution to research in creativity through musical sound exploration and in broadening the music curriculum to include the study of instruments from around the world is even more unique.

Music: The "Universal Language"

The concept of music as a "universal language" arose along with the new emphasis in education on "international relations" in the years immediately following World War I. While general educators found that lessons in world friendship also fostered better understanding among the various cultures in their own classroom, music educators attested to the power of music in uniting the immigrant populations in their performing groups and began to employ music in correlated lessons to foster world understanding. Music came to be seen as a nonverbal method of communication between populations who often could not understand each other's spoken languages.[109] The fact that many of the European folk music traditions are based in the Western music system, and that many European classical composers found their inspiration in the folk musics of their respective countries made it easier to accept the idea that all people should be able to understand each other's music. This reasoning led to the belief that music could be used to help unify the world by providing a common ground upon which all peoples could meet. That some people came from cultures which did not use the Western music system was apparently not considered, and if it was, it was not deemed important. In Clark's vision, world brotherhood through music would occur as follows:

> When that great convention can sit together—Chinese, Hindu, Japanese, Celt, German, Czech, Italian, Hawaiian, Scandinavian, and Pole—all singing the national songs of each land, the home songs of each people, and listen as one mind and heart to great world music common to all and loved by all, then shall real world goodwill be felt and realized.[110]

SUMMARY

Throughout this period, music educators saw four purposes for implementing folk songs and dances in the curriculum: music instruction, Americanization, correlation with other academic subject areas, and the fostering of world understanding.

Folk dancing was especially popular in the schools prior to World War I, and was employed for movement and rhythmic exercises as well as ethnic representation. Following World War I, music educators fully accepted European folk songs in the curriculum, primarily as song material for their classes. Text was secondary to melody, and the melodies were chosen because they were beautiful and at the same time offered good examples for studying such concepts as melodic contour or intervals. Since the songs were always sung in English, they were also a way to promote Americanization for the first- and second-generation immigrant populations. Given that these European folk songs were all based in the Western music system, and any folk songs outside this system were "Westernized," Western music came to be considered the "universal language" that could help build cooperation and friendship in the world.

In the development of a receptivity toward musics from many cultures, the dissemination of information through the music organizations of the period cannot be discounted. The MTNA, MSNC, and NEA all offered lecture/demonstrations of folk musics at their meetings and, although few in number, these presentations broadened the teachers' knowledge of these musics. For those music educators who could attend all three meetings regularly, they probably had a cumulative effect.

From 1900 to 1928 the school music curriculum gradually moved from the near exclusivity of the German music tradition to the acceptance of songs and dances from many countries in Northern and Central Europe. By 1928, the music curriculum included folk songs from nearly all Northern and Central European cultures, a few African-American and Native American songs, and some songs from Eastern and Southern Europe and East Asian countries. Though these folk songs provided only limited representation of their respective musical cultures, and often contained inaccuracies, the fact remains that their inclusion in the music curriculum was the first step taken toward full acceptance of the musics of many cultures in the schools of what was then a heavily segregated society. It is because of this that the period from 1900 to 1928 might be said to mark the first stirrings of multicultural music education.

Conclusions, Implications, and Questions

Folk dancing, along with its accompanying songs, was the first form of multiculturalism admitted in the music classroom. This methodology has survived in the music curriculum until the present day. Participatory and experiential in nature, folk dancing remains one of the primary avenues of access to another music culture for students. Given its status as the oldest viable multicultural methodology, should pre-service students have experience both learning and teaching folk dances? Would folk dancing fit an undergraduate's schedule best in conjunction with undergraduate physical education requirements? As a component of music education classroom methods classes?

Professional conference presentations can become catalytic experiences for the teachers who attend them. Since its inception in 1907, the MENC has been particularly successful in bringing together music educators to share new methods, techniques, and materials. Music educators gained at least a predisposition to employ African-American spirituals in the classroom from the inclusion of a concert performance of spirituals at the MSNC 1918 and 1922 conventions. Since the latest state-of-the-art materials and methodologies for music education are displayed at professional conferences, it is important for music educators to attend these conferences in order to remain current in the profession. What other benefits could be derived from attendance at such a conference? Should attendance at a local, state, or national music education conference or convention be required, or at least highly recommended, for pre-service teachers? In-service teachers?

The idea of music as a "universal language" is still current, although ethnomusicological research has refuted the statement. The 1996 International Society for Music Education conference even had the phrase as its main theme. Why would this respected organization use this phrase if it is inaccurate? How do you think this phrase is defined today? How does the general public define it?

CHAPTER 4

The International Movement: 1929–1953

Music speaks to the hearts of all.
—MENC RESOLUTIONS, APRIL 2, 1942

Both domestic and international events influenced education during the period from 1929 to 1953: immigration restrictions, the Great Depression, World War II, and the Cold War. Because of these, and encouraged by both federal policy and the desire for world peace, general education and music education continued to develop "international relations in education," a program begun earlier in the 1920s. At the same time, intercultural education taught understanding of the cultures within the United States, and music education began to employ more of the musics from these cultures in the classroom.

HISTORICAL CONTEXT

Immigration and Cultural Pluralism

In 1929, the last of the provisions of the Immigration Act of 1924 went into effect. This Act established a quota system for immigration based on the national origins of persons seeking to enter the United States. The new regulations not only restricted the total number of immigrants to be allowed in, but also established a formula to determine the number of immigrants allowed from any given nationality.[1] Although the ceilings and quotas changed over the years, the restriction based on "national origins" remained until its repeal in 1965.[2]

By the end of the 1920s, many Americans believed that these restrictions would create a more stable society, and those immigrants already in the United States would, given time, assimilate by way of the "melting pot" and become "regular Americans." However, Horace Kallen, who had first voiced the principle of cultural pluralism several years earlier, continued to speak against assimilation and to advocate a society made up of many coexisting cultures.[3] In the 1930s, writer-journalist Louis Adamic added his voice to Kallen's. Adamic believed that all Americans should seek to understand and appreciate the uniqueness of all other Americans.[4] Reflecting on the role of the schools, he said, "The central educational effort should not be toward uniformity and conformity, but toward accepting and welcoming diversity, variety, and differences."[5]

The Depression, the Works Progress Administration, and the Federal Music Project

The Depression that began in 1929 was a terrific shock to the national psyche. In an effort to reaffirm themselves, Americans cultivated and displayed their national identity and common culture throughout the 1930s. This was the era of the novels *Gone with the Wind* and *Grapes of Wrath*, radio broadcasts of *Superman* and *Dick Tracy*, lavish movie musicals, *The Beer Barrel Polka*, and big bands.

As the Depression deepened in America, President Franklin D. Roosevelt sought to provide employment relief through the establishment of many programs, one of which was the Works Progress Administration (WPA). The WPA provided employment in many areas, including the arts. Federal Project One was the name given to the WPA program for assistance for artists, writers, dramatists, and musicians. Within Federal Project One, the Federal Music Project (FMP) provided funds for music teachers, concert performers, composers, copyists, research studies, and both urban and rural folk festivals.[6] In addition, although limited in focus, some ethnic performing groups were also funded by the FMP and selected to perform in the schools.[7] As a result of many of the efforts of the FMP, by the late 1930s, Americans were learning to appreciate their own folk musics.

Foreign Affairs: The "Good Neighbor" Policy

At his inauguration in 1933, President Roosevelt established a policy of the "good neighbor" in foreign affairs.[8] This was a dramatic change of policy from those of military intervention and "dollar diplomacy" of preceeding administrations. Though intended to encompass all the republics of the Americas, the Good Neighbor Policy was directed most particularly toward the countries of Central and South America, and the Caribbean. These countries were often grouped in the all-inclusive term Latin America.

By 1936, the government was aware of the political changes in Germany and Italy, and the fact that these countries were exporting their culture, particularly to South America. It became imperative that the United States also have a cultural policy.[9] In 1938, Roosevelt created the Division of Cultural Relations within the Department of State.[10] The primary purpose of this unit was to administer the travel grants necessary for teacher/student exchanges, to provide means and methods for cultural exchange between the United States and Latin American countries, and to encourage understanding between these nations.[11] Education and the arts were considered the best means of cultural exchange. Many educators and artists from Latin America came to the United States at the invitation of the State Department, and many persons and organizations from the United States (including music educators) went on exchanges and goodwill tours to South America before World War II cut severely into these plans.[12]

The Postwar Period

With the end of World War II, there was a general sense of relief in American society, and an intention of keeping peace in the world. Congress ratified United States membership in the United Nations (UN) in 1945, and the next year agreed to full participation in the United Nations Educational, Scientific and Cultural Organization (UNESCO). In addition, the United States continued its support of international exchanges for scholars with the passage of the Fulbright Act in 1946 and the Smith-Mundt Act of 1948.[13]

Unfortunately, after the cessation of hostilities, the nations that had fought together against the Axis powers found themselves disagreeing about the future of Europe and Asia. In the Cold War that developed, Americans saw communism as the enemy and became obsessed with its evils. The Berlin Blockade (1948), the Chinese Revolution (1949), the start of the nuclear arms race (1949), and the Korean conflict (1950–1951) all escalated the situation.

The world grew smaller throughout World War II. Both the media and returning servicemen and -women brought information about foreign countries and a broader worldview into the homes of America. Now, through intense media coverage, the Cold War made Americans more conscious of international interaction with other cultures.

This period also set the stage for the future civil rights movement. Although African-Americans had been seeking equal rights for years, the postwar period formed the conditions that would direct actions against racial segregation and discrimination. With the fight against communism, there was a growing interest in racial justice as Americans began to fear that their stance for world democracy would be tarnished by the unequal treatment afforded some of its citizens.

Even with the Cold War and the beginnings of civil unrest, the United States experienced postwar prosperity. With employment high and inflation low, this period of prosperity encouraged the educational climate. Continued government spending made public funds available for veterans' benefits, especially for education under the GI Bill. As the standard of living rose for the majority of the population, the national birth rate began to increase, and money was allocated for highways, housing, and schools.

EDUCATIONAL CONTEXT

International Relations and Intercultural Studies

Two instructional programs established in American general education after World War I, international relations and intercultural education, continued to grow during this period. The first, international relations in education, was prominent during the late 1920s and throughout the 1930s, and focused on world peace and understanding. Lessons centered on the League of Nations, international friendship, and the contributions of all countries to the world community.[14]

Similar to this program, but developing out of the Good Neighbor Policy, was the increased attention to Latin America in the school curriculum. Schools participated in "fiesta" days and in Junior Red Cross projects with Latin American countries.[15] There was a need for more and better materials on Latin America, and for teacher training to include a greater background in Latin American studies.[16]

The second program, intercultural education, focused on the need for understanding among the cultures found within the United States, especially those of the second-generation immigrants in the schools. In order to give these students a sense of pride in their heritage, and to enable the rest of the school population to better appreciate the cultures of the immigrant students, school programs began to emphasize the many contributions of these various cultures to the United States. The Service Bureau of Intercultural Education, partially funded by the WPA, was among the first organizations dedicated to developing materials to help teach this concept through school assembly programs and pamphlets.[17]

International/intercultural education was implemented in many schools during the 1930s. Music and folk dancing were often part of intercultural education programs; in particular, school pageants were very popular.[18] All subject areas, including the arts, were supposed to teach for intercultural understanding.[19]

The philosophy of cultural pluralism espoused by Horace Kallen and Louis Adamic is reflected in the intercultural education movement. However, since Kallen and Adamic did not discuss the Americanization of Hispanics, African-Americans, Asian-Americans, or Native Americans, the Service Bureau addressed the contributions of these minorities to some extent in its programs. The Pan American Union, China Institute, Japan Society, and Friendship Press also provided the schools with materials for intercultural education.[20]

At the end of World War II, the theme of world peace through education was reiterated.[21] Education was expected to build a *new* world, a changed society. This society would value world citizenship, cooperation, and interdependence among nations. The phrase "intercultural education" began to mean education for understanding between the United States and world cultures as well as among the cultures within the United States.

MUSIC EDUCATION

International Conferences

Reflecting the trends in general education, music education also followed the theme of "international relations." In 1928, Percy Scholes, a British music educator, visited the United States and was a guest at the MENC biennial convention in Chicago. No stranger to the United States, Scholes had first voiced his wish in 1914 for a working relationship between music educators in England and the United States.[22] This time, he was able to make that wish come true. Through his efforts and the cooperation of the MENC, a one-day "Field Day for Music Educationists British and American" was held in London in 1928, and that meeting fostered a resolution to establish an Anglo-American Conference.[23]

In 1929, and again in 1931, music educators from the English-speaking world met in the First and Second Anglo-American Conferences for Music Educators, both times in Lausanne, Switzerland.[24] The internationalism that began with these two conferences was cut short by the economic strain of the Depression. However, music educators tried again, and the First International Congress in Music Education (ICME) was held in Prague, Czechoslovakia, in 1936. At this conference several sessions featured folk musics. One reason these sessions were included in the program was the fact that composers such as Béla Bartók, Zoltán Kodály, and Anton Dvořák were incorporating folk music in their compositions. This factor, and the resulting folk music sessions at the Congress provided encouragement for the inclusion of folk music in the music education curriculum.[25]

Although these international conferences were curtailed by the changing political climate in Europe, perhaps their greatest contribution to music education is the fact that they provided opportunities for music educators from different countries to meet, to become open to people from other places, and eventually to become curious about their musics. They not only encouraged an international view of music education for the educators who attended, they also firmly established internationalism in music education, and after 1936 especially, actually began to influence the addition of more folk music in the curriculum.

Folk Songs in School Music Texts

In the late 1920s and early 1930s, the folk musics in the school curriculum focused primarily on songs from Northern and Western Europe. However, with folk and ethnic musics encouraged by the American social climate and the ICME in Prague, by the mid-1930s folk musics from Eastern European countries began to be included in the school music curriculum and published in music textbooks. In *The World of Music* (Boston: Ginn and Co., 1936), nearly a quarter of the songs at each grade level are of Eastern European origin, though none appear with the foreign language text.[26]

Throughout the 1930s, school music texts generally ignored the folk musics of the Americas, North and South.[27] The musics of African, Asian, and Middle Eastern cultures were also unrepresented for the most part. Nonetheless, it is important to note that, although few in number, these musics were gradually being included in the music series texts. Most of these songs were found in *The American Singer*, *New Music Horizons*, *Singing School*, and *The World of Music*.[28]

Folk Songs in Curriculum Correlation

The "correlated curriculum" was a major emphasis in the writings on music education throughout the 1930s and 1940s. Folk songs and dances of many European cultures were part of the music class and integrated with units in history, geography, literature, and even nature study.[29] Folk dancing was often coordinated with physical education.[30]

In their texts for teacher training, Karl Gehrkins, Lilla Belle Pitts, Will Earhart, and Peter Dykema all recommended the use of folk songs as means to learn more about the people and history of a country. According to Gehrkins, folk songs frequently gave "a true picture of the civilization that existed in various countries at different times."[31] Dykema concurred with Gehrkins, saying that folk music was "illuminating regarding the people and country of its origin."[32]

Lilla Belle Pitts echoed Dykema's writings in her work with junior high school students. Pitts was among the first to utilize the concept of a "unit of study" in the junior high, each unit focusing on the music of one particular area of the world or historical period. She included both listening and reading lists in her suggestions for materials, although she often gave Western classical compositions as examples of musics from non-Western cultures.[33] Hardly authentic by today's standards, the use of Western compositions as examples of ethnic music was probably the best way known then to teach both national characteristics through folk music and the "quality music" required in the school curriculum. To Pitts's credit, some of her listening recommendations appear to be more authentic. Among the Victor recordings she listed were "War Dance" (Cheyenne Indian), selections by a Chinese orchestra, and "Ala Kefak" (Arabic native song).[34]

Folk songs of good quality were considered essential material in the music textbooks of the period. Gehrkins and James L. Mursell both emphasized the need for teachers to closely scrutinize the folk song element when selecting a music text for use in the classroom.[35] However, in examining the folk songs in the school music texts of the times, it is evident that even in the "quality" songs authenticity often suffered. Songs were sung in English rather than the native language, translations were often poor, and in many cases, entirely new words were put to the melody. This was often owing to the fact that the text of the songs in music class had to reflect "proper" sentiments and high ideals.[36]

While the text had to be appropriate for students to sing, it was often subordinate to the melody itself. Accurate translations were simply not considered an important point when compared to the didactic functions of the music, for example, teaching intervals or rhythmic patterns.[37] Besides this, stylistic changes for didactic purposes were common. Transcriptions often adjusted rhythms, provided folk songs with piano accompaniments whether appropriate or not, and often set songs in choral arrangements, even if the original was a unison song. As Domingo Santa Cruz, a Chilean music educator, said about the authenticity of the Chilean music he saw in a music textbook in the United States,

> I looked for some Chilean songs and found four so labeled. One was not Chilean at all, and two of the others represented dance forms of Chile but were written and harmonized as four-voice part songs in the very serious form of a Protestant chorale. Of these four songs, there was only one that retained the original Chilean character and flavor.[38]

His assessment of authenticity is also accurate for the musics of other cultures represented in the music texts of the period.[39]

American Unity Through Music

With folk and ethnic musics encouraged by the WPA and the ICME (1936), it is not surprising that in 1941, the MENC announced a new policy: "American Unity Through Music." This was a two-part program: Part One was based on American folk music and titled "American Songs for American Children"; Part Two, titled "Music to Unify the Americas," was international in scope and reflective of the Good Neighbor Policy, as it focused on the musics of Latin America. Though publicized in the *Music Educators Journal* (*MEJ*) since 1941, it was the 1942 MENC biennial conference in Milwaukee which officially presented "American Unity Through Music" and showed its possibilities to music educators.[40]

American Songs for American Children

The MENC and the Library of Congress jointly presented "American Songs for American Children." Alan Lomax researched the ten songs published in a brochure and given to each participant at the conference; Charles Seeger wrote the Foreword. The conference offered lectures and demonstrations of folk singing, and concluded with a sing-along of American folk songs, with "So Long, It's Been Good to Know You" as the finale.[41]

After the conference, the MENC quickly established a Committee on Folk Song. This committee published American folk songs in the *MEJ* along with lesson plans for teaching each song and suggestions for ways to implement it with integrated units.[42] In their first article, the committee said, "Because folk music, like folk tradition generally, is part of the world stream, there is no conflict between being 'at home' with our own music and giving a home to the music of the rest of the world."[43]

As a result of all this attention, school music texts were quick to incorporate American folk musics. Songs originating in the United States were included in the music texts throughout the 1940s. *The American Singer* (New York: American Book Company, 1944–1947) series in particular had a high concentration of American folk songs.[44] This series also included African-American and Native American songs, although they comprised only a small percentage of the songs representing the United States.[45]

Music to Unify the Americas

In 1939, the U.S. State Department Division of Cultural Affairs sponsored a conference on Inter-American Relations in Music. Topics ranged from lectures on the importance of folk and popular musics, to teacher and student exchanges, to radio programs.[46] Following this conference, Charles Seeger, now the Chief of the Division of Music of the Pan American Union (PAU), saw the role music education could play in inter-American relations, and asked for the support of the MENC.[47] In the summer of 1941, as part of the teacher exchange program overseen by the Division of Cultural Affairs, and under the sponsorship of the PAU, two prominent music educators, John Beattie and Louis Woodson Curtis, were sent on a fourteen-week goodwill tour of Central and South America.[48]

Beattie and Curtis's trip centered on the need to establish an exchange of ideas about music education with the seven Latin American countries they visited, and the potential incorporation of Latin American musics in the schools of the United States.[49] The *MEJ* published the itinerary and travelogue of their experiences in five successive issues throughout 1941 and 1942 and also translated and distributed these articles throughout Latin America.[50]

By 1942, the State Department's Division of Cultural Relations and the PAU invited nine Latin American musicians and music educators to the United States. The government planned their travel throughout the United States, and various universities and institutions hosted their stay. The MENC not only invited them to attend the 1942 biennial conference in Milwaukee (see Figure 4.1), but arranged for them to participate in the program.[51]

The 1942 conference resulted in several resolutions adopted by the MENC. Among them, recommendation 7 read in part:

> The presence at this Conference of musical representatives of several Central and South American countries has been, for us of the north, an agree-

Figure 4.1 Educators from Central and South America with other guests and members of the MENC at the MENC biennial conference, Milwaukee, 1942. From "Official Report of the 1942 Biennial Convention," *Music Educators Journal* 28, No.6 (1942). Copyright 1942, Music Educators National Conference. Used by permission.

able and stimulating experience. Such interchange of musical leaders attending National Conferences should be encouraged. We adhere firmly to the conviction that through exchange of music and other forms of art expression, individuals and nations have a friendly, helpful approach which can surmount difficulties caused by differences in language or custom. Music speaks to the hearts of all men.[52]

Following the conference, Antonio Sá Pereira, Director of the National School of Music, University of Brazil, Rio de Janiero, and Domingo Santa Cruz were appointed editorial associates of the *MEJ*.[53] Guests from Latin America and Canada became frequent visitors at MENC conferences throughout the 1940s. In addition, every conference featured sessions on intercultural relations, and included times for the Latin American guests to meet with each other.[54]

Many of these educators from South America began to write articles for the *MEJ* telling how music was taught in their countries.[55] These articles were among the first published in the *MEJ* on comparative music education.[56] As music educators began to perceive a wider perspective of music education in the world, the *MEJ* also carried articles on music education in the U.S.S.R., China, and Sweden.[57] However, it was not until the 1950s that articles began to appear explaining the music of various cultures to music educators in the United States.[58]

In 1944 the MENC "loaned" Vanett Lawler to the PAU's Music Division. The PAU sent her on a trip to South and Central America for the purpose of laying "the organizational groundwork for international cooperation in the field of education."[59] The *MEJ* published several articles describing her trip to fourteen Latin American republics.[60]

All this interest in Latin American music made it necessary to provide materials for music educators to teach these musics. There was an urgent demand for Latin American music materials from schools and colleges, and numerous requests for authentic recordings and resources for native instruments, folk dances, festivals, and dramas.[61] The Library of Congress and the PAU quickly assembled and disseminated sources for available materials. The PAU provided lists of recordings of Latin American songs and dances.[62] The Library of Congress produced a *Bibliography of Latin American Folk Music*[63] and worked with the PAU to prepare a list of Latin American music obtainable in the United States. This list included not only music for use in the general music classroom, but also chorus, band, orchestra, and small ensemble arrangements.[64] A cooperative editorial project between the PAU, MENC, and U.S. publishers resulted in the publication of more than 150 music selections for school use.[65] Publishers produced books containing songs from many Latin American countries.[66] Of equal importance is the fact that the MENC notified teachers of these sources as soon as they were published through letters,[67] book reviews, and advertisements in the *MEJ*,[68] and also disseminated information through the MENC Committee on Music Education in Intercultural Relations.[69] School music textbooks began to include increasing numbers of Latin American folk songs (see Figure 4.2).[70]

Figure 4.2 Fifth and sixth graders performing an Argentine Handkerchief Dance. From James L. Mursell, *Music in American Schools* (New York: Silver Burdett Company, 1943). Copyright 1943 by Silver Burdett Ginn, Simon and Schuster Elementary. Used by permission of publisher.

Pillsbury Foundation Studies

Musical creativity was another of the new avenues explored by interested music educators. From 1937 to 1951, the Pillsbury Foundation Studies, under the direction of Gladys Moorhead and Donald Pond, focused on the way children learn music.[71] They observed the creative performances (song, dance, and instrumental improvisation) of young children (aged $1\frac{1}{2}$ to $8\frac{1}{2}$ years) at the Pillsbury Foundation School in Santa Barbara, California. The unique environment Pond prepared allowed the children to encounter music and showed the effects of a growing world view in music. He supplied the children with a wide variety of instruments from around the world on which to improvise. Henry Eichhelm, a California composer/conductor, generously loaned part of his private collection of instruments to the school, including a Balinese *saron* (metallophone), Chinese drums, Indian *tabla* (drums), Burmese gongs, maracas, Japanese wood blocks, and Tibetan bells (see Figure 4.3). Pond and Moorhead provided these instruments because they believed that the way children perceive the world of music is simply too vast to be limited by the preconceived notions of one cultural system.[72] The researchers found that the child's

> primary interest is in *sounds* as things in themselves. . . . The child should hear much music, interesting in tone color, short and rhythmically dynamic, played by many kinds of instruments. . . . He should hear not only the instrumental and vocal music of our culture, and especially our folk-music, but also that of the Balinese, Javanese, Siamese, Chinese and Japanese peoples, and the instrumental music and songs and chants of primitive races.[73]

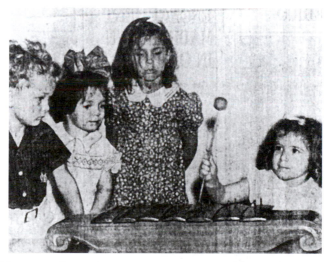

Figure 4.3 Young students playing a Balinese *saron* at the Pillsbury Foundation School, 1937. Photograph courtesy of the *Santa Barbara News Press*.

They also believed that if given a broad experience of sound and sound possibilities beyond one cultural music system, children would "be able to appreciate the music of other cultures," be open to contemporary music, and
maintain their own musical creativity.[74]

When introducing the children to a new instrument, Pond showed them
how to handle the instrument carefully, and how it was played. He also told
them its history and how it was used in the culture from which it came. The
students were then given free access to investigate the instrument as they
chose.[75] In this sense, the Pillsbury Foundation Studies follow upon Satis
Colman's work with creativity in music.

The students of the Pillsbury school not only had instruments on which
to play, but also recordings of musics from around the world both for listening and movement. There was a large record library from which to draw including music "from plainsong to Hindemith and the folk music of 28 different countries."[76] It was not unusual for the children to hear an Egyptian 'oud
(lute) one day, Chinese theater music another, and *Peter and the Wolf* on a third.

Music for World Peace

With World War II nearing its end, and the pending ratification of United
States membership in the United Nations, American music educators experienced an increase in world-mindedness. Following the trend to incorporate
intercultural education in all subject areas, the music education curriculum
could now include the musics of "all peoples and nations" along with a "properly balanced proportion of American music for American children, in order
to bring about understanding of other nations and accord with other peoples."[77] The MENC began to consider extending its contacts through the Division of Cultural Relations beyond Latin America to other countries in the
world, especially China and what was then the country of Russia.[78]

The seeds of multiculturalism that were planted in the peace movement
following World War I grew in the era following World War II. As early as
1943, Henry and Sidney Cowell predicted that

> when our soldiers return, they will have heard a great deal of music hith-
> erto unknown to most people in this country. . . . We find that we have been
> trying to live in a far too narrow a musical world. . . . If we can steep our-
> selves as educators in the richness of multi-cultural experience, the effort in
> seeking out the music of many peoples will reward us many times over.[79]

According to David McAllester, this is indeed what happened when the service personnel returned. He explained it as "the growing up of America in
World War II. The fact [was] that we had people all over the world [in the
armed forces], and some of the ones who were musical came back wonder-
ing about the people they had met."[80] The returnee's curiosity about the musics of other peoples also led to an increase in courses in ethnomusicology,
and eventually to application in music education.[81]

MENC was quick to urge Congress to ratify the participation of the
United States in UNESCO. In the MENC Declaration of Faith, Hope and

Action adopted at the MENC 1946 conference in Cleveland, Resolution 10 reads:

> Music is the universal language and should be utilized at its highest potential power to help win and sustain world-wide peace.
>
> We, the members of the Music Educators National Conference, therefore, urge the adoption of the bill now pending before Congress authorizing the cooperation of the United States in the United Nations Educational, Scientific and Cultural Organization.
>
> We further urge that our Executive Committee . . . use their every effort to see that music is adequately represented on the proposed commission and the proposed committee to be appointed by the Secretary of State.[82]

An offer of assistance to UNESCO quickly followed.[83]

The International Society for Music Education

In 1949, UNESCO approved the foundation of the International Music Council (IMC) "dedicated to the ideal of fostering understanding between nations through music."[84] One of the objectives of the council was to "encourage the inclusion of all forms of music in general education and promote the exchange of views upon the various methods of musical instruction."[85] Within a year, the IMC and UNESCO set up a commission to discuss the possibility and practical aspects of a proposed International Conference on Music Education. As the logistics became clear, the date of the conference was set for June 29 through July 1, 1953, in Brussels, Belgium. In the spring of 1953, in anticipation of this event, Vanett Lawler and Walter Arnold, members of the Conference Preparatory Commission of UNESCO, presented addresses on the coming International Conference at the MENC Eastern Division conference.[86]

At the International Conference that June, several speakers focused on music and international understanding, or folk music in the schools. The insularity of the existing music curriculum came under criticism; folk music was acknowledged both as a musical genre in its own right and as a "social binding force on the international level."[87] At the end of this First International Conference in Music Education, Charles Seeger presented a resolution recommending the foundation of a permanent International Society for Music Education (ISME).[88] The participants enthusiastically accepted this resolution. There was finally an international organization for music education, as had been envisioned in the conferences of the 1930s.

SUMMARY

Throughout the period from 1929 to 1953, there was a gradual increase in the numbers of musics taught in the American school curriculum. By the mid-1930s, songs from Eastern European countries were added to the musics from Northern and Western European countries already in the curriculum. The inclusion of these songs in the music texts was probably due to a combination of factors, among them social recreational preferences, the intercultural education movement, and the emphasis on folk musics at the First International Congress in Music Education. In addition, leaders in the MENC, such as Dykema, Pitts, Earhart, and Gerhkins, stressed the inclusion of folks songs and dances in the music curriculum in their teacher training texts.

Aided by the Good Neighbor Policy, and the fact that World War II curtailed communication and travel to the east and west, Latin American studies developed in general education during the 1940s. Reflective of this, the musics of Latin America began to be emphasized in the schools, with a resultant increase in these musics found in the school music texts of the period. The MENC program, American Unity Through Music, played a major role in this change in the music curriculum, from documenting Curtis, Beattie, and Lawler's trips to South America to hosting international contacts at conferences. The MENC kept members fully apprised of its activities in international relations, cooperated with the publishing and disseminating of authentic materials for classroom use, and provided resource lists to encourage classroom implementation. The *MEJ* chronicled these events and reported further information from national and divisional conferences.

It is primarily through the work of Vanett Lawler, both as leader and catalyst, that the MENC entered so fully into the international music education conversation, making contacts with musicians and music educators around the world. Her representation gave the MENC a direct, active role in the UNESCO/IMC and the establishment of ISME. It is largely because of her efforts that, following the International Conference on Music Education in Brussels, the IMC reported "we accustomed ourselves this summer to think truly internationally and no longer exclusively in terms of occidental music."[89]

Conclusions, Implications, and Questions

The growing internationalism in music education that finally flowered in ISME reflected itself in American music education. It found its expression in the increased number of folk musics from around the world in music textbooks and the recommendations in teacher training texts for the careful selection of folk songs for school use. However, music educators did not receive help to enable them to teach any of these musics in an authentic manner. Since these musics are based in the Western music tradition, the expectation was that Western-trained music educators should be able to teach them. Today, music education still needs to address adequate training for multicultural/world music teacher education. What do pre-service music educators need to know regarding the musics of other cultures in order to fulfill their duties as a music teacher? How can that be presented within the confines of the undergraduate program? What is already being done?

During the period 1929 to 1953, internationalism in music education helped American music education break from the insularity of a Western European tradition to include Eastern European and Latin American musics. Is internationalism in music education as important for music educators today as it was in the 1930s and 1940s? What effects has internationalism in music education had on American music education? Why should music teachers be aware of the international music education scene?

CHAPTER **5**

Pivotal Changes:
1954–1967

Music of all periods, styles, forms, and cultures belongs in the curriculum.

—Tanglewood Declaration

Change pervaded the period from 1954 to 1967. Like general education, music education was abruptly awakened from the complacency of the early 1950s by social reforms resulting from desegregation, the launching of *Sputnik 1*, and the civil rights movement. General education answered these challenges with new methods and content in the curriculum. Music education dealt with these societal pressures by an ever widening acceptance of the musics of all cultures in the school music repertoire.

HISTORICAL CONTEXT

The Cold War

The Cold War that developed following World War II escalated throughout the 1950s. The United States viewed the Soviet Union with deep suspicion, and the Korean Conflict (1950–1953) added further to this growing distrust; the fear of nuclear war was foremost in American minds. In October 1957, the Soviet Union shocked the world by successfully launching *Sputnik 1*. The Russians had put the first satellite in space and Americans were dismayed. Overriding this was a sense that somehow the United States was no longer the superior power in the world, that it had been lax in developing research scientists and mathematicians, and that Russia was beating the United States in the Cold War.

The reaction in the United States was immediate; if the Russians had gotten to space first, it had to be because the American educational system had failed.[1] The federal government and private foundations both began to fund programs that would improve American education. The National Science Foundation and the Physical Science Study Committee gave impetus to the development of new math and science curricula, respectively. In 1958, Congress passed the National Defense Education Act, which provided federal funds for the development of science, math, and foreign language study in both higher education and the secondary schools.[2] By the 1960s, the National Aeronautics and Space Administration (NASA) was founded, President John F. Kennedy had declared the United States would put a man on the moon, and the "space race" was underway.

Civil Rights

Side by side with the Cold War was the growing discontent of African-Americans with unequal treatment under the law. After years of work by African-American reformers in various litigation actions across the nation, the issue of segregation in the public schools came before the United States Supreme Court. In 1954, the case of *Brown v. the Board of Education of Topeka*, firmly declared the unconstitutionality of "separate but equal" facilities in public education, a doctrine established since 1895 with *Plessy v. Ferguson.* Holding that "separate educational facilities are inherently unequal" and that "such segregation is a denial of the equal protection of the law,"[3] *Brown v. the Board of Education* set in motion efforts to desegregate the public schools that continue to the present day.

At the same time the civil rights movement to end all forms of racial discrimination continued to build throughout the 1950s and 1960s as African-American leaders, particularly Martin Luther King, Jr., brought the issue of civil rights before the public. In 1964 Congress passed the Civil Rights Act, which provided for equal employment opportunities and the desegregation of public facilities. It made clearer the regulation for desegregating public schools, and provided funds for personnel to assist in these desegregation efforts.[4] The following year the Voting Rights Act of 1965 established equal voting rights for all persons regardless of race or color.

The civil rights movement gave rise to "black power" in the mid- to late 1960s. Led by Stokely Carmichael and Malcolm X, black power was the culmination of efforts extending back to the early 1900s and the writings of W. E. B. Du Bois and Marcus Garvey. Black power and its resulting "black pride" brought a consciousness of African-American culture to American society. Because of this attention focused on African-Americans, by the end of the decade, Native Americans, Hispanic-Americans, Asian-Americans, and European-American ethnic groups also began to demand recognition for their cultures. The melting pot gave way to the metaphor of the "salad bowl" or the "mosaic." Americans were beginning to recognize the pluralistic nature of their society—a coexistence of many cultures.

Government and Education

In 1965, Congress passed three acts that had far-reaching implications in education: The Elementary and Secondary Education Act of 1965 (ESEA), the Higher Education Act, and the National Foundation on the Arts and the Humanities Act. The ESEA (1965) and its amendments (1966) provided federal funds to local educational organizations to assist in educating children of low-income families. This law allocated funds for educational research and training of teaching personnel, for supplies and materials for many subjects, including music, and for the establishment of "exemplary elementary and secondary school educational programs to serve as models for regular school programs."[5]

The Higher Education Act encouraged colleges and universities to broaden their teacher preparation programs, and provided assistance to persons with low incomes desiring postsecondary education. In the National Foundation on the Arts and the Humanities Act, Congress declared that encouraging scholarship in the arts and humanities was an appropriate concern of the federal government. It provided funding to institutions of higher learning for research and teacher training that would "strengthen the teaching of the humanities and the arts in elementary and secondary schools."[6]

The International Education Act of 1966 further aided multicultural education. This act gave financial support to institutions of higher education for research, program development, and teacher training in international studies. It also appropriated monies for the establishment of collegiate-run institutes "for teachers in secondary schools in order to give them a broader understanding of international affairs."[7] With this incentive, colleges and universities began to establish centers for the study of comparative education.[8]

Secularization and Immigration

The 1960s were a time of upheaval in the United States. Not only was there controversy over civil rights, but discord also surrounded the acceptance of varying lifestyles, the sexual revolution, the acknowledgment of atheism, and the removal of prayer from the public schools.[9] The latter two events in particular acted as catalysts, and the secularization of America that had begun slowly at the turn of the century, and had been building since World War II, began to gather momentum.

In 1965 Congress passed "An Act to Amend the Immigration and Nationality Act," which effectively repealed the "national origins" restrictions in effect since 1921, although there remained a ceiling on the total number of immigrants allowed in the country each year.[10] The resultant increase in immigration, particularly from Asian and Latin American countries, to some extent abetted secularization, as these immigrants brought their various religions, many of them outside of the Judeo-Christian tradition, to the United States.[11] Slowly, along with changes in demographics and lifestyles, Americans began to accept the presence of many religions, or no religion, in society,[12] and also, partly because of this multiplicity, to keep religion more and more separate from public institutions, especially the public schools.

In addition to its effects on secularization, immigration during this period also began to influence public education. The easing of the immigration laws compounded the changes in school populations already caused by desegregation, and brought about radical changes in the demographics of the public schools. Educators were faced with multicultural classes, and while this had occurred many times previously in American history, it was the first time that such a large mix of cultures, both American and immigrant, was acknowledged.

EDUCATIONAL CONTEXT

The Cold War and Desegregation

With the launching of *Sputnik 1*, public education underwent a major reevaluation. Since some curricular redesign in science and math had already begun in 1956, with the added impetus from *Sputnik 1*, it did not take long for schools to adopt the "new math" and the "scientific inquiry" methods in the schools. The National Defense Education Act of 1958 made possible language centers and graduate fellowships in foreign language teacher preparation. In 1959, the Woods Hole (Massachusetts) Conference, convened by the Education Committee of the National Academy of Sciences and supported by the Rand Foundation, discussed other possibilities for improving education. From this conference came the concept of a "spiral" curriculum based on Bruner's belief that "the foundations of any subject can be taught to anybody at any age in some form."[13] Education began to restructure the content of nearly all subject areas, music included, to focus on the fundamental concepts of the subject in ever deepening complexity across several grade levels. Federal funds were available for research and development in education, model programs, and teacher training. So much curricular change occurred during this period that Usher termed it an "age of ferment."[14] Adding to the turmoil was desegregation in the public schools.

While the Cold War prompted some reform in discriminatory practices, it was the Supreme Court decision of *Brown v. the Board of Education* that directly affected the public schools. As African-American and European-American students began to share classrooms, intercultural education programs, developed at the end of World War II, came into use more and more frequently. Following the intergroup dynamics or "contact hypothesis" of Allport,[15] intercultural education worked to reduce prejudice, and encourage cross-cultural understanding and "an acceptance of the real dignity and worth of all groups and individuals."[16] To accomplish these goals, the objectives of intercultural education included learning about other cultures, developing sensitivity to another culture's feelings, values, and attitudes, training in problem solving within group relations, and developing and implementing social skills with which to function in intergroup situations.[17]

Attention throughout the 1950s was focused on desegregation in the public schools and the school systems' varying degrees of compliance.[18] At the same time, school reformers also began pointing out prejudices in textbooks used in the schools which included disparagement of racial, ethnic, and religious groups that was overt, implicit (for example, ethnocentric stereotypes), or nonverbal (pictures).[19] The increasing need for relevance in the education of minority students, combined with textbook criticisms, led to the beginnings of the multicultural education movement.[20]

As desegregation progressed and diversity in the classroom increased, the curriculum, especially in higher education, also came under examination. In 1964 the Association of Higher Education of the National Education Association (NEA) addressed the issue of general education in colleges and universities:

> Our urgent need for a global outlook and the ability to learn about the world and its peoples, to say nothing of the vast universe surrounding us, is barely reflected in what we study. . . . Increased, informed awareness of world affairs and of at least one major, literate culture in addition to one's own should be the goal of any general education program. The reasons are clear and basic. First, every major cultural tradition is intrinsically worth study as an expression of man's creative genius. Next, study of another culture based on prior, serious, and critical study of one's own civilization provides an indispensable perspective on that tradition.[21]

The report presented a series of twelve points to be found in successful programs employing intercultural studies. These included recruiting teachers with bicultural competence, and assisting existing faculty to extend their competence to another culture.[22]

Concern for the addition of studies outside the formal Western tradition grew in the early 1960s. This was the period of "area" studies, or what were sometimes referred to as "ethnic culture" studies. Non-Western areas received particular attention. With the rising emphasis on African and African-American cultures, African history became a popular area study. Other area studies focused on cultures from South and East Asia, Latin America, Russia, and Eastern Europe.[23]

At the same time, elementary and secondary educators were finding effective methods, such as role playing, and school/community or interdepartmental projects to implement intercultural concepts. There were educational techniques for combating prejudice applied to nearly every subject area. Educators particularly valued the arts in intercultural education because their creative and participatory nature provided an activity in which all members of a class could take part.[24] Researchers often cited the study of jazz as a good example of a music unit that would lend itself to intercultural study.[25] Strange as it may seem, while education saw the value of jazz as a subject through which intercultural concepts could be taught, music education as a profession had not yet accepted jazz as a subject through which musical concepts could be taught.[26]

MUSIC EDUCATION

Jazz Education

With the rising interest in African-American culture, and the growing numbers of African-American children in the public schools, white music educators gradually became aware of African-American musics. Though African-American music educators had been teaching these musics in the segregated schools,[27] except for spirituals, the majority of white music educators were unfamiliar with them. In particular, jazz was regarded as anathema in the music curriculum.[28] As late as 1964, Harry Allen Feldman asked, "By what ratiocination are directors of such institutions [colleges and schools of music] persuaded that this [jazz] is material benefiting the dignity of an institution dedicated to the higher disciplines?"[29] However, musicians gradually began to realize the importance of African-American music to American culture and to music education,[30] and jazz slowly came to be accepted as one of the first musics outside the Western classical and folk tradition to be taught in music classrooms. First adopted as college/university jazz band programs, it expanded in the 1950s and 1960s to include entire jazz studies programs.[31] It was not until these programs began that jazz made its way to the elementary and secondary music education methods classes.[32]

Early articles on jazz in the *Music Educators Journal* (*MEJ*) presented jazz historically and in an unprejudiced light, and provided music educators with the first practical information on methods for bringing jazz to the general music class.[33] In 1960 and 1962, the Music Educators National Conference (MENC) biennial conferences presented demonstrations and discussions on jazz in the schools.[34] Events such as these show a gradual acceptance of jazz in the music curriculum, but as Lawler pointed out in 1960, "the door of this trend is barely open at the present time. . . ."[35] It would not be until the 1968 MENC biennial conference that jazz was not just talked about, but performed in concert and accepted.[36] What is important is that it was often through these initial contacts with jazz that many music educators first became acquainted with African and African-American musics.

Ethnomusicology

In 1953, while the attention of music educators was focused on the International Conference on Music Education and the foundation of the International Society for Music Education (ISME), another organization, the Society for Ethnomusicology (SEM), quietly established itself through an informal newsletter correspondence between ethnomusicologists.[37] Ethnomusicology, the study of music in, and as, culture, had been the subject of ongoing research since the turn of the century. It was a small but active field, and had fostered both national and international organizations. Though successful, these organizations had ceased to function under the double strains of the Depression and World War II.[38] The SEM formalized its organization in 1955.[39] With a professional journal to disseminate its scholarship, the field of ethnomusicology, and the ethnomusicologists themselves, began to be better known in academic circles and to have far-reaching effects on multicultural music education.

Charles Seeger's continued close collaboration with music education set the precedent for cooperation between music education and ethnomusicology. Ethnomusicologists such as Mantle Hood at the University of California at Los Angeles, David McAllester at Wesleyan University, and William Malm at the University of Michigan, became the experts the music education profession called on for information about what was then called "musics of the world." They, and other ethnomusicologists, were often invited to speak at ISME or MENC conferences, and it was their view of "music in, and as, culture" which would eventually be adopted in teaching music from a multicultural perspective.

MENC Conferences

The International Relations Committee of MENC remained active in planning and presenting sessions at all the national conferences throughout this period. International participants still came from Latin America, but because of United States membership in ISME, now countries around the world also sent representatives to the MENC national biennial conferences. In the years from 1954 to 1960 alone, the MENC conferences hosted visitors and participants from fifteen countries as far-flung geographically as Norway, Japan, Indonesia, and the Union of South Africa.[40] Special features at the conferences from 1958 to 1966 included the first performances of both Japanese *gagaku* music and Greek music, a display of international materials for classroom use, an international folk song "sing," and a recital of American folk songs by John Jacob Niles, a Kentucky folk singer.[41] In addition, MENC divisional conferences during this period tended to reflect the activities of the national organization.[42]

ISME Conferences

Even though music educators were becoming acquainted with the musics and music educators from other countries through the activities of the MENC, the real push for an international scope in music education during the 1960s came from ISME. The awareness of other music cultures, which began at the First International Conference in Brussels, continued to grow with each ISME meeting. In Vienna, 1961, Gerald Abraham, then president of the Society, expressed this continuing growth best in his opening address:

We occidentals recognize now that it was a comically narrow and provincial view that our own music was the only music that mattered; today we at least realize the validity and wealth of the great musical cultures and languages of India, of China, and of the Arab lands—to take only three.[43]

The Tokyo conference in 1963 emphasized the worlds of oriental and occidental musics in music education. In his summary of this conference, Frank Calloway said:

Speaker after speaker has been challenging us to reconsider our whole concept of music education, and there is now ample evidence that a worldview of music as an art practiced by all people but in their own distinctive ways, is rapidly emerging.[44]

The ISME Interlochen meeting in 1966 focused heavily on teacher training and on the need to include multiple music cultures in music instruction at all levels. Since this meeting followed closely upon the International Conference on Teacher Education held at Ann Arbor (discussed below), it is not surprising to find many of the same topics reiterated at Interlochen. Regarding teacher education, Calloway pointed out the fact that

the widened scope of the modern music curriculum demands a re-evaluation of the content of our teacher-training courses in music for as we know no curriculum can be taught adequately unless the teachers are firstly convinced of the importance of their mission and are then furnished with the required musical knowledge, performance skills and teaching techniques.[45]

At this same conference, it was evident that the ethnomusicological idea of music as an expression of culture was beginning to become a part of music education. Karl Ernst voiced this clearly:

If we are to use music as a means toward international understanding, we must come in direct contact with many kinds of music, and to approach strange music with an understanding of the culture which produced it.[46]

The Interlochen conference concluded with six recommendations, each with a general educational objective and special music educational objective. As Egon Kraus outlined them, four of the six recommendations apply directly to multicultural music education:

#2. The most important objective of music education is to establish the prerequisites for a co-existence of musical cultures.

#3. Appreciation and understanding of the values of foreign musical cultures does not imply the devaluation of one's own musical culture.

#4. The superiority complex of western civilizations should be abolished through a deeper penetration into the significances which lie in the musical languages of other civilizations.

#6. Music is not a universal language, but rather a universal medium of expression which finds many varied forms.[47]

(See Appendix B for complete text of the recommendations.)

The general educational objectives, though intended internationally, follow closely on the recommendations of the Association for Higher Education of the NEA.

For those American music educators who could attend, the ISME conferences must have been musically expanding experiences. These educators not only had the opportunity to meet music educators from other countries, but also listened to the musics of other cultures in concert and heard lectures about research in these musics by ethnomusicologists and other authorities in the field. The conference displays of books, music, and musical instruments from many countries were an invaluable resource.[48] Upon their return, the participants often shared what they learned with their colleagues. Ever since Walters and Lawler had described the foundation and goals of ISME to MENC membership at the 1954 Chicago MENC conference,[49] the MENC regularly reported the activities of ISME at MENC "international relations" sessions. Both the *MEJ* and ISME's journal, the *International Music Educator*, printed many reports and speeches from the ISME conferences in full, thus reaching countless other music educators in the United States. These ISME reports were primary in setting the stage for the acceptance of the musics from all countries in the music curriculum.

Music Textbooks

During this period, music textbooks continued to reflect an increasing number of songs from various cultures. Along with Latin American songs, there were increases in the number of songs from Africa, Australia, Canada, Eastern Europe, the Far East and Middle East, and the Pacific Islands in many of the music texts, many included with foreign language texts.[50] There was also a corresponding increase in not only the numbers of African-American songs included in the texts of this period, but also the types of African-American folk songs, such as work songs, play-party songs, and sea chanties.[51] *Together We Sing* (1955–1960), edited by Krone, Wolff, Krone, and Fullerton, contained a high proportion of American folk songs, as well as songs from Africa, Ceylon, China, India, and other countries of the Far East.[52]

The teaching texts also began to incorporate some of this growing world view of music. As early as 1950 Louise Meyers had included an entire chapter on oriental musics in her text *Teaching Children Music in the Elementary Schools*.[53] Teachers of music education and researchers in ethnomusicology also began to cooperate. *Toward World Understanding With Song*, a songbook compiled by Nye, Nye, and Nye, followed ethnomusicology's emphasis on studying music in culture.[54] This songbook focused primarily on the common uses of music in and across cultures rather than the elements of music itself.

Even with the increased numbers of songs from a variety of cultures in the music texts, musical authenticity was still a problem. Charles Fowler argued against simplified Western arrangements, and issued a plea for authenticity, since "Only authentic ethnic music, presented with its own indigenous accompaniment, its own language, or its own dance, will provide fair representation to another culture."[55] The participants of the Yale Seminar (discussed below), "particularly those who knew about Bartók's works, and who knew about a folk song repertory which was much more sophisticated, vital and lively"[56] complained about the lack of authenticity in school music materials, and researchers warned teachers to beware of inaccurate sources in both texts and recordings.[57] Even in the late 1960s, African-American songs still contained inappropriate changes in rhythm (syncopation frequently eliminated), text (dialect often changed to standard English), and texture (homophonic arrangements created for unison songs).[58] These discrepancies, along with the often negative representation of minorities in the music composed for the texts, gave false impressions of the music to the majority students, and, as Marvelene Moore said, possibly created "a conflict between music in school and music as they [the minority children] knew it at home and in the community."[59] Though Moore was discussing African-American musics, her conclusion is accurate for the musics of other minorities as well.

At the international level, Siegried Borris complained about the "boring and tasteless examples" which still filled schoolbooks, and Ernst warned that exported examples of folk music from distant countries were often not authentic. Much work was needed to provide access to the musics of each nationality.[60]

There are other such inadequacies in source materials, but in fairness, there were also sources available to teachers that were (and still are) authentic sources. The Nyes' songbook, *Toward World Understanding With Song*, correlated with Folkways recordings in order to assist learning authentic timbre, pronunciation, and rhythmic patterns.[61] *Folk Songs of the Americas*,[62] a songbook published through the IMC and UNESCO, contains all original language texts with English translations. The songs are unaccompanied, with the exception of a few songs that have guitar chords indicated. Besides the Folkways record collection,[63] Capitol records carried the UNESCO collection of folk music, and Columbia records included both selections of American folk music and the "World Library of Folk and Primitive Music." The Library of Congress recordings of African-American and Native American folk music were also available.

In answer to the pressures from society, the music textbook companies began to make efforts to present folk songs in a more authentic manner. To do so, they hired authorities in the various musics as consultants for the selection and presentation of folk musics in their texts. Starting in the 1950s, both the American Book Company and the Silver Burdett Company had "African-American authors, board members, and representatives associated with their series."[64] The Follett Publishing Company employed the services of Charles Faulkner Bryan as a consultant for American folk music, and the Holt, Rinehart and Winston Company and the Silver Burdett Company employed consultants on the musics from foreign countries, especially for their junior high school texts.[65]

The Yale Seminar

In the mid-1960s, the issue that came to the forefront of discussion was the immediate need for improvement in elementary and secondary school music. Seeking to answer this need, the Panel on Educational Research and Development (PERD), an advisory body that reported to the U.S. Office of Education and the President's Science Advisory Committee, sponsored the Yale Seminar on Music Education (Yale Seminar). Although it also encouraged curricular redesign in English, mathematics, foreign languages, and the sciences,[66] in the early 1960s the panel had targeted a "lack of balance in Federal assistance to the arts as compared to science."[67] The Yale Seminar was designed to see if "curricular reform as it developed in science education could be applied to education in the arts,"[68] and followed the prototype for this kind of developmental seminar, the Woods Hole Conference. In June 1963 thirty-one musicians, scholars, and educators gathered at Yale University to discuss the problems of music education and recommend some solutions.[69]

As Charles Gary recalled the story he was told by Harold "Bud" Arberg of the U.S. Office of Education, PERD had already refused a grant proposal to fund a meeting for musicologists from Claude Palisca at Yale University when the decision in favor of a seminar on music education was made. PERD did not "have time to get another request for proposals out."[70] So Palisca was called and asked if he would host a music education seminar at Yale instead of the musicological meeting he had proposed, and the panel would

> use his request for a proposal for a grant. He said he would host it. And that's probably why it [Yale Seminar] had such a peculiar mix of personages ... the music educators were added as a kind of afterthought. [They thought,] if we're going to talk about music education, maybe we'd better get some [music educators]. So, they added them, more as observers than anything else.[71]

Even though those attending were a "peculiar mix," the seminar was unique in that it "brought together for the first time . . . leading representatives of the many disparate elements which comprise the field of music."[72] Their diversity notwithstanding, the members did all share a concern about what was happening in music education.

Commenting on the current educational scene in music, the seminar noted that the school repertory was restricted to certain classics of Western music and composed school music and that "non-Western music, early Western music, and certain forms of jazz, popular, and folk music have been almost altogether neglected."[73] The seminar recommended the expansion of repertory, including music from all periods of Western music history, as well as jazz and folk music, for use in the public schools, both for performance and for listening experiences.[74] The inclusion of authentic folk musics from many cultures was justified by the recent progress made in ethnomusicology. The final report stated:

The pervading opinion of not many years ago was that the musics of Africa and Asia were primitive and to be classed as varieties of ingenuous folk expressions. A large number of people in favored metropolitan centers today recognize that many ethnic groups . . . possess highly sophisticated and articulate musical cultures, in which, moreover, music is much more closely integrated with the life of the people than it is in ours. Any program of music instructions in the schools that does not find a place for at least sample studies in depth of some of these musical cultures and their music is turning its back on one of the most compelling realities of our times.[75]

The report continued:

Jazz has attained international recognition as an American art product with distinctly native roots, expressive of our particular mixture of cultures. . . . It is the present heir to a precious national heritage, and the best of the past and present repertory should be part of every American's musical experience and education.[76]

These two statements are hardly surprising, given the influence of Mantle Hood and Mercer Ellington, who were chair and member respectively of the music repertory panel.[77] In fact, Allen Sapp, secretary for this panel, said the group was "really focused on these two things: Mercer Ellington's jazz, and Mantle Hood's . . . proposals for non-Western music."[78] The panel further cited the problems in elementary and secondary music education as not only due to restricted scope, but also to the inauthenticity of music selections. They said the repertoire "is corrupted by arrangements, touched-up editions, erroneous transcriptions, and tasteless parodies to such an extent that authentic work is rare."[79] Such strong language was slightly modified by suggestions for improvement. The panel felt a good part of the existing repertoire could be used if monophonic songs were presented as such, and if the original text and language of the songs was left intact. Relying on specialists for their knowledge and critical regard for authenticity would also help in song selection and presentation.[80]

The panel recommended that the structure of the entire repertoire be redesigned, and offered Seeger's divisions of musical types (art music of the West, popular, folk, tribal, hybrid, and non-Western musics) as a way to begin.[81] As a possible suggestion for how this would work, the panel outlined a junior high school course entitled Music of the Peoples of the World. The course included a sequence of units on jazz, Spain and Latin America, Africa, Java, and France and Germany. "The purpose of each unit would be immersion in the authentic music of a people through study and mastery of a small number of selected examples."[82] The materials for teaching this course ranged from original recordings and films to show the social context of the music, to slides of native instruments and musicians, and transcriptions of original music for class performance. Though the course was full of lofty expectations for both the teacher and student, it did represent what the panel thought could be the curricular content for a junior high general music class. The panel further acknowledged the need for teacher training to implement these materials effectively,[83] and recommended an artists-in-residence program to bring performers and composers into the schools.[84]

While a newspaper account of the seminar indicated friction between the musicians who favored emphasis on the "great Western tradition" and those who felt it important to expand the repertoire,[85] Allen Sapp, secretary for the music repertory panel, reported no such real conflict surrounding the principle of adding new musics to the school repertoire. He said that the resistance that occurred came from those who wanted to know who would teach these musics in the schools, even if materials were available.[86] It was unfortunate that the Yale Seminar did not include many persons actually involved in music education. Though there were some seminar members who were music teachers and administrators, there were only two (one participant and one observer) from the offices of the MENC, a fact that caused some initial "hard feelings" in the music education profession.[87]

Nonetheless, the seminar has had far-reaching effects in music education. As Sapp said, "The most important part was to shake up the formal [music] education establishment, and the hard-hitting, rough, uncompromising attitude of much of the Seminar" was deliberately aimed so as to cause a reaction.[88] Charles Gary agreed with this observation: "If it [Yale] did nothing more than irritate the music educators when the report came out, it served a good purpose because it got us 'off the dime,' as Bob Choate used to say."[89] Perhaps the seminar's greatest contribution according to Palisca was "the acceptance of the idea that non-Western musics should have a place in general music education."[90]

The Juilliard Repertory Project

The first outgrowth of the Yale Symposium was the Juilliard Repertory Project (JRP). In a direct response to the Yale Seminar's strong stand on the need for an improved school repertory, the Juilliard School of Music submitted a grant proposal to the U.S. Office of Education "which would enable it to research and develop a large body of authentic and meaningful music materials to augment and enrich the repertory available to the teachers of music in the earlier grades."[91] The grant was approved and research for the JRP began in 1964. That this proposal should come from Juilliard was hardly surprising given that Gid Waldrop, Dean of the Juilliard School of Music, was one of the members of the Repertory Section of the Yale Seminar. The JRP involved the cooperation of composers, music educators, performing artists, and musicologists, perhaps one of the first times such collaboration was successfully undertaken for the sake of improving music education.

As stated in its preface, the purpose of the JRP was "to enrich existing materials and provide works of greater variety relative to historical era, ethnic validity, and musical scope."[92] The project contains no jazz or popular music selections. When questioned about this, the project directors replied that they felt these musics were "just not ready for inclusion as part of an organized study," hence the omission.[93] However, there was an entire section of folk music.[94] These songs, game songs, and lullabies came from many different countries and cultures.[95] All were authentic folk songs collected, transcribed, translated, and field tested in the public schools before final publication. Authenticity was strictly adhered to, unaccompanied songs remained unaccompanied, and texts were in native languages with pronunciation guides and English translations provided. The broad scope of the Repertory Project's selections, and the varied backgrounds of the project's participants led Wiley Housewright to make this comment: "The changes of our times and our own curiosity about musics of other times and other places now lead naturally into collaborations that few segments of the professions were willing to undertake even a generation ago." The proposed anthology was a "welcome addition to our [music educators'] resources."[96]

Research

At about the same time that Juilliard was involved in research for the Repertory Project, other music educators were experimenting with the music from various cultures in the classroom. One of the first of these research studies was carried out by Elizabeth May and Mantle Hood. Working with first- and fifth-grade students in Santa Monica, California, they taught Javanese songs accompanied on a set of tone bells tuned to the Javanese scale.[97] Larson, Campbell, and Anderson introduced their classes in Penfield, New York, to selections from the musics of Africa, China, India, Indonesia, and Japan through activities including listening and both vocal and instrumental performance in these musics.[98] May and Jones taught the music of Australian aboriginals to classes in Perth, Australia, and May repeated this experiment with students in Santa Monica, California.[99] Employing an intercultural approach, Hartwig used jazz as the unifying element, in a program designed to introduce African music to American children and European art music to African children.[100] While research efforts in the early 1950s had focused on ways to implement the folk songs of specific cultures in general music, and had extended somewhat to both choir and instrumental programs,[101] these music educators, alone or in collaboration with ethnomusicologists involved students directly with the music from other cultures.

Teacher Training

School systems and state boards of education began to realize the need to include the musics of various cultures in the overall music curriculum. The *Curriculum Guide, The Elementary Program* of the San Diego City Schools contained an early (1953) view of the need for world musics in the elementary music program.[102] In 1966, the New York State Education Department recommended the inclusion of the study of musics from other cultures in its seventh- and eighth-grade general music syllabus.[103] Although the suggestions for the teacher were limited in scope and contained inaccuracies, this syllabus provided a much more detailed attempt at presenting a variety of musics both as music and as an expression of culture than had been done previously.

Some teachers were already attempting the presentation of jazz and ethnic musics in their classes. However, with only a knowledge of the Western music tradition, they often unintentionally promoted misconceptions about these musics and the people who make them. Their students often found musical comprehension difficult if not impossible.[104] Since music educators were expected to teach these musics in their classes, it was becoming obvious that they would need training in the cultural context, analysis, and performance of the musics of various cultures.

While the Yale Seminar acknowledged the need for teacher training to implement a more global curriculum, it was the International Seminar on Teacher Education held at the University of Michigan, Ann Arbor, in 1966[105] that actually addressed the issue of preparing music educators to use the music of not only their native culture but other cultures as well. At this seminar, ethnomusicologists and music educators reinforced the idea that the time had come to open the doors of music education to all the musics of the world. As David McAllester pointed out, "music education can no longer afford to be precious in its definition of what is worthwhile in music."[106] In this endeavor, Kwabene Nketia emphasized that "ethnomusicology can be the handmaiden of music education," and went even further to say that "music education and ethnomusicology cannot afford to live apart."[107] Explaining the type of preparation a music teacher needed to bring to the classroom, William Malm said:

> The most fundamental attitude we attempt to impart to our students is that music is *not* an international language. A view of the total of world music reveals a large number of equally logical but different systems, many of which are as different from each other as they may be from the more familiar western system. . . . Rather we can seek to introduce into our teachers an aural flexibility which will enable them to hear each music in terms of its own special logic and then, hopefully, impart some of this logic into their students when the opportunity arises.[108]

Malm elaborated this point by saying:

> My primary goals in preparing the teacher are to give him a general aural experience in non-Western music, provide him with a vocabulary with which he can speak about non-Western concepts of music to Western students, and instill in him a musical flexibility which will allow him to listen to and enjoy each music of the world in terms of its own logic and beauty.[109]

Elizabeth May described how this could be accomplished. Her suggestions included course work in ethnomusicology and summer workshops encompassing a survey of three or four cultures involving the teacher-student in academic study, performance techniques, and the cultural context for each culture. She outlined how teachers could use recent publications in ethnomusicology, television, and community resources to help themselves learn more and present the music culture more accurately in the classroom.[110]

Group discussions generated recommendations which were presented to the entire assembly. Among them were two that touched directly on a multicultural perspective for teacher education. Group 2, chaired by Donald Shetler, summarized the feelings of several participants by stating:

> Music education in every country must be based on the musical tradition of its culture, including its own current folk tradition and contemporary musical phenomena.

> We encourage the selection and study of indigenous folk music of quality from the native culture and from foreign cultures.[111]

Led by McAllester, Group 4 specifically addressed the use of musical instruments in music teaching. Among their recommendations were two pertaining to a world view on instruments for classroom use:

> c. We recommend that music educators learn to broaden their definition of "musical instrument" to include the world inventory. . . .

> d. We recommend that one aspect of teacher training in music education be the development of imagination and ingenuity in finding indigenous instruments or inventing unconventional instruments to meet particular needs. We recommend the institution of special workshops for this kind of training.[112]

The participants at this seminar all spoke about *music cultures*, not just folk songs from a culture. The ethnomusicological concept of music in culture and as an expression of culture, which had slowly begun to take hold in music education throughout the 1950s and 1960s, was fully recognized at this seminar. However, because this conference was of an international nature, the views expressed were also international, and perhaps could be considered avant-garde for American music education. While it is true some music educators had already included various ethnic musics, jazz, and popular musics in their classes, the music education profession in the United States had not yet accepted all musics in the school music curriculum.[113] Nonetheless, this conference, and particularly the Yale Seminar and the Juilliard Repertory Project that preceded it, acted as catalysts. The next year, the MENC responded with the Tanglewood Symposium.

The Tanglewood Symposium

In the summer of 1967, a symposium entitled Music in American Society met at Tanglewood, Massachusetts. Under the auspices of the MENC, the purpose of the Tanglewood Symposium was a major self-evaluation of the profession and its goals for music in the schools through the year 2000. Like the Yale Seminar, the participants included music educators and musicians, but the MENC went one step further and asked scientists, labor leaders, sociologists, and representatives of corporations, foundations, and government to take part. To stimulate national thinking on the symposium's topics, the planning committee developed a series of questions for each area to be discussed, and published them in the April 1967 issue of *MEJ*. They asked music educators to voice their opinions as input for the discussions before the symposium began so that all concerns might be included. Among the questions asked addressing Music in Our Time, some dealt specifically with the musics from a variety of cultures in the schools.

> Polycultural curriculums are developing rapidly. Should music of other cultures be included? For what purposes? Few centers exist in this country for such studies. What are the implications? . . . Insularity, rigid departmentalization, and adherence to tradition characterizes many schools. Would music and society be better served by a greater mutuality of concern and interests of theorists, composers, musicologists, educators, ethnomusicologists, and performers?[114]

The Tanglewood Symposium itself then responded:

> There are different kinds of music existing side by side with relative degrees of aesthetic values. Separate musics have separate functions; and the functions are multiplying. . . . They pose the problem of value judgements, not only of the quality of the music, but quality within the function of the musics. Can we and should we assign a hierarchy to various musics?[115]

David McAllester's speech at Tanglewood pointed out the rapidly shrinking world as one of the forces shaping music education. He asked, "How then can we go on thinking of 'music' as Western European music, to the exclusion of the infinitely varied forms of musical expression in other parts of the world?"[116] He cited advances already being made: (1) the existence of several multicultural performing groups at various universities; (2) the use of African and Israeli songs in popular folk singing; (3) popular performing groups, such as the Beatles, adding the sounds and instruments from other countries to their performances; and (4) the existence of a program for children in the public schools of Brooklyn to experience authentic Native American songs and dances.[117]

Youth music (popular, jazz, and rock musics of the day) was also a topic which received much attention at the symposium. While music educators were inclined to disregard these musics (rock and roll was considered even more improper than jazz for study in the schools), they listened attentively to articulate presentations by young musicians.[118] As McAllester recalled it, "These young fellows, with beards and long hair, lectured all these music educators on what the rock texts and music meant in a very intelligent way. It made a big impression."[119]

At the end of the symposium, committee reports recommended that the curriculum be broadened to include all types of musics,[120] and that teacher education include competence in teaching "a multiplicity of musics."[121] As Allen Britton wrote in a summation following the symposium, "World con-

ditions demand that the musical repertory be expanded considerably. . . .
We must somehow come to terms with rock and roll, with the music of the
avant garde, with various folk and art musics of our own and other lands."[122]

The final declaration of the symposium has become a landmark document in multicultural music education. It placed all musics into the school
music curriculum with one sweeping statement:

> Music of all periods, styles, forms, and cultures belong in the curriculum.
> The musical repertory should be expanded to involve music of our time in
> its rich variety, including currently popular teen-age music and avant-garde
> music, American folk music, and the music of other cultures.[123] (see Appendix C for the complete text of the declaration.)

The November 1967 issue of *MEJ* provided a full report of the Tanglewood Symposium. Charles Fowler's editorial confirmed and supported the
declaration and the need for studying world musics:

> If the huge melting pot of music is for everyone to enjoy, then understanding
> all the ingredients is a natural pursuit of any education in music. Music education, by latching on to diversity, by being comprehensive in its coverage of the musics of the world, will insure that the tastes of the public are
> based on choices made from acquaintance with all that constitutes the art
> of music.[124]

SUMMARY

Across the thirteen years from 1954 to 1967, the music education profession
shifted from a position that still questioned the value of some musics (for
example, jazz) in the curriculum to a declaration that all musics belong in
the music curriculum. This change showed in many ways. There was a progressive inclusion of musics from many cultures in the music texts, and the
textbook companies began to employ experts in the various musics as consultants for the selection and presentation of the folk songs in their texts.
Research efforts dealing with the musics of other cultures developed from
studies that offered ways to implement folk songs in the curriculum, to actually teaching authentic music from a specific culture to students outside
that culture. As jazz studies, the results of research, and anthropology and
ethnomusicology classes slowly began to have an effect at the collegiate level,
music teacher education moved from an awareness of the need for changes
to suggestions for how this could be accomplished. As a result, in thirteen
years, the perspective in music education changed from one which saw Western music taught through the exemplar of folk songs and dances from many
cultures to one which viewed the presentation of many authentic music cultures as a way to learn about music as a human expression.

In 1957, as the MENC celebrated its fiftieth anniversary, Vanett Lawler
presented several predictions for the future of music education. Among them

she said, "World-mindedness and world-consciousness will be automatically an important part of the MENC program of the future as well as of the private endeavor of members of the profession."[125] Given the changes in music education in the ten years following this statement, it appears Lawler was more of a prophet than perhaps even she realized in 1957.

Conclusions, Implications, and Questions

Today most music educators see the Tanglewood Declaration as the basis for what is known as multicultural/world music education. The Tanglewood Symposium was designed to orientate music education toward the year 2000. Though it was intended as music education's answer to the criticisms leveled by the Yale Seminar, in effect it affirmed the seminar's recommendations for expanding the curriculum to include all musics in the school music repertoire, and for making changes in music teacher education to accommodate full implementation of these musics. As the millennium approaches, it is tempting to review just how far music education has gone to accomplish the goals set forth at Tanglewood for multicultural music education. How has Yale or Tanglewood made a difference in music education classrooms today?

Music education needs to consider the gap between the ideals of the leadership and the slow implementation of its ideas in the schools. If our profession's leadership has moved with Tanglewood, have the general ranks of teachers kept step? What is needed to help them do so?

CHAPTER 6

Multicultural Awareness: 1968–1990

A music educator must build bridges of knowledge and understanding not only between local traditions, but also between the musical cultures of the world.

—J.H. KWABENA NKETIA[1]

The years from 1968 to 1990 were a period of growing awareness of the pluralistic nature of American society brought about by increased immigration and the pressures from various ethnic groups for equal recognition and representation. In education, the need for multicultural approaches to learning, which generated bilingual/multicultural education programs, echoed this awareness. Music education likewise felt the changes in society, and, impelled by the recent Tanglewood Symposium, set about implementing the musics from many cultures in the school music curriculum.

HISTORICAL CONTEXT

The period from 1968 to 1990 was one of public "consciousness raising" regarding ethnic diversity in the United States. Inspired by the civil rights and African-American "black power" movements of the 1960s, various other "power" movements quickly established themselves as Native Americans, Hispanic-Americans, Asian-Americans, and European-American ethnic groups all began laying claims to the public's attention. This wave of "new ethnicity" was particularly evident during the decade from 1968 to 1978. Extensive media coverage, especially through television, not only increased awareness of the concerns of these groups but also brought aspects of their culture before the American public. As people became more comfortable with overt expressions of ethnicity, ethnic folk festivals once again became a popular way of sharing culture.

Ethnicity was "in"; novels such as Alex Haley's *Roots* set the trend for ethnic literature, ethnic cookbooks became bestsellers, plays and poetry celebrated ethnic heritage, and research into various aspects of ethnicity flourished.[2] The wave of ethnic awareness that engulfed the 1970s was fully reflected in the 1980 Census when nearly 85 percent of the population identified one or more cultures in their heritage.[3]

This period was also one of controversy as continuing arguments regarding the implementation of federal civil rights regulations for integration in the workplace and desegregation in the schools filtered down to state and local levels. Affirmative action policies and court-ordered school busing became facts of life, but though the need for both was generally acknowledged, there was also a fear that reverse discrimination would develop.

Some scholars began looking at the possible implications of uncontrolled ethnic self-interests within the American democratic framework, and warned that instead of cultural pluralism producing "unity in diversity," too much diversity could "disunite" the country.[4] There were also heated discussions over the idea that cultural pluralism (now often called "multiculturalism") extended beyond race, ethnicity, and religion, to include gender, age, handicapping conditions, socioeconomic status, and even sexual orientation. Besides all this, a reevaluation of American culture and particularly the educational system, forced by economic retrenchment and a "back-to basics" movement during the 1980s, also proved controversial.[5]

Immigration

A new wave of immigration came to the United States following the passage of the Immigration Act of 1965. When all the provisions of this law were finally implemented in 1968, a noticeable shift in the ethnic makeup of the immigrants from Europeans to Asians and Latin Americans began to take place. In particular, large numbers of Puerto Ricans, Mexicans, and Cubans came to the United States during this period and augmented the Spanish-speaking population of the United States.

Though there were still limitations on the total number of immigrants allowed into the United States yearly, this number was often exceeded because the law allowed family members of legal immigrants to enter the country. A great many exceptions were also made to accommodate political refugees, many of whom came to escape the war-torn countries of Southeast Asia and Central America, or the political turmoil of the Middle East.

The Refugee Act of 1980 limited those seeking political asylum in the United States to fifty thousand a year but allowed for presidential exemptions based on humanitarian concerns or emergency conditions. Although there had been many other refugee acts with similar provisions, the 1980 Act was unique in its impact on education because it ordered that plans be developed to provide these refugees with English-language training. In 1986, Congress passed the Immigration Reform and Control Act to help control the entry of illegal aliens. This Act adjusted the process of legalization for aliens, provided for the legal immigration of migrant workers, and granted legal status to aliens who had entered the United States unlawfully prior to 1982.[6] Federal funding helped the states cover the educational expenses incurred because of this influx of newly legalized immigrants.

Because of immigration, the overall demographics of the United States changed considerably, as the Hispanic, Asian, and Arabic populations increased dramatically. This new ethnic diversity was most noticeable in the large urban centers where the influx of new immigrants was coupled with a continuing migration of the white population to the suburbs.

Government and Education

With the new immigrants came an increase in the numbers of children in the schools whose primary language was not English. In response to increasing public concern for the education of these children, Congress passed the Bilingual Education Act of 1968 as Title VII of the Elementary and Secondary Education Amendments of 1967. The Bilingual Education Act acknowledged the special needs of children with limited English-speaking ability and provided monies for schools to develop and carry out new programs designed to meet these needs, for pre-service training, and for the acquisition of teaching materials.[7] Bilingual education was further defined in the Bilingual Education Act of 1974, and these Acts, along with the 1974 Supreme Court ruling in *Lau v. Nicholas*, formally affirmed the rights of all children to an education in their native language. In addition to these overall governmental provisions for bilingual education, the Refugee Education Assistance Act of 1980 specifically funded bilingual programs intended to help the children of Cuban, Haitian, and Indochinese (Cambodian, Laotian, and Vietnamese) refugees.

In 1972 Congress passed amendments to the Elementary and Secondary Education Act (ESEA) of 1965. The Education Amendments Act of 1972 reflected the growing emphasis on ethnic awareness in the country, and had a far-reaching effect on what was slowly becoming known as multicultural education. Title III of the Amendments, known as the Indian Elementary and Secondary School Assistance Act, dealt specifically with Native American educational needs.[8] The growing impact of other ethnic interests was acknowledged in Title IX of the ESEA of 1965, the Ethnic Heritage Program. The opening statement of this amendment gave a clear indication of the growing emphasis on ethnicity and cultural pluralism.

> In recognition of the heterogeneous composition of the Nation and of the fact that in a multiethnic society a greater understanding of the contributions of one's own heritage and those of one's fellow citizens can contribute to a more harmonious, patriotic, and committed populace, and in recogni-

tion of the principle that all persons in the educational institutions of the
Nation should have an opportunity to learn about the differing and unique
contributions to the national heritage made by each ethnic group, it is the
purpose of this title to provide assistance designed to afford to students opportunities to learn about the nature of their own cultural heritage, and to
study the contributions of the cultural heritages of the other ethnic groups
of the Nation.[9]

The Ethnic Heritage Program provided funding for programs to develop
curriculum materials for elementary and secondary schools, disseminate
these materials, provide training for persons to use the materials, and cooperate with ethnic community groups to promote these programs relating
to the "history, culture, or traditions of that ethnic group or groups."[10]

In addition to providing for bilingual education and ethnic studies, Title IX of the Education Amendments of 1972 prohibited sex discrimination,
guaranteeing both males and females equal educational opportunities. In
practice Title IX broadened the concept of diversity to include the viewpoints
of both genders. This concept was further extended in 1975 to include the
handicapped when Congress enacted the Education of All Handicapped
Children Act.[11]

The Global Marketplace

Advances in technology, especially the development of almost instantaneous
communications media, produced the concept of a shrinking world or global
village. People became more aware of what was happening in other parts
of the world. Telecommunications and computers effected changes, not only
in international affairs, but also in work, research, and the marketplace.
Many businesses grew beyond their domestic boundaries and became multinational corporations with global strategies for a world marketplace. These
corporations prized persons capable of working in multicultural and intercultural settings in order to be better able to sell in the world market.[12] This
concern that the United States be able to compete in a world economy added
further weight to the need for multicultural education in the schools.[13]

EDUCATIONAL CONTEXT

Desegregation and Immigration

Throughout this period, controversy raged over desegregation in the public schools. Americans, particularly in urban areas, found themselves faced
with court-ordered school redistricting and student busing to achieve a balanced population of majority (white) and minority students in all their
schools. In many school districts busing was viewed with disfavor, sometimes even causing civil discord as it did in Boston in 1974.[14] Upper- and
middle-class white populations responded by placing their children in pri-

vate schools or moving to the suburbs in great numbers. As a result, in many large urban school districts the population balance between majority and minority students reversed itself, presenting new difficulties for districts struggling to maintain a balanced school population.

Changes in the demographics of the student population were not only due to desegregation. Just as immigration affected the public schools at the turn of the century, so now large numbers of Hispanic and Asian immigrants and refugees added to the multicultural mix in the schools. Teachers had barely adjusted to dealing with African-American and white ethnic cultures in the newly desegregated schools before great numbers of children with limited English-speaking ability from many different cultures came to their classes.

Bilingual Education

Until 1968, English was the only language taught and spoken in the public schools, except for the individual foreign language classes (such as French, German, and Spanish). However, the combined effects of increased immigration, ethnic awareness, equal rights in education, and the Bilingual Education Act produced great changes in the schools as state boards of education took up the challenge of implementing the federal government's new laws. Bilingual education programs were one result.

Because of the numbers of Spanish-speaking students in the schools, the first bilingual programs focused heavily on Spanish. Following the 1968 Bilingual Education Act, these programs expanded across the nation and began to include many languages, Aleut, Arabic, Chinese, Greek, Navajo, and Vietnamese among them.[15]

The intent of bilingual education was to help bring children with limited English-speaking ability into the mainstream of American education. Much like the "ethnic" language classes advocated by Addams and Dewey in the early 1900s, the fundamental purpose of bilingual education was to enable children to function effectively in school. By the 1970s, the methods used to accomplish this goal had changed. Where once English was intended to supplant the native language of the child, bilingual instruction became a way both to teach English and retain the original language.[16] Several program models were developed for effective bilingual education, among them English as a Second Language (ESL) and "two-way enrichment" in which native English speakers and limited-English speakers help each other to learn their classmates' respective native languages.

Bilingual educators often suggested music as a means to assist language learning. Considered as a functional medium in bilingual classes, music helped teach pronunciation, grammar, and vocabulary. Folk songs taught about culture and regional differences through the social, historical, and geographical contexts of the songs and helped students better understand the people whose language they were learning.[17] However, some researchers warned against using songs only as a "show and tell" cultural activity.[18] In an observation that could as easily have been addressed to music teachers, they explained:

> Music should be taught in all its forms so that students recognize the dynamic rather than static nature of culture as represented in songs. This means, for example, that class activities involving U.S. music should include not only folk songs, children's songs, and European classical music but also current rock, jazz, blues, gospel, country and western, soul, bluegrass, and whatever forms of music continue to be developed by groups of people. Most important of all, students should discover the great variety of music produced by the varied ethnic communities surrounding their school as a part of their exploration of and increasing sensitivity to neighborhood social patterns.[19]

Since these were admittedly nonmusical goals, they highly recommended correlation with the regular music class for further understanding.

Multiethnic/Multicultural Education

Under the impetus of the new wave of ethnicity in America, "ethnic studies" began to develop out of the "area studies" of the 1960s. Since desegregation most heavily affected large urban school districts, it is not unusual to find the literature in the late 1960s referring to the needs of urban education (or inner-city education) both in the classroom and in teacher training. The growing awareness of African-American culture in America, and the need to help inner-city students develop a positive self-image combined as schools developed the first African-American studies programs.

By the early 1970s, ethnic studies could be found across the nation from elementary to collegiate levels. These first studies focused exclusively on, and were offered only to, the ethnic populations in the schools. For example, Japanese and Chinese studies could be found in schools on the West Coast, and Hispanic and Native American studies in the Southwest, while, as mentioned above, schools offered African-American studies primarily in large urban districts. In higher education, students of specific ethnic backgrounds were often the only ones taking the ethnic studies course.[20]

In 1974, the National Institute of Education (NIE) under the United States Department of Health, Education, and Welfare conducted ten conferences on bilingual/multicultural education.[21]

> The ideas discussed covered a wide range of issues but when reviewed across groups showed a strong pattern of interest in professional participation, cultural pluralism, and a number of specific research issues associated with assessment, language acquisition, curriculum development, and teacher preparation.[22]

Of these topics, curriculum development was the most often addressed as teachers began to deal with the practical applications of teaching for cultural pluralism in their classrooms.

Following the passage of the Ethnic Heritage Act, the focus changed from one in which ethnic studies were offered to enhance the self-esteem of particular ethnic groups to the need for all students to learn about all cultural groups in a "multiethnic" curriculum. Individual school districts and education associations received research grants under the Ethnic Heritage Act to develop methods and materials for multicultural education. The most common procedure for dissemination of these materials (basically, "what" and "how to" information) was through in-service meetings or professional conferences, teacher workshops, and summer classes.

These first resource materials were culture-specific units of study, often including complete lesson plans and bibliographies.[23] Many of these units focused on African-American culture. The next most available units were for Hispanic-American and Native American studies, with Asian-American materials among the last to be developed. These units were generally intended to be added to the existing curriculum, and not integral to the entire school program.

As federal and state funding became more available, school systems across the country developed various methods for implementing multicultural education. As opposed to the first ethnic studies, which were independent units of study, most of these new programs were interdisciplinary in nature, especially coordinating social studies, language arts, and the arts (visual arts, music, and drama).[24]

By the mid-1980s, this interdisciplinary approach had become the usually accepted model and the term "infusion" described the fact that every subject area was to be taught from a multicultural perspective. As the concept of multiculturalism broadened to include gender, such topics as women's studies and sexism appeared in the classroom curricula. In addition, both bilingual classes and education programs for the handicapped employed multicultural approaches.[25] A shift toward a broader world view for multicultural education began to take place in the mid-1980s, and, by the 1990s, the terms "global education" and "global perspective" often implied multicultural education.[26] This extended the concept of multiculturalism beyond the cultures within the United States to include the entire world.

Throughout this period international/intercultural education continued to grow, often paralleling the development of multicultural education. Teacher and student exchanges between the United States and foreign countries became regular occurrences, and colleges and universities promoted courses in intercultural education. Because multicultural education frequently involved cultural interactions in the classroom, as the numbers of migrant, immigrant, and refugee children increased, teachers often employed intercultural education techniques in multicultural education. In some situations, "intercultural education" and "multicultural education" even became interchangeable terms.

Research

It is beyond the scope of this chapter to do more than mention the topics discussed in the extensive amount of research dealing with multicultural education which was published from 1968 to 1990. This literature included rationales and theoretical models for multicultural education, teaching methodologies and materials, bibliographies and resource lists, model programs, multicultural teacher education, and textbook/materials evaluation.[27] The vast majority of research produced "concept materials"—methods, materials, source books, curricula and syllabi.[28] It is unfortunate that for all the research that generated these materials, as of 1985 very little was found on the implementation of multicultural education in the classroom, or its effects on students.[29] However, research since 1985 has shown that multicultural education has a positive impact on students' attitudes toward, and knowledge about, other cultures.[30] These studies have been especially pertinent in the light of the increasing number of state and professional mandates for multicultural education.

Multicultural Education Mandates and Teacher Training

Individual states established mandates for multicultural education in teacher training as early as 1973 in Montana, where undergraduate and/or in-service training was required in Native American studies. By 1990, thirty-seven states and the District of Columbia required multicultural education experiences in some form or other to qualify for teaching certification.[31] Multicultural teacher education became even more necessary as state boards of eduction began to adopt a program of competency-based education or outcome-oriented curricula, and included multicultural education in their expectations.[32]

Along with these regulations for teacher certification, state boards of education also mandated multicultural education for the curricula throughout the state school system. By 1973, thirteen states required some form of ethnic studies in their curricula.[33] In 1979, Iowa mandated that diverse cultural perspectives be taught in all classes.[34] New York, Delaware, and Minnesota followed Iowa's lead, in 1984, 1989, and 1990, respectively.[35]

Because of state mandates for certification, it became imperative that teacher education institutions offer training in multicultural education. The first official commitment to multicultural education from within the education profession came from the American Association of Colleges for Teacher Education (AACTE). In one short statement accepted by the board of directors in 1972 and disseminated to membership in 1973, AACTE placed its approval on both multicultural education in the schools and on teacher training, saying "If cultural pluralism is to become an integral part of the educational process, teachers and personnel must be prepared in an environment where the commitment to multicultural education is evident." AACTE cited a multiethnic/multiracial staff, diverse student body, and a "culturally pluralistic curriculum" as evidence of this commitment. Reaching beyond methods courses, AACTE said this commitment must "permeate all area of the educational experience provided for prospective teachers."[36]

In 1979, The National Council for Accreditation of Teacher Education (NCATE) added multicultural education to its standards. In its revisions in the 1980s and again in 1990, NCATE dropped multicultural education as a separate standard and incorporated it within several others. In the 1990 standards, the professional studies component criteria included preparing teachers to be knowledgeable about various cultural influences and learning styles, to be able to apply appropriate teaching strategies for culturally diverse and exceptional populations, and to have experienced a professional studies component which itself was taught from multicultural and global perspectives.[37]

MUSIC EDUCATION

The Goals and Objectives Project

Following the Tanglewood Symposium, one of the immediate concerns of the MENC was the implementation of the Tanglewood declaration. To accomplish this, during 1968 and 1969, the MENC undertook a national review of goals and objectives for both music education and the organization toward the year 2000. To investigate "the musics of non-Western cultures and their uses in education,"[38] the steering committee of the Goals and Objectives (GO) Project established GO Project Committee 18, chaired by William P. Malm, an ethnomusicologist with deep interests in music education.

Committee 18, composed of both music educators and interested ethnomusicologists from across the nation, had as its primary goal "to suggest procedures and prepare materials for use in presenting different musical systems of the world as integral parts of the music education curricula in American elementary and secondary schools, colleges, and universities."[39] To this end, the committee asked its members to gather information to help answer two key questions:

1. What understandings and values about ethnic music should MENC advocate as a desirable part of public school education?
2. What new steps should MENC take to meet critical curricular needs? In what ways will MENC be most efficient?[40]

In the final report presented to the steering committee, Committee 18 emphasized that "the world of music consists of many equally logical but different systems" and "music is *not* an international language." For these reasons, the committee recommended that the MENC should join forces with the Society for Ethnomusicology (SEM) to provide authentic multimedia materials for use in the classroom. The committee also recommended that MENC work to (1) create "multi-media resources and textbooks in world musics;" (2) help change the basic teacher education curriculum to include instruction in world musics for both collegiate and in-service teacher train-d (3) share its knowledge of acquiring federal funding to help schools .... performances by native culture bearers to help establish world musics in school/community life.[41]

In 1970, MENC accepted and published its new goals and objectives. Among the objectives marked "for priority attention" were:

> To lead in efforts to develop programs of music instruction challenging to all students, whatever their socio-cultural conditions, and directed toward the needs of citizens in a pluralistic society.

> To advance the teaching of music of all periods, styles, forms, and cultures.[42]

Organizational efforts toward the full implementation of these goals for multicultural music education included the establishment of the MENC Commission on Minority Concerns (later the Multicultural Awareness Commission), numerous in-service conference sessions on various music cultures, sponsorship of both the 1984 Wesleyan and 1990 Multicultural Approaches to Music Education symposia, publication of multimedia resources, and closer working ties with SEM and the Smithsonian Institution.[43]

Urban Music Education

At the same time that the MENC was establishing its long-term goals and objectives, music educators were faced with the more immediate concerns of daily teaching, and most particularly in reaching discontented urban students. The atmosphere in the urban general music classrooms of the 1960s was one where students were "fighting against the music teachers because the students were doing more interesting music outside the classroom than they were inside. They learned about the music of various cultures and of their own music in spite of their teachers, not because of them."[44] Singing from the available music series textbooks was a virtual impossibility since students found the songs in these books "square" and unappealing.[45] Traditional music education failed in the inner city because, as Allen Britton said, "The music used does not sound like music to the children. Rather, it is heard by them as the music of another culture with which the children are in fact in conflict."[46] Music educators found themselves unprepared to teach these students, both in knowledge of musical styles and of the students' cultures. James Standifer described the shock these early years of desegregation had on music teachers:

> After these schools were desegregated, we [African-Americans] took our music and our ways of behaving into the schools and, aside from intimidating most of the teachers as well as some of our peers, it required that the teacher training program reevaluate itself because teachers were going to schools, and couldn't cope with, or couldn't focus on, the kind of music that the black students were doing.[47]

They had to learn quickly.[48] Music education in the inner city was the profession's first attempt to address the needs of a multicultural society, a newly desegregated school population, and the youth of the 1960s.[49]

In order to reach urban youth, music educators found themselves learning to employ the very musics that had been so long withheld from music education classes: jazz, popular and rock music styles, and various ethnic musics, particularly African and African-American musics. In fact, because jazz and many popular music styles were derived from African-American sources, and most of the inner-city students were African-Americans, Standifer called the phrase "urban music in the inner-city" a "euphemism for Black music."[50] In an effort to assist its readership with understanding urban music education, the *Music Educators Journal* (*MEJ*) focused specifically on that topic in its January 1970 issue.[51] The articles addressed urban culture, the classroom uses of rock music, African musics, and a "musical concepts" approach to discovering how various musics work.[52]

Like the African studies that were the first ethnic programs in general education, African and African-American musics were the first ethnic music areas employed in music education. In November 1971, the *MEJ* published a special issue devoted entirely to African-American music. This issue covered research, the impact of music and African-American culture, and a program in African music established at Howard University.[53] The issue also included a selected resource list for studies in African-American music. This was the first time the *MEJ* made such assistance available to its readership.[54]

In 1972 Barbara Reeder and James Standifer published a major resource for teachers wishing to employ African and African-American musics, the *Source Book of African and Afro-American Materials for Music Educators*, made possible through the Contemporary Music Project (CMP).[55] In 1968 and 1969, CMP awarded Reeder a grant to explore the possibilities of a comprehensive musicianship approach in a Sub-Saharan African Music Program for the Seattle Schools and also funded Standifer's syllabus and curriculum models for teaching comprehensive musicianship in urban education.[56] Standifer and Reeder presented the results of their research at MENC conferences and CMP workshops around the country; the summation of their research is found in the *Source Book*, which was intended "as an impetus to teachers to use these materials and musical traditions in the classroom."[57] It contains background information, resource materials, and sample lesson plans that had been tried "on the front lines" in the inner cities. As Standifer described it, "Anything that didn't work, we threw away, so what you've got there is what actually works."[58]

Jazz, Popular, and Rock Musics in the Schools

Following the coverage given to the foundation of the National Association of Jazz Educators (NAJE) and the "jazz night" concert at the Seattle convention in 1968,[59] jazz concerts and sessions on the teaching of jazz became a mainstay at both national and divisional MENC conferences. The *MEJ* also lent its support to jazz education in the schools through its publications, especially the November 1975 special focus issue on jazz and jazz studies, and the January 1980 special issue on improvisation, which contained a section on both vocal and instrumental jazz improvisation.[60] Though grateful for the support given to jazz education, jazz educators were often concerned that the creativity of jazz improvisation would be lost in the flurry to "play from the charts."[61] Noting that jazz and music education "are a real collision of cultures," Gunther Schuller said what was needed were "music teachers who can translate from the jazz world to the Western world."[62]

Support for popular music in the schools also came early as "music educators searched for methods that would use the pervasive influence of popular music to sensitize students to the common elements of music."[63] In 1969, the *MEJ* issued a special report on the use of popular musics, including rock, in the classroom. Although there were a few scattered articles on popular music over the next years, in 1979 the *MEJ* carried several more articles focused primarily on popular music styles.[64] Paralleling this reduced emphasis on popular musics, there were fewer sessions devoted to popular musics at MENC conferences, though beginning in the 1980s, "show choirs" performing popular music repertoire became more common. However, during this period, music teachers often supplemented the music series textbooks with currently popular music which they purchased themselves. As a result, the music series texts began to include more popular music and Broadway show tunes, especially for the sixth through eighth grades.[65] Rock music simply did not receive the same attention as jazz and popular styles either in the *MEJ* or at MENC conferences. After the emphasis given rock music in the special reports on "youth music" and "urban music education" of 1969 and 1970, respectively, the *MEJ* published few other articles on rock music in the schools until its special focus issue in 1991.[66] Although jazz and popular musics were generally accepted by most music educators, even with this affirmation, some teachers still felt that rock music had no place in the music classroom.[67]

Music Series Textbooks

Along with the increased attention given popular music in the school music texts, the music publishing industry was also becoming more responsive to the requests of minority groups for greater representation of their musics in the music series texts. The Minority Concerns Commission brought music educators and music publishers together at the 1974 MENC conference at Anaheim. This session enabled the publishers to personally answer the teachers' questions regarding the authenticity of the music presented, and the need to include the music of Native Americans as well as the music of minority composers. Since the music industry publishes what will sell, publishers began to respond to the teachers' requests for more music of minority composers, and more authentic representative examples of the musics from specific cultures in the music series textbooks.

Beginning in 1970, and throughout the 1980s, the percentage of folk songs in the music texts from Western Europe declined to about 20 percent of the total number of songs included, with a corresponding increase in the percentage of songs from various minority cultures. African-American songs showed the greatest increase, followed in order by songs of Caribbean/Latin American origin, Native American songs, and songs from several countries in Asia.[68] The number of different cultures represented also increased. In 1990, the Master Index of Silver Burdett and Ginn's *World of Music* (grades K–8) lists folk and composed songs from sixty-six countries or geographic regions.[69]

Not only the numbers of songs, but also the authenticity of the musics increased during this period. Music publishing companies had often employed experts in various musical areas as special contributors and consultants; now they turned to ethnomusicologists and music educators with experience in specific cultures. Representative of this trend, William Anderson (Chinese, Japanese, Korean musics) contributed to *New Dimensions in Music* in 1970, and Dorothy Gillett (Hawaiian musics) and Alan Lomax (American folk musics) were among the consultants for the 1975 edition of *Exploring Music*.[70] The Silver Burdett Company employed the services of Louis Ballard (Native American musics), Judith Becker (Southeast Asian musics), Tilford Brooks (African-American musics), Robert Garfias (Latin American musics), William Malm (Japanese musics), and David Reck (Indian musics) for its 1978 edition of *Music*.[71]

Besides more authentic music, there were also more songs included with foreign language texts, and all the music textbooks began to include photographs, art reproductions, poetry, and descriptions of musical instruments from many cultures. These helped students gain a better understanding of the musics they were studying, and the place these musics held in each different society.[72] The music textbooks also presented sections that focused on composers from other cultural backgrounds.[73]

The recordings that accompanied the music texts for listening lessons also began to include authentic examples of folk music from an assortment of cultures as well as the music of minority composers. While the earlier recordings contained as many inaccuracies as the music texts, such as simplified melodies, and arrangements that did not reflect authentic performance styles, there was a general improvement over this period.[74] In addition to the recordings supplied by the music publishers, music teachers also had available to them an enormous amount of authentic recordings (records, cassette tapes, CDs), films, and videos made possible through the advances in technology and the continuing research of ethnomusicologists. Teachers had access to literally the whole world of musics. Along with the needs of multicultural music education, the competition from this influx of authentic musical material encouraged publishers to provide a more accurate pre-

sentation of music cultures in the music series texts and their accompanying recordings.

There were still inaccuracies in the musics as presented in the music
textbooks, however. Song origins were sometimes mislabeled; accompaniments did not always match the style of the culture. As in the past, song selections continued to be governed by propriety, and as a result, some of the
songs did not fully represent the music culture. As Ricardo Trimillos said
after examining the Japanese, Chinese, and Mexican songs in the 1988 Silver Burdett and Ginn series, "The songs were interesting; they were nice little songs and had been cleaned up, but had little to do with the way folk
music was styled and what people were actually doing." The songs in the
texts, though intended to represent Mexican-American or Asian-American
culture, "were not the [music] cultures they [children] were experiencing at
home," and somehow it was still "school music" with its own repertoire.[75]
In addition, Anthony Palmer indicated that "one of the problems with the
textbook series is that they teach from a Western point of view, even when
they include authentic recordings. . . . [For example,] oral traditions are put
down in notation." He felt that oral traditions taught from notation, "when
we could kind of re-create their [the culture's] mode of behavior in learning
music," superimposed a Western teaching methodology on the original culture.[76]

Minority Concerns/Multicultural Awareness Commission

In the early 1970s, music education, like general education, felt the urgent
demands for minority representation. "Disenchanted over what they saw as
a lack of black participation in the MENC,"[77] African-American music educators brought their charges to the MENC following the 1972 biennial convention in Atlanta. These concerned African-American music educators cited
MENC for a "lack of visible participation of black people, insufficient use of
black resources," and a conflicting conference schedule that they felt put
African-American music sessions at a disadvantage. They presented MENC
with a statement demanding that (1) the MENC be more active in seeking
out African-American music educators to participate in its conferences, (2)
African-Americans be better represented in the MENC, especially in policy
and decision-making positions, and (3) African-Americans be included in
planning and implementing programmed objectives of the MENC.[78]

This impromptu meeting in Atlanta quickly led to the organization of
the National Black Music Caucus (NBMC), which committed itself to "making the national organization [MENC] more responsive" to the needs of
African-American music educators.[79] Gradually, the NBMC became an advisory organization within the MENC, identifying and promoting both
African and African-American and other minority music experts, African
and African-American musics in education, and sponsoring MENC conference sessions. The NBMC also encouraged research, and published resources
to assist music educators with implementing African-American musics in

the classroom.[80] The organization officially became an affiliated member organization of the MENC in the later 1980s, the only such organization within MENC to promote a specific music culture.[81]

The charges leveled by the Black Music Caucus in Atlanta were taken seriously by the MENC. In July 1972, the National Executive Board passed a motion to create a national Minority Concerns Commission (MCC) appointed by the MENC to "make a study of minority concerns as they apply to music education in the United States."[82] Where the NBMC focused specifically on African-American musics, the MCC was "dedicated to alerting the MENC membership to the concerns of *all* minority groups."[83] As the MENC realized,

> It is no longer appropriate that those individuals in control of the classroom be concerned only with educating within the context of their own cultural background or cultural experience, regardless of their ethnic origin. Today's teacher must be sufficiently knowledgeable to function with children from a variety of ethnic backgrounds. In addition, he or she needs to be able to assist in helping these children relate to their own culture as well as that which emanates from the Western traditions.[84]

In July 1974, the NEB accepted the following statement drawn up by the MCC as its official affirmative action policy statement:

> In recognition of the heterogeneous composition of the nation and of the fact that in a multi-ethnic society a great understanding of the contributions of one's own heritage and those of one's fellow citizens can contribute to a more harmonious, patriotic, and committed populace, and in recognition of the principle that all persons in the educational institutions of the nation should have an opportunity to learn about the differing and unique contributions to the national heritage made by each ethnic group,"* it is therefore recommended that all units of MENC—state, local and national—when planning programs and classroom activities, make every effort to include individuals and representative music from the various ethnic groups that comprise our nation. This type of consideration would thereby reflect the pluralistic nature of our society.[85]

The issues addressed by the MCC during the 1970s were threefold: the almost desperate need for instructional methods and materials, the need to see the MENC actively include persons from minority groups in conferences (performances, music industry presentations, public relations, etc.), and the need for multicultural music teacher education at undergraduate, graduate, and in-service levels.[86] To these ends, the MCC encouraged multicultural music education through publications, development of resource lists and suggested lesson plans, conference sessions, promotion of both pre-service and in-service teacher training, and research in multicultural music education.[87]

---

*Elementary and Secondary Education Act, Title IX, Section 901.

In 1977, the NEB "authorized the change of the name of the MCC to the National Minority Awareness Commission (MAC),"[88] but in order to be current with changes in multicultural education, and because the work of the commission moved into "the broad spectrum of music from various cultures and visible ethnic groups throughout the country,"[89] the name was changed again in 1979 to the Multicultural Awareness Commission (MCAC). In 1982 the NEB restructured its committees and the MCAC ceased functioning as a commission within the MENC. Instead the national chairperson for Multicultural Awareness represented the state Multicultural Awareness coordinators on the National Council of Chairs.[90]

Research[91]

Research in multicultural music education, so strongly urged by the MCC, increased dramatically from 1968 to 1990. With the impetus of the reports from the Yale Seminar and Tanglewood Symposium, and the availability of generous federal funding, a number of interested music educators began to develop programs, projects, methods, and materials to implement various specific ethnic musics in the classroom. Much of this curricular research took the form of lessons, units of study, teacher's source books, and even complete course outlines; many of these were untested collections of materials. Other research tested students' musical achievement in, or attitudes toward, the music from a given culture.[92]

While most research projects focused on the general music curriculum, some extended multicultural music education into the instrumental and choral programs, and a few even were intended for application in higher education.[93] In addition to this research, several studies focused on the future implementation of these materials through teacher training.[94] As in general education, the research recommended more effective multicultural music teacher education.

While methodologies, materials, and teacher training were major concerns, other researchers tried to provide a philosophical basis for multicultural music education. Anthony Palmer's and Abraham Schwadron's research placed multicultural music education in the context of aesthetic education, which was the generally accepted philosophy of music education during this period. Both researchers defined the aesthetic goals of multicultural music education, Palmer through acknowledging the intrinsic aesthetic value of each music, and Schwadron through viewing the aesthetics of several cultures comparatively.[95] To these ideas, Paul Burgett added the viewpoint of the African-American aesthetic, which was later seconded by Marvin Curtis.[96]

In the late 1980s, David Elliott introduced a praxial philosophy of music education. In a close parallel to Pratt's research in general education, Elliott presented his concepts of multicultural music education and, like Pratt, recommended a "dynamic multiculturalism model." He concluded that such a model combined the "widest possible range of world musics and a world view of musical concepts," enabled students to achieve the ability to "discriminate and appreciate the differences and similarities among musical cultures," developed bimusicality, and offered the "possibility of developing appreciations and new behavior patterns not only in relation to world musics, but also in relations to world *peoples*."[97]

Along with this philosophical research, there was also some evaluative research focusing on how well multicultural music education had been implemented over the two decades since Tanglewood. This research showed that in twenty years, progress in fully implementing multicultural music education had been slow, in spite of the wealth of available materials.[98] The authenticity of the materials themselves was also subject of evaluation, with studies examining both the songs of various cultures represented in the school music textbooks, and the recordings that accompany these texts.[99]

ISME Conferences

Throughout the period from 1968 to 1990, three areas of multicultural music education research were frequently reflected in the papers presented at the International Society for Music Education (ISME): methodology, philosophy, and music teacher education. Though many sessions offered various methods for accessing the musics of the world in the classroom, the use of the commonalities found in various musics was a recurrent theme. In 1972, Robert Werner was among the first to propose an international music curriculum employing a cross-cultural approach based on the elements of music (such as melody, rhythm, and form), an echo of the Brunerian "concepts" approach developed in music education in the early 1960s.[100] In a similar vein, Kwabene Nketia recommended looking for "universal recurrences." He explained further:

> While recognizing the uniqueness of each musical culture, an inter-cultural music education programme would take particular interest in the study of universals in music in recognition of our basic humanity and the common patterns of human response that persist everywhere in spite of variability of culture. . . . The music educator can use it [study of universals] for handling musical materials cross-culturally in terms of identities, similarities and differences or in terms of alternative mode of musical expression [or] Aesthetics.[101]

In 1986 Leon Burton described a comprehensive approach to studying the musics of diverse cultures based on the commonalities of conceptual framework, musical process, melody, functions, and performance practices.[102]

As the 1980s proved to be a period of reflection and evaluation in general education, likewise music education stood back from the first rush of interest in world musics to take a look at multicultural music education, what it should do for the student, and how it fit within a philosophy of music education. The papers presented at the ISME conferences of the 1980s tended to focus on a broad world view of music education, often citing the educational benefits of multicultural music education in a diverse society. Students who learn about the musics of other cultures would extend their own musical expression, appreciate diversity, develop tolerance and respect for others, see the interrelatedness of all the arts, and develop a global perspective both of society and of various music systems.[103] This broadening view became the theme of the 1988 ISME meeting in Canberra, Australia: "A World View of Music Education."

At the Canberra conference, Nketia called this world view "a nonparochial approach to the music of other cultures" but he also warned that without this global view, multiculturalism "can lead to separatism rather than integration."[104] To make sense of diversity, music educators will be required to find

> some way of facilitating the sharing of musical experience through programmes in which musical cultures are made to complement each other, or programmes in which students from different backgrounds become involved in reciprocal learning and mutual responsiveness ... [in order to] build bridges of knowledge and understanding not only between local traditions, but also between the musical cultures of the world.[105]

At the same time that multicultural music education was changing to accept a global perspective, the philosophy of music education was undergoing a change as well, as David Elliott presented his ideas on a "global philosophy of music education." In his praxial philosophy, Elliott viewed music as performance, as "human internalization," and looked to answer "why musical experience is universal, fundamental and necessary to man."[106]

Overriding all of the discussions at these ISME meetings was the topic of music teacher education. Nearly every presentation on multicultural music education mentioned the need for teachers trained in the musics of a variety of cultures. In 1976, Brenner presented a challenge to music education by saying "if school music is to have relevance for the general populace, the education of the music teacher will include experience with many forms and styles of music and a sensing of the essence and the cultural forces in folk, popular, and ethnomusics at a level of familiarity traditionally confined to 'Western art music.' "[107] Music teacher education in 1984 was faced with the twofold problem of preparing teachers "to teach their own indigenous music, as well as the musics of other cultures."[108] The challenge of training new teachers in multicultural approaches proved difficult enough, but there were many in-service teachers who had had no such training. In 1984, Schwadron noted that "many teachers-in-service are neither musically or pedagogically prepared to meet the needs posed by a curriculum charged with the world of musics. They are simply not ready either to conceptualise nor to teach others about different systems of musical communication, values, meanings, functions and performances."[109]

Teacher Training and Multicultural Mandates

The music education profession acknowledged this pressing need for teacher training in multicultural music education. As research had shown, though materials on the musics of various cultures were quickly being made available, prospective teachers were not being trained in how to use them. The National Association of Schools of Music (NASM) standards of 1972 indicated that all undergraduate music curricula should provide "a repertory for study that embraces all cultures and historical periods." NASM also showed an awareness of the social changes taking place in the country at the time as the standards also recommended "experimentation with curricular patterns and modes which might lead to . . . areas of exploration which appear in response to a changing society."[110] In 1974, NASM redesigned its standards, reflecting the trend toward competency-based teacher education that was sweeping the county. These new competencies added specifics to the general broad repertory in the 1972 recommendations include the following:

> Students should have opportunities through both performance and academic study to deal with music of various historical periods, cultural sources, and media. Students should have experience with Western concert music, contemporary "pop" music, music of non-Western cultures, folk music of Europe and America, and Western art music since 1950.[111]

In addition to these general requirements, the baccalaureate degree in music education should prepare students "to relate their understanding of musical styles and principles to all types of music, including 'pop' and folk music" in their teaching. In acknowledging the population a music educator faced daily, the standards also recommended that the undergraduate music educator give evidence of the ability "to maintain positive relationships with individuals of varied social and ethnic groups."[112] These standards are still in effect.

In 1980, the MENC Commission on Graduate Music Teacher Education followed NASM's lead and recommended that along with the basic requirements, the master's degree also include

> Basic knowledge of music literature, including jazz, popular, ethnic, and non-Western music
>
> An acquaintance with instructional materials for multicultural needs
>
> Techniques for motivating and relating to students of diverse cultures.[113]

In addition to these professional mandates and recommendations, there were also state and local multicultural education regulations for curricula and music teacher certification. Many states required the same multicultural education experiences mandated for elementary and secondary teacher certification for music teacher certification, though a few began to require that music teachers have a knowledge of both Western and non-Western musics.[114] In addition to certification requirements, in the 1980s, some state boards of education began to be more specific about the multicultural content within the school music curriculum.

Colleges and universities had to comply with both state certification requirements and college accreditation mandates for multicultural music education. Some made introductory courses in world musics, and/or non-Western performing ensembles available to music education students, while others offered courses in ethnomusicology, and many added summer workshops in the musics of specific cultures.[115] While some schools of music had exemplary courses in multicultural music education,[116] most continued to emphasize the Western European art music tradition, almost to the exclusion of other musics except perhaps for jazz.[117]

While colleges and universities struggled with incorporating world musics in the music teacher education program, the MENC began to address the problem of teaching in-service music educators about a variety of musics through its conferences and publications.

MENC Conferences

It did not take long following the Tanglewood declaration for the MENC to incorporate musics from various cultures around the world in its national conferences. Designed around the recommendations of the Tanglewood Symposium,[118] the 1968 conference in Seattle set the precedent for the inclusion of the musics from many cultures in successive conference programs. At this conference, the University of Hawaii presented a program of songs and dances illustrating the diverse heritage of the Hawaiian islands, and Barbara Reeder, then with the Seattle Schools, directed her students' performance of music from African countries south of the Sahara.[119] According to Charles Gary, "She put on a program with dance and costumes and intricate African rhythms. It just knocked everybody's socks off!"[120]

Not only were performances of Polynesian and African music featured at this conference, but for the first time, a jazz concert was scheduled at a general session evening concert. The atmosphere at this concert was electric, as a standing-room-only crowd provided ovations for the young jazz performers.[121] As Allen Scott noted in retrospect, this concert marked "the beginning of an acceptance of jazz in education," or, put a little more bluntly by guest composer Meredith Willson at the end of the concert, "the old gal has finally become legitimate."[122]

Beginning in the 1970s, MENC conferences really tried, as Anderson said, to bring "a broader study of world musical traditions into the curriculum."[123] An Ethnic Musics Institute was organized by O. M. Hartsell for the 1970 Chicago conference, inspired by the success of an "Institute on the Music of Asia and Oceania" presented at the 1969 Western division conference in Honolulu.[124] Following a format similar to that developed for the Western division, each session featured a lecture and demonstration of specific music cultures (Japanese, Native American, Pacific Islander, and South

Indian) by a specialist in the field; the concluding session was devoted to a presentation of various teaching resources.[125]

The 1972 conference in Atlanta also included multiple sessions of both ethnic musics and the history of jazz.[126] Because of the input from the newly formed Minority Concerns Commission and Black Music Caucus, there was a real concern that the 1974 conference in Anaheim be reflective of the musics of the entire country. This conference presented twenty-four sessions with musics from various cultures, ranging from a demonstration by an African drum ensemble, to choral and instrumental performance practices in various parts of the world, to jazz education.[127]

The MENC national conferences during the late 1970s and throughout the 1980s continued to offer sessions to assist music educators with the implementation of musics from various cultures. Representative of these many sessions were African-American music (Miami Beach, 1980),[128] a viola lecture/recital of music by Spanish and Latin American composers (San Antonio, 1981),[129] diverse approaches to teaching multiple music cultures in the classroom (Anaheim, 1986, and Indianapolis, 1988),[130] and ensembles from Hungary, Australia, Taiwan, and Canada (Washington, D.C., 1990).[131]

Throughout this period, MENC divisional conferences reflected the trend toward multicultural music education seen in the national meetings. Like the national conferences, the divisional programs included sessions that featured information about the musics of various cultures, and methods and materials to help music educators implement these musics in their classrooms. Notable among these were the extensive sessions of the Institute for Ethnic Musics at Honolulu (California/Western Division, 1969) and the entire Eastern Division (1989) conference with its multicultural/international theme. The latter not only offered mini-institutes on African-American and Russian/Jewish musics, but also required that all performing groups include at least one selection of music from a culture other than the Western classical tradition (such as folk, jazz, and non-Western) in their program.[132]

Multicultural Music Education and the *MEJ*

Throughout the period from 1968 to 1990, the *MEJ* published articles which provided music educators with background knowledge, resources, and teaching methods about the musics of many cultures. The first articles published from 1968 to 1972 provided basic information about various musical cultures, but gradually more were included on how to use these musics in the classroom. Many of these dealt with African-American music, hardly unusual in light of the growing awareness of African-American culture in the United States.[133] Informative articles also appeared on the music of India and Hudson Bay Native Canadians, and another on Native American music in the classroom.[134]

From 1972 to 1990, the *MEJ* continued to include articles about musics from many cultures. The topics were eclectic, ranging from Eskimo string-figure games,[135] to Scottish pipe and drum bands and how to make a Tsonga xylophone;[136] from Appalachian traditions, gospel music, and the blues, to the training of Indian musicians.[137] The *MEJ* brought the musics of Argentina, China, Tibet, and Native America to the attention of music educators.[138] Along with these more explanatory articles, there were some thought-provoking essays on the balance between attitudes and strategies when working with world musics and the social foundations of the music of African-Americans.[139]

As music educators gradually started to employ their new knowledge of various music cultures in their classes, they wrote articles to give their colleagues ideas about what worked for them. Some told of their methods for incorporating a world perspective in their music classes, while others offered examples of how they employed specific folk musics.[140]

A multicultural perspective was starting to pervade other areas of music study as well. The *MEJ*'s January 1980 special focus issue on improvisation devoted an entire section to world musics, addressing improvisation specifically in the musics of Latin America, West Africa, the Middle East, and Korea.[141] In a similar crossover, the topic of musical creativity was viewed from a cross-cultural perspective.[142]

The emphasis during the later 1980s tended to be twofold. Multicultural perspectives in music not only increased students' knowledge about the musics of other peoples, but increased understanding about the people who made these musics. Articles stressed the fact that teachers cannot teach understanding if they themselves do not understand. Through multicultural music education, teachers could provide "windows" to cross-cultural understanding.[143] In addition to these regularly occurring articles, the *MEJ* published two special focus issues on multicultural music education during this period.

MEJ Special Focus Issues, 1972 and 1983

Following on the successes of the 1969 Western Division Conference in Hawaii, and the Ethnic Music Institute at the 1970 Chicago meeting, the October 1972 issue of the *MEJ*, subheaded Music in World Cultures, was "a further step in trying to make information about the musics of different cultures available to the profession-at-large" and a reflection of the more global thinking of the early 1970s.[144] Barbara Smith, guest editor of this issue, further explained:

> The intent of this special issue was to provide materials for teachers, . . . some examples of application, and, we hoped, some stimulus [for teachers] to look around their own particular area to create new materials [and] to bring good performers from their local resident traditions into the schools.[145]

Designed as a resource for music educators, this issue was divided into three sections, the first of which presented an overview of world musical cultures. Beginning with an introduction by Margaret Mead,[146] the articles progressed through the musics of Northeast Asia, Southeast Asia, South Asia, the Middle East–North Africa, Africa south of the Sahara, European folk traditions, the Americas, and Oceania, providing basic information about these various music cultures.[147] A unique aspect of this issue was the inclusion of two soundsheets with musical examples from cultures representative of each of these world regions. The listening guide that accompanied the soundsheets contained pertinent information about the source, context, and content of each selection.

The second section contained articles explaining the need to employ these musics in the schools, and suggesting some ways to use musics from a variety of cultures in the classroom.[148] A compilation of resources for classroom music teachers made up the third section of this issue. With the exception of the resource list on African-American music published in 1971, there had not been another effort like this one. The issue contained a glossary of terms, a bibliography, a discography, and a filmography of available materials for many cultures. There were also nearly ten pages of pictures of musicians and instruments from around the world.[149]

The book review column of this particular issue is well worth noting.[150] Up to this point there were few, if any, books reviewed that had anything to do with multicultural approaches in music. This was owing in part to the scarcity of such books, but also to the fact that the *MEJ* published reviews of books that its readership would find useful. Up until 1967, the musics from cultures around the world were simply not very high on the "useful" list for most teachers. However, all the books reviewed for this issue dealt with some facet of these musics. These reviews became a further resource for the teacher looking for more depth on the subject of various cultures, or ethnomusicology in general. From this issue onward, the *MEJ* either reviewed publications about world musics, or listed them in the Book Browsing or Study Shelf columns, and since 1989 has supplemented these with Video Views.[151]

While the 1972 special issue had focused on acquainting music educators with musics from around the world, the May 1983 special issue, subheaded The Multicultural Imperative, emphasized the fact that music educators needed to teach music from a multicultural perspective. This issue had four main topic areas: the multicultural imperative, educational tactics, tools for teaching world musics, and selected resources. The articles in the first section all stressed the fact that no educator could ignore the cultural diversity within the classrooms of the United States.[152] The second and third sections of this issue offered assistance with classroom applications.[153] In addition, there were ideas for using the community as a resource, annotated resources for Hawaiian and Samoan musics, and especially pertinent reviews in both the Book Browsing and Study Shelf columns.[154] The issue concluded with a selected resource list, which, though not as extensive as the bibliographical type of listing found in the 1972 special issue, included reports, committee results, and coming events such as the 1984 ISME conference and the Wesleyan Symposium.[155]

The Wesleyan Symposium

The MENC, Wesleyan University, and the Theodore Presser Foundation jointly sponsored the Wesleyan Symposium on the Application of Social Anthropology to the Teaching and Learning of Music (Wesleyan Symposium) in August 1984. The MENC invited anthropologist/ethnomusicologist David McAllester to organize and chair the symposium, the emphasis of which was on "exploring practical implications of research findings in other cultures for U.S. music teachers in their daily instruction."[156] Because the symposium was well funded through the Presser Foundation, McAllester was able to bring "ethnomusicologists from all around the world, from Germany, from Ireland, from England, as well as all over this country to talk about the role of world music in music education."[157] There were several presentations on the transmission of music and dance in various cultures (African, Bulgarian, Hopi, Iranian, and Polynesian). Other discussions centered on music education and social inclusion as a process of transmission, and the use of ethnomusicology as a teaching tool.[158] The Wesleyan Symposium "was the first such conference to focus principally on a transcultural approach, seeking information from musical practice and thought, world-wide."[159] Though it did not deal specifically with curricula for classroom use, it was the first time the MENC sponsored a gathering of anthropologists and ethnomusicologists for the purpose of a face-to-face exchange with the music educators who would use the results of their scholarship.

Ethnomusicology and Music Education

The increasing acceptance in music education of the ethnomusicological view of "music as, and in, culture," influenced in part by the Wesleyan Symposium, led many music educators to join the growing Society for Ethnomusicology (SEM). Their interest, and the fact that the leadership of MENC increasingly approached SEM for help with presentations of ethnic music for its conferences and publications led to the formation of the Music Education Committee of the SEM in 1968.[160] This committee was formed as a liaison between SEM and MENC and any other educators interested in teaching the musics of various cultures.

Besides this committee, the growing cooperation between ethnomusicology and music education produced several forms of collaboration. Ethnomusicologists presented lecture/demonstrations at MENC conventions, and music educators presented educational applications of musics from around the world at SEM conferences. Action research, texts, and other resource materials for multicultural music education have resulted from ethnomusicologists, sometimes working alone, but more often collaboratively with music educators.[161]

One publication best illustrates this expanding association between music educators and ethnomusicologists: *Multicultural Perspectives in Music Ed-*

ucation.[162] Edited by Anderson and Campbell and published by MENC in
1989, this book provided music educators with information about a variety
of music cultures as well as practical assistance for presenting these musics
in the classroom. Many chapters consisted of an introductory section on the
musics of a specific culture-region written by an ethnomusicologist whose
expertise in this culture area was well known, followed by lesson plans prepared by a music educator who was likewise familiar with the music culture. It is this balanced approach, along with a general discussion of music
in culture in the opening chapter, which proved so valuable to music educators.[163] The largest book ever published by MENC at the time, *Multicultural Perspectives* represented a major commitment to multicultural music education on the part of the organization, and as the first major publication of
its kind, it may prove to be one of the pivotal books in music education history.[164]

Another type of collaboration took place at the 1990 Multicultural Symposium in Washington, D.C., where ethnomusicologists teamed with music
educators and native culture bearers to present approaches for multicultural
music education in the classroom. Though registration was restricted to a
limited number of music educators, the information available at this three-
day symposium reached many more through a text and videos compiled
from the proceedings and disseminated through MENC.[165]

The Multicultural Symposium

The MENC presented the Multicultural Symposium: Multicultural Approaches to Music Education in cooperation with the Society for Ethnomusicology, the Smithsonian Institution's Office of Folklife Programs, and
MENC's Society for General Music. Originally proposed at the 1988 SEM
meeting in Arizona, the symposium, under the direction of William M. Anderson, was planned "to promote a great national discussion among music
teachers on the importance of a broad multicultural curriculum in music at
all educational levels." Noting that "in the past, school music has often been
a separate phenomenon from the music with which our children grew up,"
the planning committee, comprising ethnomusicologists, music educators,
and representatives from the Smithsonian Institution sought to "put our
classrooms in contact with the real world."[166]

The symposium targeted the culture and music of four general cultural
groups: African-American, Asian-American, Hispanic-American, and Native American. An ethnomusicologist, performers from the culture, and a
music educator well versed in that musical tradition joined together to present each music culture and to give suggestions for classroom implementation.[167]

The speakers at the symposium provided much for music educators to
reflect upon.[168] Bernice Reagon from the National Museum of American History, Smithsonian Institution, stressed the need to help students "understand

the relationship between people and their music."[169] Along the same lines, ethnomusicologist David McAllester said, "We need to learn how to live together even though we belong to different cultures."[170] Perhaps even more powerful was the following statement by Edwin Schupman, a consultant with ORBIS Associates:

> I believe the potential role of a music educator has not yet been realized in terms of broadening the multicultural horizons of their students, of promoting human understanding, and tolerance for racial and cultural differences. [171]

All the presenters at the symposium pointed out the fact that each large music tradition is itself multicultural, each encompassing a great variety of musics. Because of this multiplicity of music traditions, Reagon stressed how important the challenge of multicultural music education is for music educators, saying:

> We must struggle to understand how, as music educators, we can begin to validate the music that comes into our rooms the first time a child enters school. We must begin to understand that there are almost no human beings who come into our space who are not loaded down with powerful music traditions - and sometimes many music traditions.[172]

At the close of the symposium, a Resolution for Future Directions and Actions was adopted by the participants. This declaration, partly quoted below, forms a statement of commitment to multicultural music education for not only the MENC as an organization, but for all music educators.

WHEREAS:

Americans are increasingly exposed to other world cultures through travel and media,

Demographic data document the increasing multicultural nature of the United States,

American schools now contain large percentages of students from various cultural backgrounds,

Organizations such as the Music Educators National Conference, the Society for Ethnomusicology, and the Smithsonian Institution have placed increasing emphasis on the importance of learning and teaching a broad array of musical traditions,

BE IT RESOLVED THAT:

We will seek to ensure that multicultural approaches to teaching music will be incorporated into every elementary and secondary school music curriculum,

Multicultural approaches to teaching music will be incorporated into all phases of teacher education in music,

Music teachers will seek to assist students in understanding that there are many different but equally valid forms of musical expression,

Instruction will include not only the study of other musics but the relationship of those musics to their respective cultures; further that meaning of music within each culture be sought for its own value,

MENC will encourage national and regional accrediting groups to *require* broad, multicultural perspectives for all education programs, particularly those in music (see Appendix D for the complete text).[173]

SUMMARY

With the reports of the Yale Seminar and the Tanglewood Symposium acting as catalysts, music education moved quickly to incorporate all musics in the curriculum. Reflecting the tenor of the times, the MENC recognized that music education had to serve "the needs of citizens in a pluralistic society," and directed its resources toward encouraging a multicultural perspective for music education. Musics from cultures around the world and within the United States, including jazz, popular, and rock music styles, found a place in music education, particularly in urban areas. Efforts to counter the need for in-service educators to gain experience with these musics included conference sessions (sponsored by both MENC and ISME), journal articles, summer workshops, symposia, and increased contacts between music education and ethnomusicology.

The immediate result of accepting the musics from a variety of cultures in the curriculum was a plethora of resource materials, both about the various musics, and how to implement them in the classroom. In addition to these new resources, the school music textbooks began to include more authentic songs from a greater variety of cultures than ever before, supplemented with photographs, art reproductions, and poetry from these cultures.

Despite the fact that all musics were accepted in the music curriculum, by 1990 there was little evidence that schools of music had incorporated multicultural approaches in music theory, history, or even music education methods. Researchers throughout the period found that compliance with both professional and state multicultural education mandates was slow; the one point upon which they all agreed was the continuing need for adequate multicultural music teacher education.

The MENC worked to enable in-service educators to gain experience with these musics, in particular co-sponsoring a national symposium on Multicultural Approaches to Music Education with the Society for Ethnomusicology and the Smithsonian Institution in 1990. The combined presentations of ethnomusicologists, native culture bearers, and music educators at this symposium gave evidence of how far multicultural music education had developed since 1968. The final resolution of the Multicultural Symposium officially committed music education to a broad multicultural perspective. Allen Sapp called it "the hope of the future."[174]

Conclusions, Implications, and Questions

The first materials for ethnic music programs often focused on a one-culture, one-unit approach. Although this method remained viable throughout the period, music education soon began to use the world's musics as exemplars for the basic elements of music (such as melody, rhythm, form, and timbre). Both are currently accepted modes of incorporating a multicultural perspective in the classroom. However, with the current emphasis on infusion across the curriculum, the one-unit approach is losing favor, and questions have been raised about the exemplar approach. For instance, can we always look at the musics from another culture in terms of the structures of Western art music? Should we? Would an approach based on geographic regions offer a better way to present all musics accurately? How might a "topics" approach such as the role of the performer, or the place of music in the culture present more possibilities?

Throughout this period, general music programs were the first to incorporate a multicultural approach; choral and instrumental programs had only begun to implement the musics from a variety of cultures by 1990, though there had been some research in this direction. Historically, however, this has not always been so. Jazz was first primarily the domain of instrumental music education before it was adopted by the choral and general music practitioners, and spirituals quickly found favor in the choral program. Yet a balanced school music program implies the need for a multicultural approach in all areas of music education, general, choral, and instrumental. In what ways could this be achieved?

CHAPTER **7**

Since 1990

*I believe the potential role of a music educator has not yet been
realized in terms of broadening the multicultural
horizons of their students.*

—Edwin Schupman[1]

The 1990s ushered in a period of economic recession. Stricter budgets forced
retrenchment in all areas from business to government to education. Cor-
porate downsizing became a fact of life, and school systems operated on
austerity budgets.

At the same time that educational systems began belt tightening, the
public began demanding reforms. The chief reforms came under the head-
ing of exit competencies or educational standards, but other topics such as
accountability, authentic assessment, and site-based management paralleled
them in importance. Education and music education alike have had to strad-
dle the line between cost cutting and program development. Multiculturalism is in the midst of this balancing act, and cannot be ignored. It is now a
part of the fabric of the entire country—as pride of heritage, raised consciousness, political correctness, and sometimes as blatant racism. There is
no longer a question of whether education and music education would employ a multicultural approach in the curriculum. The question now was, and
is, how a multicultural or world perspective could best be fostered through
the curriculum.

HISTORICAL CONTEXT

Goals 2000: Educate America Act

At the federal level, the issue of improving education has been high on the agenda in the past few years. The interest in national goals for education had its origins in the six National Education Goals agreed to in 1990 by President George Bush and the state governors. Soon after this, the National Council for Standards and Testing published *Raising Standards for American Education* (1992), which represented one of the first national efforts to raise educational standards.[2] This report led to the development of national standards in several subject areas. Influenced by this report, and others such as the Secretary of Labor's Commission on Achieving Necessary Skills and the National Commission on Time and Learning,[3] Congress passed the Goals 2000: Educate America Act in 1994. This law outlined eight goals for education throughout the nation, to be accomplished by the year 2000. Along with goals to improve preschool education and attendance, this act set high achievement goals for all students. Students would exit grades four, eight, and twelve "having demonstrated competency over challenging subject matter including English, mathematics, science, foreign languages, civics and government, economics, *arts* [italics added], history, and geography."[4] Under the section containing the objectives that would lead to the accomplishment of this goal, one specifically had an impact on multicultural education in all subject areas. Objective six reads: "All students will be knowledgeable about the diverse cultural heritage of the Nation and about the world community."[5]

These goals and objectives were outlined at the federal level, but the law placed implementation at the state level. Federal grants to the states provided the funding necessary to begin work on state projects to bring these national goals to fruition.

At the same time that the federal government was encouraging education with lofty goals and grant funding, there was ever stronger pressure to balance federal and state budgets. This has led to severe reductions in spending, including lowered support for education.

Desegregation

Desegregation continues to be an issue in public education. It has been further complicated because of the 1995 Supreme Court decision *Missouri v. Jenkins*. In reversing a prior district court decision, the Supreme Court curtailed federal judges' authority in school desegregation cases by restricting their judgments only to issues of segregation. They could no longer pressure school districts into improving educational opportunities for minority students in ways that would both attract and keep majority students in the school system. Justice Rehnquist's decision stated: "The District Court's pur-

suit of the goal of 'desegregative attractiveness' results in too many impon-
derables and is too far removed from the task of eliminating the racial iden-
tifiability of the schools."[6] This decision had a direct bearing on desegregation cases still pending, affecting everything from maintaining magnet
schools to pay raises for teachers and staff.

Court decisions also effected affirmative action at both the federal and
the collegiate level. In *Adarand Constructors Inc. v. Peña*, the Supreme Court
limited the use of racial preferences in federal programs, and in *Hopwood v.
Texas*, the U.S. Court of Appeals for the Fifth District barred the University
of Texas Law School from considering race as a "factor in deciding which
applicant to admit in order to achieve a diverse student body."[7] The questions of desegregation and reverse discrimination have not yet been settled,
but both *Hopwood v. Texas* and *Missouri v. Jenkins* will have direct impact on
population diversity in the schools.

EDUCATIONAL CONTEXT

Goals 2000: Educate America Act

Goals 2000 has been as influential on education as the legislation of the 1970s,
and possibly is more far reaching: "At the heart of Goals 2000 is the effort
to raise academic standards."[8] In response to Goals 2000 and the reports surrounding it, various academic organizations began drawing up national
guidelines or standards for their subject areas. The National Council of
Teachers of Mathematics released standards for mathematics in 1989. The
Center for Civic Education and the National Geographic Society published
their standards for civics and geography in 1991 and 1994, respectively.[9] The
history standards were first presented in 1994, but there was such controversy over them that they were withdrawn and are now being revised.[10] *National Standards for Arts Education* was completed in 1994, and the standards
for science and English were released in 1996.[11]

Goals 2000 gives formal sanction and incentive to standards for all subject areas at the state and local level. These are voluntary standards, and are
"not established or reviewed by any federal agency."[12] The state response
has been impressive. In the first year since the act's passage, 47 states have
taken advantage of federal funds to begin projects for educational improvement, including the development of their own academic standards or
frameworks.[13] Often these state standards have been based on the existing
national standards.

Reduced funding for education has impacted heavily on the arts. Budgetary cutbacks have forced reductions in programs at all levels of education. Unfortunately arts education has gained the reputation of a "frill" in
the curriculum, and has most often been the first area cut when budgets are
tightened.

MUSIC EDUCATION

National Standards for Arts Education

The *National Standards for Arts Education* includes standards for dance, music, theater, and the visual arts. It was developed by the Consortium of National Arts Education Association: the American Alliance for Theater Arts, MENC, the National Art Education Association, and the National Dance Association. In compliance with the recommendations of Goals 2000, these standards include the study of culture and history, and as such, all have implications for multicultural education in the arts. For example, content standard 5 for dance ("Demonstrating and understanding dance in various cultures and historical periods") includes proficiency in folk dancing and/or classical dances from various cultures in grades K–8, and develops an advanced competency in dance in high school such that students can "compare and contrast the role and significance of dance in two different social/historical/cultural/political contexts."[14]

For music, content standards 1 and 2 ("Singing, alone and with others, a varied repertoire of music" and "Performing on instruments, alone and with others, a varied repertoire of music") both imply a repertoire that includes diverse genres and styles. Even more specifically, content standard 9 ("Understanding music in relation to history and culture") refers directly to multicultural music education. This standard focuses on aural identification of various musics for all levels, on distinguishing characteristics of genres and styles and understanding the role of music and musicians in various societies or historical periods for grades K–4 and 5–8, and at the advanced level in high school on identifying and describing "music genres or styles that show the influence of two or more cultural traditions [and] the historical conditions that produced the synthesis of influences."[15]

Although the dance and music standards have the most direct impact on multicultural music education, because of the interrelated nature of the arts in various cultures, music educators can also employ segments of the theater and visual arts standards. For example, content standard 4 for the visual arts ("Understanding the visual arts in relation to history and culture") at the elementary and junior high levels focuses on identifying works of arts from specific cultures and understanding how the historical-cultural context influences art. In high school, students are to recognize the differences in "characteristics and purposes of works of art" and explore "the meaning of specific art objects within varied cultures.[16] Content standard 5 for theater ("Researching by evaluating and synthesizing cultural and historical information to support artistic choices") is most directly intended for grades 9–12.[17] However, since drama and music cannot be isolated from each other in many cultures, music educators at all grade levels will need to teach contextual information for both the musical sounds and the dramatizations.

"The visual, traditional, and performing arts provide a variety of lenses for examining the cultures and artistic contributions of our nation and others around the world." For music to be such a lens, music educators must not only "attend to the artistic elements and aesthetic responses" in music but also to "issues of ethnicity, national custom, tradition, religion, and gender."[18]

While the national standards offer a wide-angle view of musical competencies, those at the state level tend to present a narrower focus, designed for their specific populations. In the New York State *Learning Standards for the Arts*, for example, standard 4 states: "Understanding the cultural dimensions and contributions of the arts. Students will develop an understanding of the personal and cultural forces that shape artistic communication and how the arts in turn shape the diverse cultures of past and present society."[19] Examples of how this can be demonstrated in dance, music, art, and drama include learning folk dances, developing a performance and listening repertoire of various musics, understanding how the visual arts can represent the views of people around the world, and learning how theater reflects life in various societies.[20]

The national standards are succeeding as an exemplar for standards at the state and local level. As of July 1996, 44 states already had standards in the arts based on the national standards, and 2 more states had plans to do so within the near future.[21]

The *MEJ* 1992 Special Focus Issue: Multicultural Music Education

In 1992, the *Music Educators Journal (MEJ)* offered its third special issue on multicultural music education. Teachers who had learned about other cultures in 1972, and of the necessity of classroom applications in 1983, now were challenged to incorporate the music from many cultures into all their music classes, choral and instrumental as well as general music. This issue was not divided into sections as were the past issues. Following Anthony Seeger's opening article of encouragement for multicultural music education,[22] each article had an individual focus. There were several pedagogical techniques to foster the infusion of musics from a variety of cultures in the general music curriculum,[23] a multicultural resource list,[24] and two articles that examined the possibilities of incorporating a multicultural perspective in the instrumental and choral programs, respectively.[25] In the concluding article, William Anderson argued for multicultural music teacher education, saying that if students are to be taught music from a multicultural perspective, then music teacher education also needs this perspective.[26]

The Society for Ethnomusicology and *MEJ* Series

Following on the practical needs of in-service teachers to both know about and implement world musics, the education committee of the Society for Ethnomusicology (SEM) presented a series of articles in the *MEJ*. The format for each article was the same: an interview with an ethnomusicologist (respected for his or her knowledge of a specific music culture) that included information about the music culture and a discussion of how music educators could select music from that culture for classroom use. There were also accompanying lesson plans for immediate use. The cultures introduced to music educators in these articles included Navaho, Iranian, Amazonian Indian, Thai, Chinese, Yoruba, African-American, and Latino.[27]

In addition to the articles supplied by the SEM education committee, other music educators began to share their knowledge of multicultural/world musics and their classroom applications of those musics with the *MEJ* readership,[28] and new publications from MENC focused on the needs of practicing teachers. *Specialized Ensembles*, a book in the MENC *Strategies for Teaching* series, focused on the practical aspects of employing diverse musics through the ensemble experience. A second edition of *Multicultural Perspectives in Music* continued to provide a combination of contextual knowledge and practical applications for teaching musics from around the world.[29]

MENC Conferences

The MENC has continued to provide sessions for in-service teachers at its national conventions. As in the past, there were demonstrations and discussions about topics ranging from the philosophical implications of music education in a multivalue culture, to multicultural concerns in music teacher education (New Orleans, 1992).[30] Two sessions at the 1994 Cincinnati meeting in particular pointed up the broader definition of multiculturalism in the classroom. One dealt with the urban music classroom's diversity not only of cultures, but of socioeconomic status, and learning styles. In the other, Paul Winter's "Earth Music" presented one of the first sessions dealing with environmental concerns and global music education.[31]

At Kansas City (1996) the MENC scheduled two special Key Focus Sessions on multicultural music education. These in-depth sessions provided educators a mini–in-service devoted to world music cultures and classroom applications.[32] In addition, nearly every time slot scheduled for sessions offered two or more choices of topics dealing with multicultural/world musics in the classroom. There was information on a wide variety of music cultures, and discussions ranged from issues of authenticity to a critical investigation of multiculturalism in music education. Many sessions targeted the general music classroom from early childhood to secondary levels; several focused on the choral experience in elementary and middle school. However, except for jazz improvisation, multicultural sessions for the instrumental educator were still lacking.[33]

ISME Conferences

The International Society for Music Education (ISME) has continued to bring the topic of multiculturalism in music education to the forefront.[34] A primary focus for the ISME conferences since 1990 has been musics from a variety of countries. In addition, many reports have dealt with comparative music education as well as with multicultural music education in member countries.[35]

Because of its theme, Music Education: Sharing Musics of the World, the 1992 ISME conference in Seoul, Korea, merits special mention. The presentations reflected the global view implicit in the words *sharing* and *musics*, and provided a greater interchange of ideas on various topics relating to world musics in the music curriculum. Bruno Nettl's keynote address set the tone for the conference as he challenged music educators to "lead students to an understanding of music as a worldwide and varied phenomenon which will help them to comprehend all kinds of music and also provide an entry into understanding other things about the world's cultures; and to help members of all societies understand their own music."[36] Many presenters described music education in their particular countries; others sought philosophical and theoretical approaches to multiculturalism. Still others shared their strategies for teaching unfamiliar musics to their students.[37]

As music educators became more familiar with world musics, the more practical aspects of implementing multicultural music education found expression. Topics at the 1994 (Tampa) conference ranged from issues of musical authenticity versus practical application in the classroom to the implications of song translations and cultural inaccuracies. Another discussion focused on a very real problem for many music educators around the world—that of not only having to teach a variety of musics, but of having to teach them to students who themselves come from diverse backgrounds.[38]

Perhaps even more than the Seoul conference, the 1996 conference in Amsterdam dealt with multiculturalism in music education. The week-long conference was designed to highlight the world's music cultures through the theme Music, the Universal Language. Each day offered sessions and concerts focused on the musics from a different continent. Educators from around the world presented perspectives on multicultural music education from their representative countries.[39] Keynote speakers focused on the need to incorporate all musics in the curriculum and to present these musics within their cultural contexts.[40] There was also much debate as educators deliberated the possibility of universals both in music in general and in international music education.

Finally, ISME's revised constitution, adopted at this conference, makes it clear that the purpose of the organization has changed from one of helping music teachers merely to preserve "traditional national music while developing creative and competent musicians for the contemporary world" to one of assisting them "in the preservation *and teaching of the music cultures of human society* while developing creative and competent musicians for the contemporary world" (italics added).[41]

This change in purpose also reflects the work done by the ISME Panel on World Musics. In 1993, ISME established this panel for the purpose of drafting a policy statement "that would specify the attitudes of the Society in this area."[42] After citing some basic assumptions about the world of music, and identifying some specific educational issues derived from these assumptions, the policy statement offered several recommendations. The following is a partial quotation from those recommendations:

- **a.)** that any musical education, including of course the study of individual musics, repertories, and instruments, take as a point of departure the existence of a world of musics all of which are worthy of understanding and study.

- **b.)** that exposure to local musics, Western art music, and as much foreign music as possible be part of the formal music educational curricula of all nations; and further that special attention be paid to the musics of ethnic and social groups comprising the national population.

- **c.)** that a minimal background in understanding a selection of musics of the world's cultures be part of all teacher education curricula.

- **d.)** that music education methods in the teaching of the world's musics be formulated in such a way that the aesthetic integrity of the musics, and when possible their authentic processes of transmission, be fully respected.[43]

The panel's other charges included gathering information on the "state of world music" in the music education systems of selected countries, and developing a resource guidebook for teachers that would include a discussion of some of the educational and conceptual issues found in teaching world musics.[44] The panel made the completed manuscript of this guidebook public at the 1996 ISME conference. It contains philosophical perspectives on world musics, case studies, and an annotated bibliography. Perhaps the greatest contribution of this panel was "the raising of an awareness among ISME members of the importance of taking a more global perspective on music."[45]

SUMMARY

Since 1990 multiculturalism has continued as a strong force in fostering diversity in both education and music education, particularly through the recommendations of Goals 2000 and national and state educational standards. However positive this seems, some court rulings have tended to reduce support for multiculturalism, and budgetary retrenchment has forced cutbacks in arts programs across the nation.

Music education has continued to implement the recommendations of both the Multicultural Symposium and the National Standards in its efforts to encourage teaching a variety of musics in as authentic a manner as possible. Publications and conference sessions have increased the resources available to music educators. In addition, contacts with SEM and ISME have broadened the perspective of music educators to include ethnomusicological research and comparative studies of music education around the world.

Conclusions, Implications, and Questions

The 1990 Multicultural Symposium appears to be a watershed event, much like the Tanglewood Symposium, or Music for American Unity in its ability to generate changes quickly in the music curriculum. A plethora of information has resulted from articles in the *MEJ* and other MENC publications, as well as MENC conference sessions since the publication of the resolutions from that symposium. The continuing collaboration between MENC and SEM has produced useful resources for the music educator seeking to present a variety of music cultures in the classroom.

Besides the symposium, the National Standards will undoubtedly impact on music education for years to come. Multicultural music education is not just an isolated component of the Standards, it also provides opportunities for their full implementation. In what ways might teachers employ the music from another culture to help students achieve all the goals outlined in the Standards?

Goals 2000 and the National Standards for the Arts seem to assure a place for multicultural music education in the curriculum. What remains unaccomplished is implementation, and that will require teacher training and retraining. Some progress has been made; more needs to be done. In what ways are the resources available useful for in-service music educators? For pre-service teachers? What might help improve them?

CHAPTER **8**

Interlude: The End of the Beginning

The history of music teaching and learning ... has been a colorful one, replete with . . . attempts to respond to the needs of American society.

—Patricia Shehan Campbell[1]

Multicultural education did not develop in a vacuum, but has been answering the larger agenda of the American society as reflected by government actions for the greater part of this century. It was the immigration legislation of the 1920s that first affected intercultural education, and the repeal of the national origins restrictions in 1965 that resulted in large demographic changes and eventually to laws establishing bilingual education and ethnic studies programs. In addition, Supreme Court decisions such as *Brown v. the Board of Education* have left indelible marks on education in this century. Even federal foreign policy has had a role in what happens in the public schools to some extent. Music education has been found to be "more dependent on its societal context than we ever suspected."[2] The same can be said of multicultural music education.

Figure 8.1 shows the overlap between governmental and social-historical forces in both general education and music education. It should be noted that the changes in multicultural education and in multicultural music education are not hierarchical but inclusive. As each new expression of multiculturalism entered, it did not replace its predecessor but was in addition to it. With the resulting complexity caused by this constant overlap, it is not surprising that multiculturalism in education and music education is so controversial.

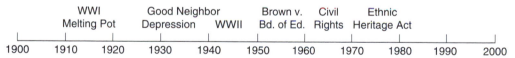

MULTICULTURAL MUSIC EDUCATION
VIEWED WITHIN EDUCATIONAL AND HISTORICAL CONTENTS

EDUCATIONAL CONTEXT

Global Education

Multicultural Education

Multiethnic Education

Ethnic Studies

Area Studies

Intergroup Studies

Intercultural Education

"International Relations"

Americanization

MUSIC EDUCATION HISTORY

Multicultural Perspective

All Musics

Latin American Musics

American Folk Musics

Eastern European Folk Musics

African-American Spirituals

Western European Folk Musics

Euro-German Classical Tradition

HISTORICAL CONTEXT

| WWI | Good Neighbor | | Brown v. | Civil | Ethnic |
| Melting Pot | Depression | WWII | Bd. of Ed. | Rights | Heritage Act |

1900   1910   1920   1930   1940   1950   1960   1970   1980   1990   2000

Figure 8.1 Designed after the graphic in James Lynch, *Multicultural Education in a Global Society* (London and New York: Falmer Press, 1989), 14.

This figure also demonstrates what appears to be a thirty-year cycle for a new idea to be introduced, disseminated, implemented, and fully accepted in the music curriculum. Eastern and Western European folk musics were the primary force in music education from about 1910 to 1940. (The exception was the acceptance of African-American spirituals.) American and Latin American folk musics were the focal point from 1940 to 1967. All musics were accepted in 1967, but commitment to a multicultural perspective on the part of the profession (through the MENC) did not occur until 1990. It is possible that music education has embarked on a new cycle and that by

2020, the multicultural/global perspective now being fostered will be accepted as commonplace with still another change underway.

Several trends are evident in multicultural music education across the century. The first, and most obvious, is the gradual increase in the number of music cultures that were accepted in the school music curriculum. A second trend is the gradual change in the reasons why music educators employed the musics from various cultures in the classroom. In the early part of the twentieth century, teachers used these musics to help assimilate the foreign-born.[3] Because they had beautiful melodies, they were also acceptable for didactic purposes: to teach melodic phrases, intervals, note reading, and rhythms.

The concept of music as a culture representative received more attention from the 1920s to 1950s, especially with the strong emphasis on curriculum correlation. So intense was the impact of curriculum correlation that Charles Gary said, "Music kind of got lost as music and it became a handmaiden to teaching social studies."[4] During the 1940s, Latin American musics became an accepted part of the curriculum primarily as a means to promote inter-American unity. In the 1950s, music education adopted an activities-based methodology. Of the five basic activities (singing, rhythmic work, performing, creating, and listening), folk musics had their place in listening experiences, singing, and rhythmic movement, still primarily for didactic purposes.

Music education changed methodologies in the 1960s to focus on the basic elements (or concepts) of music, such as melody, harmony, rhythm, form, and timbre. Music educators employed musics from a variety of cultures in the classroom as exemplars of how they demonstrated these musical elements. While this is still true in the 1990s, this is not now the only reason for inclusion of these musics in the curriculum. Studying various musics helps students to learn about the people who made them, to gain insights into self by studying others, to become open-minded toward a multiplicity of musical sounds and systems, to encourage polymusicality and creativity, to place Western art music in perspective with the rest of the musics in the world, and to encourage aesthetic development.

Third, and perhaps most important for the development of multicultural music education, was the change in perspective from which music education viewed diverse musics. Prior to the turn of the century, there was not even a mention made of folk songs as culture representatives. With the acceptance of European folk musics came the recognition that these musics were indeed the expressions of a variety of different peoples; however, music education tended to observe them distantly and through the eyes of the Western classical tradition. The phrase "primitive music" was common; all non-Western musics were "Westernized" for school use, and folk musics generally had value only because they provided the inspiration for Western classical compositions. Given this limited perspective, the musics from many cultures were presented with serious inaccuracies. (While this is unfortunately true, it is also true that these errors were unintentional on the part of the teachers who were simply doing "the best they could . . . looking for what they thought of as the best quality in music."[5]) Only a few forward-looking researchers took pains to give both historical and background information about the musics of various cultures before presenting a collection of authentic folk songs for use as a teaching resource.

This perspective gradually began to change following the Tanglewood Symposium, as music education became aware of the many other music cultures not yet addressed in the music curriculum. By 1990, music education had come to see Western art music as only one of many other equally valid musics in the world. Perhaps the most influential factor in effecting this change in perspective was the contact between music education and ethnomusicology.

Music education now advocates teaching music from a multicultural perspective where all musics "fit into a music curriculum that is based upon . . . the teaching of an understanding and valuing of music."[6] In a further extension of this perspective, Anthony Palmer described this approach as trying, through understanding music, to "get out of our own skins . . . and experience being the 'other' even for a short while," thus providing another perspective on the truth of being human.[7]

SUMMARY

Music education has often been accused of being "faddist," and too willing to jump on the next bandwagon of educational change. This certainly has been true in the past and it may appear that multicultural music education is just another item on the list of good ideas that won't last. The acceptance of each music culture in the curriculum does tend to look like the latest fad when seen separately; however, the long historical overview denies this. Multicultural music education has been slow to develop, and long in coming to fruition, but it has been undeniably a continuing force since the turn of the century. From European folk musics to American folk songs and Latin American musics, to traditional and popular musics from all around the world, there has been a crescendo of acceptance for these musics in the curriculum across the century accented by the approval of the MENC and concluding with a commitment to multicultural music education made at the 1990 Multicultural Symposium. Multicultural music education has grown from an isolated program of folk dancing in a few urban centers to become a major component of music education.

Conclusions, Implications, and Questions

American music education has transformed itself over the past ninety years. It has changed from the exclusivity of one music tradition to the inclusivity of all the musics in the world; from a narrowly defined didactic function for folk songs in the classroom to more widely defined purposes for multicultural music education; and from a Western ethnocentric perspective to a multicultural perspective that acknowledges Western art music as one of many valid music systems in the world.

However, as the literature from ISME indicates, these changes are also to be found in many countries around the world. Multicultural music education exists today in a global context; its development in the United States is only one piece of the picture. What has brought about the growth of multiculturalism in other countries of the world? Is international multicultural music education similar to, or different from, its counterpart in the United States?

CHAPTER **9**

Multiculturalism in International Music Education

We are so concerned with tending our . . . Orff tree or our game-
lan tree that we sometimes do not realise that we are only part of
the . . . international forest.

—LAURENCE LEPHERD[1]

The topic of multiculturalism has become one of worldwide concern, and many countries have addressed this issue both in education and in music education. Sometimes it is focused on the need to reestablish indigenous musics in the music education curriculum. Many countries (Zambia, Malaysia, and Nigeria among them) had their own musics supplanted by the study of Western art music during colonization and since independence have been trying to find ways to incorporate their own various music traditions in the schools. Some places (the United Kingdom, Australia, and Canada) are dealing with incorporating the music cultures of immigrant populations, much as in the United States. Still others, like Germany, are just beginning to incorporate a perspective that includes world musics in their curriculum. The development of multicultural music education in some cases runs parallel to that of the United States; in other cases, it provides contrasts.

GREAT BRITAIN

Historical Context

England, like other countries in Western Europe, encouraged immigration to help rebuild following World War II. For the most part, these immigrants

127

came from the New Commonwealth countries that had once been a part of the British empire. The British used to refer to all these immigrants as "black," whether they were from Africa, India, the West Indies, or East Asia. More recently there is a differentiation made between blacks and Asians.

In 1962 and again in 1965, Britain began to restrict immigration with the Commonwealth Immigration Acts. In 1981 the British Nationality Act not only imposed further restrictions on immigration, but also defined three classes of citizenship in Britain based on immigrant origins within the Commonwealth and removed some previously held rights of Commonwealth citizens.[2] In addition, the Immigration Act of 1988 replaced that of 1971 with even stricter regulations.[3] Although these laws discouraged new immigration, they did not address the needs of the immigrants already in the country.

As a result of the immigration restrictions of the 1960s, and the increasing families of already settled immigrants, the black population began to find its own identity. During the 1960s and 1970s, there was considerable, organized, antiracist activity. Martin Luther King, Jr., Malcolm X, and Stokely Carmichael all paid visits to England in the 1960s, and their presence added to the growing support for black power. In the 1970s, many popular and rock bands took up the antiracist cause, bringing the issue to the forefront through "Rock Against Racism" concerts.[4] As racial tensions escalated, Parliament passed the Race Relations Act of 1968, thus establishing a Select Committee on Race Relations and Immigration (SCRRI). Beginning in 1968 there was also a political shift from one of strict assimilation for immigrants to one of mutual tolerance.[5]

However, reactions to the passage of the British Nationality Act brought conditions to a boil. Black people rioted in Brixton, London, and other parts of England in 1981, and again in Birmingham and Handsworth in 1985. There continues to be a simmering undertone of racial tension.

The biggest problem in England seems to be the denial on the part of the majority population that there is a race problem.[6] A typical response when people are questioned about it has been "Oh, we don't have that problem here."[7]

Educational Context

In England, public education is primarily governed by the Local Education Authorities (LEAs) and by individual schools, under the aegis of the Department for Education (DFE, established 1992), formerly the Department of Education and Science (DES). Local autonomy was the rule until the Education Reform Act of 1988 gave more authority to the DES and Britain first began to establish its National Curriculum. Since then, the British curriculum has been organized into four Key Stages, determined by the age of the students in each stage: Key Stage 1 encompasses ages five to seven; Key Stage 2, ages seven to eleven; Key Stage 3, ages eleven to fourteen; and Key Stage 4, ages fourteen to sixteen. Students in all Key Stages must take the core subjects: English, math, and science. The foundation subjects of technology, history, geography, art, music, and physical education begin in Key Stage 1 and are continued in Key Stages 2 and 3. A modern foreign language is added to these subjects in Key Stage 3. In Key Stage 4, the only required foundation subjects are physical education, technology, and a modern foreign language; the other foundation areas may be pursued at the interest of the student. Each subject has its own curriculum and form of evaluation across the Key Stages. In addition, topics such as gender issues and multicultural education are incorporated in all subject areas across all stages.[8]

Immigration and the schools   Historically, British schools responded to the open immigration policy with a policy of assimilation. The students were to become "British" in language and manners as soon as possible. There was no allowance for language barriers or culture shock. The educational system simply treated these as "problems" to be solved.

The "problem" of immigrants in the schools became more urgent in the 1960s with the restrictions placed on immigration and the realization that the numbers of immigrant children in the schools was increasing. The schools dealt with this situation in two ways: English as a Second Language (ESL) classes and dispersal, by which students were transferred from the school closest to their homes so that no school would have more than 30 percent of its population minority students. The point of both these solutions was the same: to have the immigrant students learn English quickly and adjust to English society.[9] The DES discontinued its support for the dispersal policy in 1971.

The SCRRI report of 1969 recognized cultural differences for the first time and suggested that schools teach for a better understanding of immigrant cultures, especially through religion and history classes. These classes often took the form of ethnic or area studies, and frequently focused on the immigrants' contributions that enriched the mainstream society. The 1973 SCRRI report recommended a change in terminology. It stopped referring to "immigrants" and began speaking of a multiracial society and the need for appropriate education to live in it. The phrase "unity through diversity" came into use for the first time in this report.[10]

The 1981 Rampton report (*West Indian Children in Our Schools*) and the 1985 Swann report (*Education for All*)[11] for the first time acknowledged racism "as playing an important role in children's and adults' perceptions" and recognized "that all children in all schools should be made aware of the multiethnic nature of British society."[12] Researchers have criticized the Swann report for not going far enough and actually advocating antiracist education. The debate over the issue of antiracist education has been ongoing for the last decade with the final result that there has been an attempt on the part of some at reconciling both views, producing what is currently labeled as "antiracist multicultural education." This synthesis provides for teaching about a multiplicity of cultures, which may or may not be ethnic, and also about perspectives on ways to overcome racism.[13]

Recent changes   In 1988 Parliament passed the Education Act, which has had far reaching effects in both central and local education administration in England. This law both gave more power to the DES as a central agency and left less in the control of the LEAs. The Education Act of 1994 gave even more power to the DFE.[14] Most recently Britain has inaugurated its national curriculum for ten subject areas. The National Curricula for Art and Music (1992) were the last to be approved.[15]

Although the Rampton and Swann Reports are official documents, they are not government policy. Since 1990, funding for multicultural and antiracial education, now often seen as a "frill" in education, has been reduced. The Education Act of 1994 has continued to centralize education. Nonetheless, teachers continue to try to incorporate multicultural and antiracist practices and procedures in the classroom. They have found it can be incorporated within the national curricula for various subject areas, notably citizenship education, religious education, history, and the arts.[16]

Music Education

Although music is a required subject in Key Stages 1, 2, and 3, the place of music education in the British primary/middle schools depends almost completely on the commitment of the head (principal) and school governors to arts education. Classroom teachers are often responsible for all music education in their schools even though they frequently lack music skills,[17] although at present most primary schools have a music coordinator, who may or may not have music skills. This person helps train other teachers in the school, organizes music activities, and develops the music curriculum and assessment methods.[18] Few music specialists are employed. Where they do exist, music specialists sometimes supervise five to six schools, demonstrate master lessons, provide lesson plans, and give in-service instruction to the classroom teachers. What the classroom teachers know about music, and multicultural music education in particular, often comes only through in-service training.

The situation is different at the secondary level where music specialists not only teach music classes but also conduct ensembles or give instrument lessons, sometimes as a peripatetic (itinerant) teacher assigned to several schools. However, in 1988 lower funding for the LEAs reduced the number of positions for arts specialists, including music teachers, peripatetic instrumental teachers, and LEA advisors. Many of these people now serve as consultants and in-service teachers on a freelance basis.

Though the British music education repertoire has been, and remains, solidly founded in the European classical tradition, there is evidence of interest in musics from around the world. In the 1960s there was an "early advocacy of a serious regard for Afro-American musics, especially jazz and pop music."[19] By 1987, a survey found that in general the teachers questioned "deemed it important to engage pupils in music from different cultural backgrounds."[20] Since then, there has been a gradual increase in activity in teaching world musics. It is not unusual today to find cross-cultural music education taught in the schools in one form or another. African, Caribbean, and Indonesian musics, among others, have been employed successfully in British schools.[21] As of 1993, a few schools offered an integrated arts course; others hired peripatetic Asian-instrument music teachers for interested students. These classes included lessons in singing and dancing, and occasionally instruction on sitar or tabla. Unfortunately, these teachers were hired on a temporary basis, and if their positions are not renewed, the programs will cease functioning.

The National Curriculum for music   The National Curriculum for Music is now a reality for British schools. It did not come to be so without controversy. The National Curriculum for Music was first published in 1992. It presented two "attainment targets." The first was "Performing and Composing: the development of the ability to perform and compose music," and the second, "Knowledge and Understanding: the development of knowledge and understanding of musical history and theory, including the ability to listen to and appraise music."[22] Regarding multicultural music education, the National Curriculum indicated only "that pupils should perform and listen to music 'in varied genres and styles, from different periods and cultures.' "[23]

The controversy that developed over these two points centered first on the imbalance caused by the inordinate emphasis on the academic study of music theory and history, with only secondary emphasis on listening and music appraisal. The second argument surrounded the music examples suggested in the nonstatutory part of the National Curriculum. The planning committee that designed the curricula recommended that these examples reflect "the multicultural nature of Britain's society . . . through a balanced study which included a variety of world art and music."[24] Instead of following these recommendations, the government's Education Minister opted "in favour of an emphasis on Euro-centric art and music traditions."[25] As a result, the 1992 document contained only general references to other music cultures.

British musicians and music educators voiced such displeasure over both the Interim Report (1991) and the final form of the 1992 National Curriculum for Music that the curriculum was revised in 1993. The current document lists the two attainment targets as "Performing and Composing: the development of the ability to perform and compose music with understanding," and "Listening and Appraising: the development of the ability to listen to and appraise music, including the knowledge of musical history."[26]

While the revised National Curriculum does not specify content, it is now expected that

> the repertoire chosen for performing and listening should extend pupils' musical experience and knowledge, and develop their appreciation of the richness of our diverse cultural heritage. It should include music in a vari-

ety of styles: a) from different times and cultures; b) by well known composers and performers, past and present.[27]

The National Curriculum offers teachers a wide range of musical styles from which to select their class material. Among their choices are "European 'classical' tradition; folk and popular music; the countries and regions of the British Isles; [and] cultures across the world."[28] Student activities should lead them to "recognize that music comes from different times and places [Key Stage 1]; compare music from contrasting musical traditions . . . [Key Stage 2]; sing and play a variety of music . . . [and] relate music to its social, historical and cultural context [Key Stage 3]."[29] In addition, students who have achieved Attainment Target 2 should "begin to recognize how music is affected by time and place . . . [and] listen with attention to detail and describe and compare music from different traditions" [end of Stage 2]; and "respond to music, identifying conventions used within different styles and traditions" [end of Key Stage 3].[30] Advanced students will give evidence of "exceptional performance" in Attainment Target 2 if they can "identify continuity and change within a range of musical traditions from different times and cultures, making connections between the music and its historical, social, and cultural context."[31]

Implementation of the National Curriculum has been slow. There are few music specialists in the primary schools, and the curriculum is so new that pre- and in-service training has not yet had time to cause much change in the schools where specialists are employed. Nonetheless, some improvements have already been noted, especially regarding the increasing quality of the music lessons in the primary schools.[32] Although the curriculum has been finalized, it is only for a five-year period. Evaluation at that time may result in even more changes.

Music teacher education   For the most part British music educators graduate from higher education with largely classical backgrounds; however, they do receive some training in world musics. This training tends to be uneven, ranging from small segments within other courses to modules devoted to teaching popular and world musics, to courses in ethnomusicology, depending on the institution.[33] Some institutions also promote world musics in general education. King Alfred's College of Higher Education in Winchester, for example, offers a World Musics degree with courses open to students in the Bachelor of Education program. Students intending to go into primary education often take a class in world musics. This department has also produced a book entitled *World Musics in Education*.[34]

In addition, many boroughs offer a wide range of music workshops for in-service teachers. For example, the Borough of Lambeth has a Musicworks project that includes courses in Indonesian gamelan, rap and reggae rhythms, and jazz, along with basic notation and song skills.[35]

Despite these improvements, there remains an urgent need in Great Britain for multicultural or antiracist music teacher education. In general education, both researchers and organizations have called for better multicultural teacher education since the 1970s, but until recently, very few teachers have had any multiethnic or multicultural education in either their preservice or in-service training.[36] It is difficult enough for the committed music specialist to implement world musics in the National Curriculum. It is even harder for the relatively untrained classroom teacher. It is understandable that "many teachers find themselves bewildered and confused."[37]

Although there is agreement that schools should prepare students to live in a multiracial society, there is disagreement about how to implement this goal. It appears that some progress is being made in a few LEAs, primarily where the minority population is particularly high. Unlike the United States, where accreditation agencies insist that music teacher education programs have a multicultural component, there has been no such directive in Great Britain, the recommendations of the Rampton and Swann reports notwithstanding. Well implemented, the National Curriculum could be a step toward achieving this goal.

AUSTRALIA

Historical Context

Australia is a nation built through immigration. Except for the Aborigines, everyone in Australia came from somewhere else at one time or another. Australian immigration programs have traditionally leaned toward the permanent settlement of entire families. The primary sources for immigration were the United Kingdom and Ireland, but demographics changed in the 1950s and 1960s with higher numbers from Italy and Greece, later followed by Lebanon and Turkey. Since the 1970s, most immigrants have come from Asia, Southeast Asia, South America, and the Pacific Rim. All were considered not "guest workers" but "New Australians." The policy toward these people was one of assimilation, a policy applied for years to the Aborigines. In the 1970s, "self-determination" became the official government policy toward the Aborigines, and "multiculturalism" the official policy for those who immigrated to Australia.

The shift from strict assimilation into Australian society to a formal policy of multiculturalism began in 1972 with the Minister of Education Grassby promulgating a view of "the family of the nation." The Galbally Report (1978) followed soon after. This report identified four basic principles for immigrants: (1) equal opportunity for all, (2) the maintenance of their culture without prejudice, (3) social programs and services for all, and (4) self-help programs. In 1977, the government established the Australian Ethnic Affairs Council; its publication, *Australia as a Multicultural Society* (1977), "became an ideological blueprint for a future multicultural society . . . based on three social issues: cohesion, equality, and cultural identity."[38]

Although multiculturalism is currently the official policy in Australia, there are many cultural groupings that have maintained their ethnicity within Australian society. These culture groups—for example, the Greek population in Melbourne or the Vietnamese in Sydney—are "vibrant communities, and as such do influence the day to day running of society and the schools,"[39] official policy notwithstanding.

Educational Context

Although there is a Commonwealth Department of Education headed by the Minister of Education, the individual states have the primary responsibility for education in Australia. Schooling is mandatory up to grade 10, though most students complete grade 12.

Almost from their inception, Australian schools have had to provide for the children of immigrants. The schools were the primary mode through which the children of immigrants could assimilate into Australian society. Initially education offered no special arrangements for these children, often merely considering them "problems" to be solved. In the late 1960s and early 1970s adjustments began that would allow these children a quicker entry into the full school program. This occurred primarily through ESL, which was officially established under the Child Migrant Education Program (1970).[40] Federal funding enabled the states to develop these ESL programs, and to offer training courses for teachers, especially in areas of high immigrant density.

Educational change followed the governmental shift toward multiculturalism. The Galbally Report was "such a strong statement on cultural pluralism [that it] emphasized the narrowness of the previous provisions for sole English-language learning."[41] With the implications of this report and the overall governmental support for multicultural education, there resulted an abundance of teaching resources and literature applying a multicultural perspective to nearly every subject area throughout the 1980s.[42]

In 1979, the report of the Schools Commission Committee on Multicultural Education (*Education for a Multicultural Society*) became the basis for multicultural education programs in the country, and the states responded in kind. The situation in New South Wales (NSW) will serve as an exemplar. NSW released its first Multicultural Education Policy Statement in 1979. This statement became the foundation for a second such statement in 1983. This second statement included "intercultural understanding" and "interethnic harmony" in its aims for multicultural education. It supported ESL classes, ethnic studies, intercultural education, and multicultural perspectives to the curriculum, the latter two mandatory for all schools in the state.[43]

In 1992 the NSW Department of School Education released its *Multicultural Education Plan 1993–1997*. This five-year plan not only continues to support previous programs, it "contains a complementary and strategic shift of emphasis on greater respect for and understanding of the diverse cultural and linguistic traditions that are undeniable features of contemporary Australian society."[44] To this end, NSW committed itself to having "teachers and staff who are cross-culturally aware and able confidently and competently to impart multicultural values, curriculum and resources which reflect and promote diverse cultural and linguistic traditions," as well as to promote research, work with parents and community members, and to recognize excellence in multicultural education programs.[45]

Since the late 1980s, the economy has had a greater impact on education. In 1986, a more conservative government reduced funding for ESL by half. It also cut funding to multicultural education and abolished the influential Australian Institute for Multicultural Affairs, replacing it with the Office of Multicultural Affairs within the Department of Immigration and Ethnic Affairs under the aegis of the prime minister's office. Besides this, national priorities, along with a renewal of attention to Australian studies, took precedence over multicultural programs, especially in the years surrounding the Australian bicentennial celebration (1988).

There has also been an increasing involvement in educational affairs at the federal level, not the least of which are the Statements and Profiles for Education released in 1994. These Statements provide ten goals or outcomes upon which the individual states could build their curricula for each of eight subject areas: English, mathematics, science, technology, languages other than English, health and physical education, studies of society and environment, and the arts.[46]

Music Education

The primary influences on early Australian music education were British. The work of both John Hullah and John Curwen was popular, although Curwen's system of movable *do* supplanted Hullah's fixed *do* method by the turn of the nineteenth century. As a result, music education in Australia focused primarily on Western tonal music, especially European art music. There is some evidence of a limited use of folk musics in the schools by the 1950s. European folk dances introduced movement to music, though more often in physical education classes than music classes.[47] In addition, some European folk songs accompanied the influx of immigrant children during the years following World War II.[48] However, as late as the 1960s the folk songs of England and Scotland, and occasionally African-American spirituals, were more commonplace in school concerts. They also provided a large proportion of the repertoire for classroom singing. Although at least two state music syllabi for secondary schools (NSW and Western Australia) recommended some study in musics outside the Western tradition, until the 1970s there was very little implementation.[49] What folk songs were used were not employed to teach about other countries. Australian music education was, and still is, firmly rooted in teaching musical concepts, and whatever folk musics were included in the curriculum were there simply as another way of approaching these concepts.

Along with the changes in education toward multiculturalism in the 1970s, there was a corresponding change in music education. The increase in awareness of world musics during this period was reflected primarily in the music curriculum at the secondary level. Although there were no substantive changes in the music curriculum, the syllabi for secondary students in NSW, Queensland, and Tasmania each added an elective topic for in-depth study in folk or ethnic music. Suggestions for these studies included Music of an Asian Country, Scale Forms and/or Rhythmic Forms of Specific Non-Western Cultures, and Aboriginal Music.[50]

Education for a Multicultural Society brought prompt response from the states for curricular changes in all subject areas, including music education. In NSW, for example, the *Multicultural Education Policy Statement* (1979) provided a guideline for its implementation—including experiences through music, singing, dance, art, and drama, along with literature, history, and language.[51]

By 1984, the NSW music syllabus (K–6) directed the teaching of music through elements which the Australians refer to as concept areas (for example, duration, pitch, dynamics, tone color, and structure). This was to be achieved through listening to, performing, and creating music in a spiraling curriculum of increasing complexity. One of the aims cited for music education was "to help students develop aural competencies, understandings and skills which make possible . . . awareness and appreciation of various cultural traditions, past music traditions and present practices." There are also references to "broadly based music programs which cater for the needs, interests and abilities of all students."[52] These statements, along with the multicultural makeup of Australian music classes, provided the potential for a multicultural approach to music education.

Statements and Profiles for the Arts   Released in 1994, the Statements and Profiles for the Arts in Australian schools formalize the arts as a Key Learning Area for education nationally. For public education, "the arts" means a combination of dance, drama, media, music, and the visual arts. The Statements provide eight levels of achievement for all the arts, though each art discipline reinterprets these and adds subject-specific outcomes as needed.[53] There appears to be wide recognition of the importance of the arts in the curriculum. Today, most school systems "are now in the process of revising their syllabuses so that they conform to the outcomes stated in the Statements and Profiles."[54]

The structure of the arts curriculum consists of three basic, interrelated topics: (1) creating, making, and presenting; (2) arts criticism and aesthetics; and (3) past and present contexts. It is in the area of Past and Present Contexts that the Statements allow ample opportunity to include the study of a wide variety of musics in their historical and cultural contexts. The integrated curriculum approach "should strengthen artistic understandings and enrich arts programs by providing alternative ways of understanding and participating in the arts," a plus given the interrelatedness of arts in various cultures.[55]

Music education in New South Wales   NSW is among the most progressive of the Australian states. Its syllabi for music education, grades 7–12, have recently been revised. As of this writing, the 1984 elementary syllabus is still in effect, but a new syllabus for the elementary level is currently being developed.

This new syllabus will have outcomes emanating from the content of the syllabus rather than the National Statements. However, like the Statements, it will treat the arts (music, media, dance, drama, and visual arts) through independent but interrelated strands. The content of the music strand will include repertoire and the elements of music. Students will be expected to listen, sing, move, compose, and play instruments. The recommended repertoire will include a wide variety of musics, with special reference to Aboriginal music traditions, classical and folk idioms, popular music, and world music. Along with this repertoire, a portion of the syllabus will provide access for students to learn to understand musics from various cultures as an expression of those cultures through personal, structural, and sociocultural perspectives. For example, as of this writing, draft programming units that support the syllabus framework include material relating to Aboriginal music and attempt to present this music from an Aboriginal point of view.[56]

However, no matter how varied the repertoire, the goal of Australian music education is teaching for musical understanding through a knowledge of the elements of music. The wide-ranging repertoire is intended as the material that will enable the students to achieve this goal. Accomplishing this from a multicultural perspective will depend solely on the ability of the teacher.

The 1994 *NSW Music Syllabus (grades 7–10)* incorporates the new Statements and Profiles for the Arts. The syllabus begins with a reaffirmation of the study of music through concepts, by way of listening to, performing, and creating music. Under the listening component for Past and Present Contexts (PPC), specific competencies are expected, ranging from identifying "distinguishing features [such as, melodic or rhythmic characteristics] of music which locates it in a particular time, place, or culture," to showing "an understanding of the way music is made [for example, large or small ensemble, who sings and for what occasion] within particular cultural and historical contexts," and researching music "from a variety of past and present social and cultural perspectives."[57] More specifically, the repertoire for the PPC section should take into account "current musical practices and the multicultural aspects of the Australian community," and "must be broadly based . . . to extend and enrich students' musical experiences." This repertoire may therefore include "art music of various periods and cultures, jazz, popular musics, [and] traditional music."[58]

More in-depth experiences are available in the Additional Study Course in Music (grades 7–10). This elective course includes a compulsory segment devoted to Australian music in all its forms, including "traditional and contemporary music of the Aborigines and Torres Strait Islanders, jazz, music from Australia's diverse cultural backgrounds, and art and traditional musics." In addition, there are three elective segments within this course. One choice is an in-depth study of the traditional music of a specific culture, with "cultural context, stylistic features, notation, dance and its music."[59]

Australian high schools in NSW offer a Preliminary Course 1 in Music for grade 11 that follows the standard mandatory music classes in grades 7–10 sequentially. In this course, the PPC section of the syllabus provides for elective studies. Students may choose from topics such as music and religion, Australian music, the traditional music of a culture, popular and art musics, and medieval music.[60]

There is also a two-year music course (grades 11 and 12) leading to a Higher School Certificate (HSC) that follows the elective course in music from grades 7–10. This course is intended for those students who want to major in music. The PPC section of the HSC has a wide variety of topics for elective study, including Australian music and the traditional music of a culture, along with the individual historical periods of Western European music. Assessment may take various forms, including performance (vocal or instrumental), composition, audio or video tape, or a written essay, but must give evidence of "an integrated study into the topic."[61]

While the focus of Australian music education is element-based, it does allow for students to study how music functions in another setting, especially at the secondary level. Elective studies offer the opportunity for students to research the music of another culture and also to "reflect on how pitch, for example, is manipulated in their own music . . . through having made a specific study of another musical culture." The idea of element-based education, upon which the syllabus is founded, has indirectly supported multiculturalism.[62]

Music teacher education   Australian music educators may begin their studies by first completing a bachelor's degree in music and then continuing for an additional year to obtain a teacher training diploma. Although colleges and universities may not specifically offer multicultural studies in music education, some do give future music teachers the chance to acquire this knowledge through personal investigation combined with the study of ethnomusicology. Depending on the institution, courses in ethnomusicology may either be elective or a required component of the core music subjects for a bachelor of arts with a music major, or a bachelor of music. For example, students at the University of Sydney Music Department take two core courses in ethnomusicology, and may also choose from several electives including field methodology, Aboriginal, Indonesian and Japanese musics, and performance in a Javanese gamelan.

There is currently only one institution that provides for multicultural studies in music education, the Sydney Conservatorium of Music, University of Sydney (separate from the Music Department mentioned above). Students in the Bachelor of Music Education program are required to take one semester of multicultural studies dealing with the ethical, moral, and methodological issues involved in teaching the music of another culture. A second semester dealing with the practice of multicultural music education is elective, and many students choose to take it. Students studying for the master of music in music education can choose to major in one of three areas: curricular design, technology, or multiculturalism. At the doctoral level, it is not uncommon for dissertation topics to include research in world musics or multicultural music education.

For the future classroom teacher, instruction in world musics or multicultural music education at other institutions of higher education is sporadic at best. Some schools, such as the University of Western Sydney, Macarthur, offer courses in musics from around the world to their students studying for a degree in education. At others, students receive training in world musics only if their particular instructor at the time is interested and knowledgeable in the topic.

Not all schools in Australia have music specialists; at the primary level, it is not uncommon for the classroom teacher to be responsible for the music lessons. This fact, combined with the new emphasis on the arts in the Profiles, should put pressure on tertiary education to supply adequate multicultural music teacher education. Unfortunately, because of the amalgamation of the various art forms into one Key Learning Area, music has lost some of its single-subject status in the curriculum for future teachers in NSW. As a result, in some institutions the requirements for music education training have actually been reduced.[63]

CANADA

Historical Context

Like the United States and Australia, Canada is a nation of native peoples and immigrant populations. While the earliest settlers in Canada were predominantly French or British, since the late 1800s a wide spectrum of peoples from around the world have come to Canada. Today, nearly half the student population in Vancouver and Toronto schools speaks English as their second language.

Canada has officially been a bilingual country since the British North American Act of 1867 declared both French and English as the official languages of the Canadian Parliament and the Houses of Legislature of Quebec. The Language Act of 1969 reaffirmed this policy, although since the passage of the Quebec Bill 101 in 1977, French has been the single official language for Quebec and its Legislature. Multiculturalism in Canada is combined with official bilingualism.

In 1971, Prime Minister Trudeau promulgated a national policy of multiculturalism. In essence, this policy established four objectives for cultural maintenance within Canada. This policy states that the government will

> assist all Canadian cultural groups . . . to develop a capacity to grow and contribute to Canada
>
> assist all members of all cultural groups to overcome cultural barriers to full participation in Canadian society
>
> promote . . . interchange among all Canadian cultural groups in the interest of national unity
>
> assist immigrants to acquire at least one of Canada's official languages.[64]

This formal policy of multiculturalism has given Canada its distinctive identity among democratic societies. In 1988, Parliament passed the Canadian Multicultural Act, and backed it with sufficient funding to support initiatives to "promote harmonious race relations, . . . preserve heritage languages and cultures, [and] ensure full and equal participation of ethnic minorities."[65] With this Act, the Canadian government made its policy of multiculturalism law throughout the nation.

Even though there is continuing federal support for this policy, the Canadian population has also shifted toward a desire for "Canadianness" and the feeling that multicultural education presents a threat to national unity. This was particularly evident in the Spicer Commission Report (1991).[66]

Educational Context

The tax-supported educational system in Canada encompasses both public and parochial schools. For the purposes of comparisons with the other countries discussed in this text, only the public schools (both French- and English-speaking) are discussed here.

Education in Canada is controlled by the provinces, although some funding is provided through federal transfer payments to the provinces. During the 1950s and 1960s, the typical response to the immigrant "problem" was assimilation. English language training was the foremost gateway of entry to Canadian society in English-speaking Canada. In some cases, students were sent to special programs where they were given daily classes in English, and Canadian customs and ways of thinking. In Toronto, this was described as a "cultural immersion strategy." In some cases, immigrant students found themselves in special language programs, as educators deemed them "handicapped" by their English language difficulties.[67] French schools for English speakers also began to emerge during this period.

Today most provinces have officially accepted multiculturalism for implementation in their education programs, but each has dealt with it differently. Because of the diversity between provinces in language and religion, there is no one model of multicultural education in Canada.[68]

In 1968 Ontario guaranteed French-based education in the province. Twenty years later, the Ontario Ministry made a resource guide available that emphasized equality in a multicultural and multiracial society. In 1993 the province moved even closer to a policy of antiracist education as it "mandated all school boards to develop a racial and enthocultural equity policy and programs to implement anti-racism initiatives."[69] Today the Ontario Ministry of Education and Training supports an active educational program of multicultural and antiracist education, in particular through a thorough review process for materials on which school funds may be spent. This review process is designed to assist in selecting materials that avoid bias and stereotypical representations. Besides this, there are many after-school teacher in-service programs in a variety of languages.

There are also integrated language programs in Manitoba, Alberta, and Saskatchewan. As early as 1974, Alberta established bilingual programs, and today there are several bilingual schools, Arabic, Blackfoot, Cree, Hebrew, Hungarian, and Ukrainian among them. Saskatchewan set up a heritage-language program in 1978, Manitoba in 1979. Still in effect today, these programs teach heritage languages through bilingual classes, as core subjects, and in community sponsored after-school programs.

British Columbia adopted its multiculturalism policy in 1990 and gave final approval for the Multiculturalism Act of British Columbia in 1993. As of 1995, there was no multicultural education policy in British Columbia.[70] Quebec, with its predominant French culture and desire to promote its language and customs, prefers to term its multicultural education "intercultural education." The Northwest Territories took a step toward "self-determination" for the Native Canadians living there. Since the 1970s, this has meant a revision of the school curriculum to provide relevant courses in native culture. There has never been quite the pressure to "become Canadian" as there has been to "become American." The Canadian concept of multiculturalism stems mostly from the fact that since its foundation, the country has had a complexity of cultures, primarily French, English, and First Nations (Native Canadians). Today Canadian education has to consider

> how much diversity is compatible with social integrity. . . . Multiculturalism is not only the preservation of ethnic cultures. . . . There is no argument for teaching the young to be what they no longer are or can be. There is, however, every reason to teach them *who* they are and what they may become.[71]

Whether Canada accomplishes this through multicultural education, or antiracial education, or some combination of the two remains to be seen.

Music Education

Canadian music education has been heavily influenced by both British and American methodologies. As early as the 1850s, Curwen's tonic sol-fa system and Lowell Mason's song method were equally represented in Canadian music classes. During these early years, the approved music texts in Canada included L. W. Mason's *National Music Course*, Curwen's *School Music*, and Holt's *Normal Music Course*. At the start of the twentieth century, there was little that was truly Canadian about Canadian music education, and many Canadian music educators had already studied in the United States and were fully cognizant of the changes occuring in American music education.[72]

With increasing immigration in the early twentieth century, especially in Manitoba and Saskatchewan, music educators were faced with the same type of multicultural classes as their counterparts in the United States. Given that the role of the schools was to encourage assimilation, music educators favored patriotic songs as a means of "nation building."[73]

Over the ensuing years, publishing companies regularly offered school music texts from the United States such as *The Hollis Dann Music Course* and *The Progressive Music Series* to Canadian schools. There was often no difference between the texts beyond titles and the inclusion of Canadian rather than American patriotic songs. It would seem that at least some of the changes in American texts regarding the increase in song material from other countries should apply closely to those in Canada. While that may be so, research into Canadian music texts published in and for Canada shows that, regardless of suggestions to include local folk songs (either those of Canadian settlers or from ethnic communities), the repertoire remained primarily British.[74]

Of all the provinces, the schools in Eastern Canada preserved the closest ties to their cultural heritage, primarily French, English, Scottish, and Irish. In New Brunswick (1920s), Gibson's *Canadian Folk Songs* and *Recueil de chants acadiens* accompanied *Twice 55 Community Songs* on the list of supplementary materials for music teachers. In Nova Scotia (1930s), folk music and folk dance festivals were "viewed as a means of encouraging cooperation among schools, training students in constructive ways of filling leisure hours, and acquainting them with their cultural heritage." During this same period Quebec City held a Canadian Folk Song and Handicrafts Festival. Newfoundland has maintained its folk song traditions in the music curriculum to the present day.[75]

Phonograph recordings also had a great deal of influence in Canadian music education, and music appreciation became an important part of music lessons. The growing inventory of recordings, especially those from the RCA Victrola Company, gave teachers the opportunity to present folk songs and dances along with vocal and instrumental compositions. In spite of the music available, jazz recordings generally remained outside the music classroom until the 1970s.[76] The general curriculum may have restricted jazz studies, but jazz was not unknown in the instrumental music program. Like their counterparts in the United States, many high school bands had already incorporated jazz in their repertoire.[77]

In the 1950s, there was some interest in focusing on the ethnic musics of the country. For example, Rj Staples, a Saskatchewan teacher, taught songs from the ethnic groups who helped settle the area to his students for a special pageant in honor of the province's jubilee (1955). *Folk Songs of Canada* (Waterloo Music Co., 1954) was "one of the first folk music publications to enjoy widespread use by music educators."[78] These were more the exception than the rule, however. As June Countryman noted, "The activity in ethnomusicology in Canada had virtually no effect on school music materials up to this point [1959]." Music educators lacked "an awareness . . . of the importance of using indigenous folk materials" and school music publishers did not print ethnomusicological materials.[79] This is not unusual since ethnomusicology was not even included in tertiary music study until it was introduced in the graduate programs of the University of Toronto and the University of British Columbia in the late 1960s.[80]

Since the 1950s, the Yale Seminar, the Tanglewood Symposium, and the Comprehensive Musicianship Project in the United States, as well as the acceptance of Kodály and Orff methodologies, have all had far-reaching effects in Canadian music education. Along with adopting the spiral curriculum introduced by Jerome Bruner, Canadians "enthusiastically endorsed" comprehensive musicianship. This led to a more global choice of repertoire, including "song materials from all eras of Western music as well as selections from various world musics, North American and British popular music among them."[81] Because the Kodály methodology in particular encouraged teaching the music from one's own traditions, during the 1960s and 1970s teachers sought the folk songs of the British and French settlers and "rediscovered" the use of Canadian music, both composed and folk, in music classrooms. Articles and conference sessions frequently addressed this topic.[82]

Following the bilingual education movement, music publications for French-speaking children have increased. However, in Quebec the increase of French music materials is a result of the fact that French is the official language of the province, and not because of growing multiculturalism. In addition, since the 1970s, Native Canadian music traditions have been part of the music curriculum in the Northwest Territories. Introducing native musics in the music classroom is not exclusive to the Northwest Territories. In other parts of the country, music educators are also making efforts to include native musics and the music of native-born composers in their classes.[83] Native musics and multicultural music education are separate components of the Canadian music curriculum because Canadians tend to view multiculturalism as referring only to immigrants.

Given the strong influence of British and American music education in Canada, it is no wonder that "the oral traditions of both the immigrants and the indigenous people of Canada have generally been neglected as an integral part of music education."[84] However, this is not the only reason for the lack of traditional musics in the curriculum; other issues have contributed to this fact. One is based on the differences between world music systems, and the question whether teachers and students *can* perform musics deemed too complex for school use. A second issue is the fact that many immigrants to Canada are refugees, and they desire *not* to perform their traditional music because the sounds remind them of the unhappy conditions from which they escaped.[85]

From the late 1980s through the 1990s, multicultural music education, particularly in terms of the musics of the Canadian people, immigrant and First Nations, has become the "hot" topic. There are now workshops available to in-service Canadian music educators in these musics. Canadian ethnomusicologists have begun to work with music educators, and materials are more readily available.[86] Unfortunately, some of the older school music texts still in use do not offer a balance of musics. *Musicanada* (Holt, Rinehart and Winston, 1982) has fifty-five European folk songs in its intermediate grade textbooks, but only four Asian songs. Very few of these songs are in the original language.[87]

Music teacher education   The assortment of cultures in the music classroom is so great that sometimes "tensions arise as the literate thrust of music instruction collides with the contrasting oral perceptions of the students."[88] There is still a lack of adequate music teacher education programs to train Canadian teachers to deal with both this musical situation and the cultural diversity of students within the classroom, although some institutions are making efforts in this direction. As Robert Walker said, being a music teacher with a "highly prized technical proficiency as a performer is of little consequence when faced with, say, 35 grade seven children, most of whom cannot speak English well and whose culture at home is from the other side of the Pacific." Walker goes on to recommend the ideal music teacher education program. This training would include

> philosophical and critical abilities to enable them to understand the complex issues surrounding education
>
> a sophisticated understanding of ethnomusicology, in particular the problems of different cultural uses of sounds as powerful cultural symbols
>
> knowledge of child development, sociological and anthropological aspects on youth, culture, the media.
>
> a working knowledge of . . . technology. . . . All this in addition to musical training[89]

The question is, when will it be available? And will that learning be enough for a student teacher to develop a "perspective on *practice* that will help them cope . . . in a way that is culturally responsive," not just with a multiplicity of musics, but also with learners from diverse musical cultures?[90]

GERMANY

Historical Context

Rebuilding Germany after World War II produced a heavy demand for migrant workers. In 1973, however, Germany passed a ban on recruitment outside of the European Community. Instead of encouraging those itinerant "guest workers" already in Germany to return to their homelands, this law produced the opposite effect. The migrant workers sent for their families and elected to settle in Germany. Although technically this fact made them immigrants, the Germans continue to refer to them as migrants because of the official policy of nonimmigration in Germany. Along with the Italian and Greek workers who first came to Germany, the demographics of the country now include Turks, Serbs, Slovenians and other peoples from the former Yugoslavia. Besides these "migrants," large numbers of asylum seekers also came to Germany in the 1970s. These numbers increased dramatically after the fall of the Warsaw Pact in 1991.[91] For example, today fully one third of the population of Stuttgart is foreign born.

Since the fall of the Berlin Wall in 1989, the new German nation has been going through an identity crisis, and race relations have come to the forefront. As the Germans from east and west try to sort out who they are as a nation after years of physical and ideological separation, foreigners have become the target of choice upon which they can both agree. There are no racial equality laws in Germany so that "discrimination against minorities, with the exception of Jews, is therefore not illegal. . . . [It is termed] *hostility against aliens* . . . to be criticized but not persecuted."[92] All this makes developing a peaceful, multicultural society in Germany difficult at best.[93] Only recently has there been a shift to allow the term "immigrants" and to speak of "Turkish Germans" instead of "Turks in Germany."

Educational Context

Education in Germany is the responsibility of the individual Länder (states), overseen by the Standing Conference of Länder Ministers of Education. Although it is only a recommending body, resolutions from the Standing Conference have been accepted and incorporated in the educational laws of the Länder for many years. Education in Germany is primarily a "track" system, whereby students often as young as ten or twelve years old must make a choice for their high school education: job training, vocational, or college preparation. All the Länder require students to take German language and literature, mathematics, history and social sciences, sports, at least one foreign language for five years (usually English or French), music or art, and at least one natural science.[94]

The resultant stabilization of the immigrant population has strained the educational system. Gerd R. Hoff of the Freie Universität Berlin commented on this situation saying, "Given the large numbers of people who are unsure of how long they will remain in Germany, it is extremely difficult to define the core subjects and major goals of education."[95] Because Germany sees itself as a monocultural country, multicultural education has had little advocacy until recently. The primary policy until well into the 1970s was either separation (schooling provided for the various migrant populations) or strict assimilation. There was a policy shift in the late 1970s with the Standing Conference Resolution of 1976 (amended 1979). This resolution made very clear that the main goals of education for the "migrant" children are both integration into German society and maintenance of their cultural identity. It was built on the assumption that these children will need to reassimilate into their own cultures upon their return to their homelands. It did not consider the possibility that they would not be going back, at least not in the near future.[96] There was little attention to special cultural needs, minority issues, or antiracist perspectives. Education for foreigners related closely to special-needs education, the "handicap" being the fact that these children were not, and did not speak, German.[97]

As the permanence of these children in Germany became clear, education focused on binguality: German and the mother tongue. These bilingual classes were frequently taught by native teachers on temporary contracts, though today many universities offer teacher education courses in teaching German as a Second Language.

In the 1980s, there was some development of multicultural, or more often "intercultural," education. There was a greater focus on establishing cultural identity, an introduction to the world's major religions, and modification of the general curriculum to include "multicultural representation of values." There was a marked increase in publication on multicultural education and teacher training, and an acceptance of the "migrants' " language and cultures in the classroom. More recently there has been a move toward antiracist education.[98]

Some of the more progressive Länder require student teachers to take a course described as "work with foreign pupils in school" in order to pass their exams for teaching. Other states require additional work in a foreign language, frequently Turkish, for certification. More often these are required only for teaching in the primary schools. There is little or no multicultural training given secondary teachers.[99]

In the schools, multicultural education is most often found in experimental models of integrated curriculum programs lasting from three to five years. For example, from 1975 to 1979, the Krefelder Modell provided a model for assimilative integration. Lack of funding discontinued this highly effective model. In fact, there were few model programs, regardless of quality, that continued after their initial funding ran out. Their effectiveness really depended on the development and wide dissemination of classroom materials, as did two models in Berlin. The handbook *Von wo kommst'n du? Interkulturelle Erziehung im Kindergarten* (Where do you come from? Intercultural education in Kindergarten) and lesson booklets for multicultural education produced by these models are well known and used throughout primary education in Germany.[100]

The question for education in Germany today is whether society will demand school reforms and open the gates to multicultural education in all German schools. Until multicultural and antiracist education are "compulsory components of the curriculum for all schools, they will have little effect in preventing the growing tide of racism and nationalism in Germany."[101]

Music Education

The requirements for music teacher certification in Germany were first pre-scribed in the 1922 *Ordnung der Prüfung das künstslerische Lehramt an höheren Schulen in Preussen* (Regulations for testing the teacher's art for secondary schools in Prussia), and were still basically in effect in the 1960s. According to these regulations, school music teachers had to prove their competency in the European classical tradition through both academic and musical ex-aminations following a course of study for music teacher education, usually at a state college. In order to gain admission to these education programs, future music teachers had to perform a short recital on their major instru-ment and to sing and accompany German lieder and folk songs,[102] evidence of the strong tradition of German folk music taught in the elementary and secondary schools throughout this period. German music education focused entirely on the European classical tradition supplemented with German folk songs and dances until well into the 1970s, and, for the most part, still does so today.

At the present time, there is a great deal of interest in multicultural mu-sic education in Germany and a growing body of research literature on the subject.[103] There are also an increasing number of multicultural projects in the schools, as well as among music education students in colleges and uni-versities. For example, a teacher at a Hauptschule in Nürnberg has designed a video that employs Turkish children's songs as a means to help educate young children against Neonazism, and a student at the University of Er-langen-Nürnberg recently completed a comparative study on "Irish music in German school songbooks and German music in Irish songbooks."[104]

Contemporary German music educators are facing an increasingly mul-ticultural student population. In densely populated urban areas, a single classroom of students might include twenty different nationalities. Over the past twenty-five years, little or no assistance has been given to the music teachers, either as pre- or in-service training, to help them cope with the di-verse cultures and musics represented in their classrooms. Although there are some songs and dances from countries in Africa and North and South America in the school music texts, they have not been required in the syl-labi.[105] Jazz, rock, and popular musics have been included in most curric-ula, however, and are taught in many classrooms. These musics are often preferred by all the students, regardless of their homelands.[106]

In the last decade or so, many music teachers have begun to find their own ways to deal with this situation. Although they must still teach from the syllabus, interested teachers are learning from their students, and by in-corporating their students' musics as best they can, they bring the songs and dances of their students' cultures (for example, Turkish, Greek, or Italian) into their classes. They also seek out conference workshops, read articles, and go out to their communities seeking culture bearers who will help them. Some materials are available for use in the classroom, but there are also prob-lems finding accurate transcriptions.[107]

Music education in Bavaria   Since all educational policies in Germany
are bound to the discretion of the individual Länder, each is different. As a
result, the officially approved music curriculum for each of the Länder tends
to differ from the others, as does any inclusion of multiculturalism.

At the present time, Bavaria may be one of the most progressive Länder in Germany regarding multicultural music education. Over the past
twenty years, the state curriculum guides for music education show a gradual increase in interest in multiculturalism. Before 1976, there was no mention of any "foreign" music in the curriculum and all the recommended
songs were German for all grade levels, and even in 1977 only German, and
specifically Bavarian, songs and dances were listed in the curriculum for the
Grundschule (grades 1–4). However, the 1977 curriculum guide for the
Hauptschule (student ages 10–15) indicated the beginning of study for jazz
and popular musics in grades 5 and 6.[108]

The 1981 curriculum for the Grundschule, and the 1982 guide for the
Hauptschule both listed units of study containing songs from Germany "and
other countries" (mostly European). In the first real change from this Western framework, there was a special unit on Balkan folk music in the seventh
grade included as a preliminary study for Bartok in the eighth grade. By
1985, the Hauptschule curriculum included songs and folklore from many
"foreign" countries, with an emphasis now on both the music traditions and
the culture of these peoples for both seventh and eighth grade. Songs from
Italy, France, Poland, England, and Israel were listed with their original languages; dances included the Eastern European polka, kolo, and polonaise
as well as American square dances.[109]

Further changes occurred in 1993. The curriculum guide for the
Hauptschule now required that teachers stress the importance of "other
songs from Europe" for grades 7 and 8. In addition, rock and popular musics were listed as a unit of study, and in grade 9, jazz was introduced—this
time with a special emphasis on both its African and European elements.
The ninth grade also added depth to the "foreign songs" studied by including their cultural contexts.[110]

Most recently, the Bavarian school curriculum for the Hauptschule is
undergoing a complete revision. The proposal has been approved and the
curricular model discussed and accepted. The new curriculum will go into
effect in September 1997 for the fifth and seventh grades, and in 1998 for the
sixth and eighth grades

The greatest change will be the official inclusion of multicultural music education for the first time in the Bavarian state curriculum. The introductory section of the new curriculum goes on at length to establish
that musics from all times, styles, and peoples belong in the classroom.
The curriculum justifies this inclusion on both musical grounds (basic elements, rhythmic movement, instrumental study) and social grounds
(peace, tolerance, antiracism, intercultural exchange.) In grade 5, for example, an entire unit is devoted to "My own music—Other people's mu-

sic." There is the usual inclusion of "songs and dances from near and far," but each musical experience must now be centered in its contextual background. The unit also includes a section on the instruments peculiar to the cultures (with demonstrations as much as possible), and follows with the opportunity for students to make these instruments (or their facsimile) in class.[111]

Needless to say, this curriculum is a long way from that of 1976. In the fall of 1997, implementation will begin across Bavaria—in the schools, in the teacher-training programs, in the Akademie für Fortbuildung (offering teacher in-service programs), and in the school music textbooks. There will be a concerted effort to bring both old and new teachers into the curriculum. The hardest part will be finding the materials to help teachers implement it.

MULTICULTURAL MUSIC EDUCATION IN OTHER COUNTRIES

Just as immigration has had its effect on many countries, there are many other countries "moving away from the colonial structures of music education imposed upon them."[112] These "structures" focused primarily on Western European music and music literacy, with a rather strong disregard for indigenous musics and their aural-oral tradition. Music educators in these countries have begun to find ways of bringing their traditional musics into the classroom.

Argentina

Spanish colonization first brought Western classical and popular music to Argentina in the sixteenth century. The Indians learned to sing the compositions of Palestrina, and to build violins and organs. Western music became so much a part of the culture that when Argentina declared independence in 1816, both Western and local folk songs were already being taught in some schools. In 1884 the National Parliament passed Law 1420 and made music a mandatory subject in the primary schools of Argentina. By 1910 Argentinian songs and dances were a regular part of the primary music program.[113]

Argentina has continued to make efforts to keep up to date in music education. The National Ministry of Education issued a series of aims for music education in the 1960s. Two of these aims had implications for multicultural (or intercultural) music education:

> to improve the capacity [of students] to assess the interrelationship between music, literature, and arts, in the context of geographical regions, history, civilization, ages, and styles
>
> to increase knowledge about Argentinian music and its contribution to the musics of the world[114]

In 1993 Argentina adopted the Common Basic Contents (CBC), a general curriculum for music education. Enacted as law at the federal level, after votes of approval by all the states of Argentina, the CBC requires folk songs and dances as part of the music curriculum. The recommended criteria for repertoire from which these songs and dances may be selected are very broad and includes all musics, styles, and genres, as well as the instruments and instrumental forms characteristic of each. As of this writing, the CBC has not yet been fully implemented across the country.

Today Argentinian music educators frequently include musics from other countries of Latin America in the classroom. However, multicultural music education, in the scholarly sense of teaching world musics and music cultures, is just beginning in Argentinian music education.[115]

Indonesia

Education in Indonesia is controlled by the central government, and every Indonesian citizen has the consitutional right to formal education. The Indonesian state policy, the *pancasila*, guides educational practice. By law, this policy requires, among other things, nationalism (defined as "unity in diversity") and social justice (including cultural equality). With its myriad indigenous cultures and multilingual population, the government deliberately nurtures unity in diversity as its cultural philosophy.[116]

The arts hold a central position in Indonesian culture. It is not surprising then to find that the government "has targeted music education specifically as the means for pursuing and promoting multiculturalism within their country." Music is required during the nine compulsory years of school and in all teacher-training institutions.[117]

Unlike countries still struggling to overcome the influence of colonialism on music education, Indonesia has had some success incorporating its indigenous music within the music curriculum. In the public schools, all students learn to read both Western and Indonesian (Chevé system using numbers 1–7 for *do-ti*) notation, to begin performance on both Western and traditional instruments, and to sing a mixed repertoire that includes sixteen national songs. However, the public school music education program is primarily formulated on Western teaching methodologies.[118] In the Akademi Seni Karawitan Indonesia, students learn the traditional arts from the various regions of Indonesia in a conservatory-type atmosphere. These academies are the "high art" institutions of Indonesia, providing professional musicians trained primarily in Javanese gamelan music.[119] At the collegiate level, pre-service music educators learn Western music theory and history, but are also required to take one course in Indonesian traditional or art music, usually gamelan. With media access to the diverse cultures across their archipelago, their own regional heritage, and their formal education, Indonesian children grow up truly multicultural.[120]

Malaysia

Once a part of the British Empire, Malaysia, like many other countries, is trying to overcome its legacy of colonialism. Malaysian education has been colored by British thinking. For music education, this meant studying Western European music.

Music education has been compulsory in all elementary schools since 1983, but it is not required in the high schools. Very little attention has been paid to either Malaysian traditional music or any other music culture in the classroom. In the elite British schools of the past, folk songs were used as a way to teach the English language (or Japanese during Japan's occupation of Malaysia in World War II).[121]

Besides the British schools, there were Malay, Chinese, and Indian (Tamil) schools. These schools taught students in the vernacular rather than English, and, as might be suspected, each culture taught its own traditional songs in music class. The Chinese schools also included music reading using the Chevé system of notation in its curriculum.[122]

Today the Malay language is the national language and is taught in all the schools, with English as a compulsory second language.[123] Training for pre-service music educators still focuses predominantly on Western European music, with basic proficiency on the guitar required. It is only since 1990 that music educators have seen the importance of Malaysian folk and traditional musics and begun investigating ways to incorporate traditional music in the primary school music curriculum.[124]

Namibia, Nigeria, and Zambia

Namibia and Zambia both incorporate pan-African musical arts as well as music and dance from their resepective countries in their school music classrooms. In 1992 Namibia actually adopted an educational policy that ensures a balance of Namibian culture in the music curriculum and also pays attention to musics from around the world.[125] Unfortunately, in music teacher education the greater emphasis remains on Western European music and music literacy. In both Namibia and Zambia, however, efforts are being made to acquaint future music educators with an African philosophy of music education, traditional folk songs, African instruments, and the social and cultural contexts of African music.

In Nigeria, music education has not been considered an important subject for public school education.[126] Western music completely precluded traditional Nigerian musics in the schools.[127] However, since 1962, music educators have proposed a curriculum which would include Nigerian music in the music program. Over the past thirty-five years, limited progress has been made toward achieving this goal, progress made more difficult by the lack of the teacher training needed to be able to present traditional musics in the schools.[128]

The Philippines

Because of its double colonial heritage, the Philippines has both a history of transplanted Western music brought from Spain and public school music education established by the United States. Until 1952, the elementary schools employed the *Progressive Music Series* (Silver Burdett and Company, 1924), along with songbooks of Filipino compositions and folk songs. Music education closely paralleled the music syllabi of American educators.[129]

Since 1982, there have been significant changes in the Filipino music curriculum, not the least being minimum time requirements for study; the interdisciplinary connections between music, civics and culture, and languages (both English and Filipino); and the establishment of required music classes at the high school level. The new high school curriculum is based on Western music, but it also allows for the introduction of Filipino and Asian musics in the third year of study. The fourth-year course is called World Music, and focuses on "the historical and stylistic periods of Western Classical Music."[130]

Very few teacher training institutions are able to offer a bachelor of science degree in music education; however, conservatories and colleges of music do offer a bachelor of music in music education. For most of these institutions, music instruction is only offered in Western music. However, there are six Filipino institutions of higher education that do offer formal courses in musics from around the world. These range from programs in ethnomusicology and Asian musics, such as those taught at the University of the Philippines, to ongoing research in Filipino music, to infrequently offered survey courses in Filipino and Asian musics.[131] Since the 1980s, all music students at the University of the Philippines School of Music have been required to perform in the gamelan ensemble, and to take courses in Filipino and Asian musics along with their Western music studies.[132]

These six universities are well supplied with musical instruments, Folkways, UNESCO, and field recordings, and monographs and other printed ethnomusicological and anthropological materials. Unfortunately, "in spite of the presence and relative availablity of scholarly sources on non-western music, very little institutional effort has been made to translate such . . . information into instructional materials."[133] In addition, because of the newness of the high school courses, it will take decades to properly train teachers to present Asian or traditional Filipino musics adequately. As a result there is an intensive program of in-service instruction currently underway in the Philippines.[134]

South Africa

South Africa is a country rich in musics. It is also a country that has just emerged from a period of enforced apartheid (1994), with a heritage of a strictly segregated educational system divided into Indian, black, white, and colored schools. During all the time under apartheid, although there were different approved music curricula for the various schools, the primary focus for music education remained Western European music.

Instead of these separate systems, there is now one education department and one curriculum for South Africa, and that curriculum is currently under total revision. Because of the newly desegregated population of South Africa, by implication this curriculum will be multicultural in nature.[135]

In 1985 music educators had already begun to try to break from the exclusively Western format and to find common ground where all the musics of South Africa, black and white, could be included.[136] In an effort to do this, Elizabeth Oehrle of the University of Natal established the Network for Intercultural Education through Music and its publication the *Talking Drum*. Both are designed to bring people and resources together, to disseminate and evaluate sample lesson plans, and to develop an idea bank for intercultural music education.[137] Oehrle prefers the term "intercultural" to "multicultural" because it "is not just a belief in a plurality of separately-nurtured musical cultures, but in a free intermingling of different musics in one common school curriculum applicable to all schools."[138] Also founded in 1985 was the Southern Africa Music Educators Society, an organization providing support for music education throughout the southern part of the continent.

Some recent changes in South African music education have occurred at the collegiate level. Both the University of Natal and the University of Durban-Westville have restructured their music courses to teach African, Indian, and Western (Classical, popular, and jazz) musics. For example, the University of Durban-Westville has incorporated more of a cross-cultural focus, such as courses that teach "techniques of composition in Indian and African music and jazz styles," and performance classes on instruments from the African, Indian, and Western music cultures.[139] The University of Natal, for the first time in its history, has established an African music post. This three-year position is designed to focus on African music both in the immediate community and at large.[140] At the University of the Witwatersrand in Johannesburg, there is a new first-year course titled Music in Context, a course that brings the multiple musics of the students into the classroom and provides the students with an opportunity both to share their own music and to learn how to approach new musics with an open mind.[141] Music education students at the University of Cape Town concentrate on African musics and performance techniques in their second year, and employ these techniques in their third-year teaching experiences. Their fourth-year studies divide between an emphasis on popular and world musics and student teaching.[142]

These are among the first steps taken as music education seeks that "free intermingling of different musics" in a country seeking to unify and heal itself. It is a new, exciting, and dynamic time.

Around the World

Multicultural music education has become a concern in a great many countries. Programs are developing in places as geographically separate as Sweden and Brazil, and examples can be found in the Netherlands, Italy, Portugal, Norway, and Japan where music educators are also coming to terms with the need to address multiple musics in the classroom.[143] Sometimes it is the need to adjust the curriculum to the changing demographics of the classroom that has brought about this change; sometimes it is established through a cross-cultural program between schools. The inclusion of a variety of musics in the curriculum may be state-sponsored or teacher-initiated. Always there is the desire for improved teacher training and better materials and methodologies.

SUMMARY

As in the United States, immigration has produced great societal changes in Great Britain, Canada, Australia, and Germany. The initial response from education in all these countries was to assist in assimilating these people into the dominant culture. In music education, this was accomplished through the exclusive teaching of the Western European tradition, sometimes with the inclusion of patriotic music. It was not until the late 1960s that the peoples of minority cultures began to gain a voice, both legally in their countries, and literally in their music classes.

The exclusivity of the Western perspective is being challenged around the world. In many countries, the initial experiences offered through music education were controlled by a colonial power and focused exclusively on teaching the Western art music tradition. As these countries obtained their independence, they began to restructure their educational system. It has taken a very long time, but slowly music educators are beginning to reintroduce their indigenous musics into the music curriculum.

Although changes in multicultural music education have taken place in theory in all these countries, in actuality implementation has been slow. In many cases, music teachers are finding their own way to include the musics of the students in the music curricula; sometimes there is assistance from governmental or collegial sources. Progress has been made only recently in both pre-service and in-service music teacher education to enable teachers to work effectively with both a multiplicity of musics and a multiplicity of cultures represented by the children in their classrooms. Much more needs to be done.

Conclusions, Implications, and Questions

The histories of multicultural music education around the world have a great deal in common. Many began by using music as a means of assimilating the new immigrant populations in their countries. All have come to value the musics of all peoples as worthy of study in the music classroom. In nearly all cases, the change in perspective occurred sometime in the 1970s. What might have brought about this worldwide change in music education?

By looking at the development of multiculturalism in other countries, we can see it from various perspectives. Countries that view themselves as being multicultural, such as Canada and Indonesia, have made their concept of multiculturalism ("unity in diversity") a law. The Australians have adopted a similar concept as a national policy. In many countries, multiculturalism is based on including the cultures of the various native populations. Germany basically still sees itself as a monocultural country, in spite of the fact that its population has been multicultural for years. Although it is a law in the United States that all should have access to learning about their heritage, multiculturalism is not a governmental policy. These various perspectives can affect the attitudes of teachers in all subject areas. In what ways might this affect the way music education is taught? Does it help to know these differences? Why? Some countries have designed "multicultural" music education programs, while others function "interculturally." What are the differences between these viewpoints? How might these differences change the way American music educators teach?

In all the countries discussed here, multicultural music teacher education is of paramount importance, just as it is in the United States. In many places, teachers are already dealing with students from diverse musical backgrounds while their educational training system remains focused on the Western tradition. In others, the commitment to multicultural music education is strong at all levels of instruction. All countries acknowledge that for multiculturalism in music education to become a real part of the curriculum, there must be a change to a broader perspective in schools of music and departments of music education. In what ways might this take place? What might assist this transition?

PART
III
Implications for Music Education

CHAPTER **10**

Music Teacher
Education

The musical tapestry which makes America one of the most colorful nations in the world is both music teacher education's greatest asset and its greatest challenge.

—CARLESTA HANDERSON[1]

There is no doubt folk musics have been taught in the schools for many years; many people remember singing European and American folk songs, including spirituals, as elementary or high school students.[2] However, there was little or no training given new teachers in how to teach these musics. Colleges assumed that training teachers in Western music was sufficient to enable them to teach any kind of music. The concept of music as a "universal language" upheld this idea, as did the fact that the first musics admitted to the curriculum were European, American, and Latin American folk musics, all based on the Western music tradition. The exception to this situation was the African-American colleges and universities where the music education program regularly included the teaching of African-American music traditions along with European musics.[3]

Across the years, many have recommended that music teacher education include training in the musics from a variety of cultures. Beginning in the 1940s with Curtis's entreaty that teachers learn about the musics of Latin America, and following with the Yale Seminar, the International Seminar on Teacher Education, and the Tanglewood Symposium, educators have repeatedly emphasized that teachers need a knowledge of various musics and their social contexts. In addition, since 1967 professional recommendations along with state and local education mandates have published statements treating the need for multicultural music teacher education.

With the resolutions of the 1990 Multicultural Symposium, the music education profession, though the MENC, committed itself to actively encouraging a multicultural approach in teaching music at the elementary, secondary, and collegiate levels. The latter is most important, because until there is a change to a multicultural perspective at the collegiate level, teachers will continue to teach from the Western perspective, as they have been taught. This is the conclusion of both Navarro's and Montague's studies,[4] and history appears to justify their conclusions.

In the past, changes at the collegiate level filtered down to the elementary and secondary schools. However, in the case of multicultural music education, it may well be that it is the grass-roots elementary/secondary music teachers, especially those in highly diverse urban school systems, who are going to effect the change in the colleges and universities by demanding training in a multiplicity of musics in order to better teach their students.[5] In either case, as William Anderson said, "The most significant change will really come when we can do something with the [collegiate] curriculum."[6]

MULTICULTURAL MANDATES AND RECOMMENDATIONS

In the light of contemporary developments in multiculturalism, many state departments of education already require teachers to have training that includes multicultural education. In most cases these involve student teaching experiences with multicultural populations and/or course work in multicultural (or intercultural) awareness for certification in elementary and secondary education.[7] For music education certification, four states currently require evidence of knowledge about both Western and non-Western musics or the relation of music to culture. Seven states expect multicultural competencies in their professional education requirements for music certification.[8]

The accreditation bodies for higher education also recognize the need for broader music study. Both the National Council for Accreditation of Teacher Education (NCATE) and the National Association of Schools of Music (NASM) currently require the inclusion of multicultural studies in the programs of the students who will be exiting their accredited institutions.[9] In particular, NASM requires that "students have opportunities through performance and academic studies to work with music of diverse cultural sources, historical periods, and media."[10]

Beyond these mandates, professional music organizations have pointed out the need for multicultural music teacher education. The Music Educators National Conference (MENC), in its report *Teacher Education in Music* (1972), said, "All music educators must be able to . . . apply their knowledge of music to diatonic and nondiatonic Western and non-Western art, dance, and folk music, . . . should know how composers in various cultures combine the elements of music to elicit responses in the listener, . . . and must be familiar with the tone-production capabilities of . . . instruments of other cultures."[11] The MENC report from the Commission on Graduate Music Teacher Education (1984) recommends that those teachers exiting with a master's degree have knowledge of a variety of music cultures and how to employ them in the classroom.[12] The need for teachers broadly trained in various music cultures has also been a recurring theme in the *Music Educators Journal (MEJ)*.[13] In 1989 the College Music Society (CMS) also commented on this need, stating, "The undergraduate curriculum should begin to reflect a pluralistic perspective of our age, and goals for students' development should involve global and cross-cultural competency."[14]

THE COLLEGE MUSIC CURRICULUM

If colleges and universities are going to adequately meet the NASM mandates, they will need to provide a multicultural component in all their courses for all their graduating musicians, not just for future music educators. Incorporating a multicultural approach only in music education courses not only puts limits on the studies of *all* the students, it could promote a double standard: that world musics are fine for music educators but not for anyone else. Offering distinct courses in ethnomusicology open to all students is one solution, but this can sometimes have "a tendency to isolate the musics of various cultures and to set up a structure that presents these musics as 'foreign phenomena' with no real connection to the traditional core of the curriculum."[15]

General Music Courses

Various proposals have been presented as suggestions for redesigning the collegiate undergraduate music curriculum to reflect a multicultural perspective. Colleges have already begun to implement some of these. More and more music departments offer a world musics survey course, include world music traditions within general music appreciation courses, or offer specialized courses in African, Asian, European, and/or American folk and traditional musics.[16]

Still another suggestion that colleges could employ to introduce students to the study of music from another culture is through a two- or three-credit independent-study project. Though this probably would work best at the graduate level, it might be employed as an option in the list of humanities/arts courses that form the liberal arts core of courses at most institutions. This project is actually an extension of the kind of term projects already required as part of some courses such as music appreciation or a world musics survey. The difference is the depth of research and field work required. This independent study would be overseen by a college professor, perhaps in conjunction with a cooperating musician, but will not require further expenses in the form of more staff, or logistics such as classroom space or scheduling. The project would not have to be investigated solely on campus; in fact it would be a good way to involve the college, the students, and community members. The students would present a proposal to their professors, stating what, why, and how they would research this music, and under whom they would be working (for example, taking lessons from a community musician, participation in an ethnic music ensemble, interviews with prominent local musicians). Professor and student can then agree on the frequency and mode of evaluation. For instance, progress could be measured through combinations of conferences or written reports, and the final evaluation could be a written term paper, performance, or video presentation.

Core Music Courses

Along with incorporating a multicultural perspective in the general music offerings for all students, there are also changes occurring within the core music courses such as music history and theory. Some institutions have changed the sequence of their history courses to include a course in musics around the world designed to provide a perspective for their Western music studies. Both Kent State University and the University of Michigan, for example, require all students to take one semester of such a world musics course as their beginning foundation studies in history.

In other colleges these classes are beginning to place the events in Western music history in a broader perspective and to enhance aural and analytical skill through studying more than one music culture.[17] For example, studying the development of the Western violin could lead to discussions of the Arabic *rebab* (bowed lute), or Arabic music and its influence on European musical culture, especially in Spain and Southern France. Likewise, the concept of musical variation might be studied in a Mozart piano sonata, a Bach passacaglia, a jazz improvisation on a popular song, or a classical Thai composition. Notational systems might also be compared, for example, tabulature notation for the European lute and the descriptive notation for Chinese *qin* (zither), or even between forms of Western notation: Gregorian chant, the Chevé system, and the American shape-note tradition. Ear-training exercises can incorporate melodies and rhythms from different cultures for sightsinging and dictation. This would be especially effective if these exercises are accompanied by recordings of the authentic sources so the students get used to the timbres and tuning systems for those cultures.[18]

Performance Opportunities

Educators tend to agree that what is currently missing, and is most needed for music students, at this point is performance opportunities in a wide variety of cultures.[19] Performing the music of another culture is the only real gateway to understanding it. This experience could be gained through elective ensembles in African, African-American, Asian, or Latin American musics. Some colleges do offer these kinds of performing groups, from gospel choirs to gamelans, African drumming and dance groups to mariachi and salsa ensembles. Still others supplement their regular faculty "with distinguished performer-teachers from other areas of the world who come to the United States to work on advanced degrees, and, as graduate assistants, perform and teach music from their native musical traditions."[20] However, there are not enough such programs. Only about 19 percent of the multicultural music courses currently offered in NASM accredited institutions today provide for performance, either in ensembles or private lessons.[21]

Students need a minimum of one semester experiencing unfamiliar music to begin to understand it. One semester will not guarantee competency, but it will lay the necessary foundation for further musical explorations.[22] Because the process of learning a second music culture is so important to being able to teach it competently, performing in these ensembles should have an equal status with performing in the more traditional band, orchestra, and chorus, both in their schedules and credit hours.

These ensembles provide only a part of the performance repertoire, however. Students will also benefit from a multicultural approach in their traditional band, orchestra, and choral experiences. Directors of collegiate ensembles might begin by looking to expand their repertoire to present a balance of musical elements, historical periods, cultural sources, and composers and arrangers representative of many cultures.

Beyond this, any student who is proficient performing the music of another culture might be allowed to perform one or more selections in recital, alone or with a small ensemble. While there may not be many who qualify, for those who do, it will be of benefit for both the performer and the audience. The performer will have this music culture affirmed and will have the opportunity to teach the audience, and the audience will have a chance to hear music from another culture.

Finally, schools and departments of music can encourage a world perspective by sponsoring and presenting concerts of musics from a variety of cultures. The impact and immediacy of live performance on students far outweighs listening to a recording, no matter how good.

Music Education

According to Rosita Sands, "Multiculturalism should be the norm in all music education classes, particularly those that deal specifically with performance repertoire or pedagogical materials."[23] In music education, some departments offer a multicultural music education methods course, and others are making efforts to provide this information within the regular methods classes.

Ideally, graduating music education majors should be both knowledgeable about musics in other cultural contexts, and capable of employing these musics in their classrooms. In order to do so, they should have:

1. experienced the musics of other cultures:

   a. through guided listening
   b. through attending concerts of music from other cultures, either school or community sponsored
   c. through performing for at least one semester in an ensemble other than the traditional Western ensembles (chorus, band, orchestra) or, if no ensemble is available, through attaining a minimal performance competency in methods classes

2. learned about the basic systems, instruments, and vocal timbres of musics from other cultures

   a. through a survey course in world musics
   b. within other classes (e.g., methods, music history, theory)

3. developed the ability to incorporate the musics of other cultures in classroom music lessons

   Most of these requirements, and especially the last, could be achieved in a multicultural music methods course. Such a course would (1) allow for listening, reading, and research; (2) provide some performance experience; (3) address classroom applications (including such topics as authenticity of performance of music from other cultures); (4) include the teaching methods of other cultures; and (5) provide opportunities for developing lessons plans, units of study, and teaching practice lessons employing the musics from a variety of cultures. However, such a course may not fit into the school's guidelines for credit hours to graduation. It then becomes the task of the regular methods classes in general music, both elementary and secondary levels, and instrumental music, to include some time for addressing these issues. This ideal situation is slowly becoming reality. Some colleges do offer such a multicultural music education methods course, while others are already making efforts to provide this information within the regular methods classes.

   Educators emphasize the need for repertoire classes that incorporate as multicultural a base of literature as possible, including "arrangements and compositions that reflect indigenous folk music idioms and traditional styles."[24] Some lists are already available with the beginnings of such a repertoire. The May 1992 *MEJ* (Special Focus: Multicultural Music Education) contained suggested repertoire for chorus, band, and orchestra.[25] The New York State *School Music News* published similar lists of musics from diverse cultures for large performing organizations.[26] Other such efforts are probably available, but researchers would do well to assist in the identification and evaluation of this repertoire.

   Methods classes especially should offer students the opportunity to examine classroom materials that are multicultural in nature, to prepare them to teach in schools where there are many different cultures and ethnic groups. Pre-service students need field experiences in such schools whenever possible. This is even more important today with the requirement for multicultural experiences in current state certification requirements.

In addition to the repertoire and methods classes, multicultural perspectives need to permeate beginning courses in music education foundations.[27] Some possible ways to do this include student explorations of "basic philosophical tenets from a variety of music cultures," and the contributions of women, minorities, and ethnic groups to music education history. Classes could introduce "the topics of music perception and learning theory in a broad array of musical traditions" when learning psychological aspects of music.[28]

Added to this, music education departments can enhance the multicultural program they present through the recruitment of students and faculty from a wide range of cultural and ethnic backgrounds for music education department. As Sands explained, "Our country desperately needs a multicultural teaching force. All students benefit when they have the opportunity to develop relationships with individuals who are members of different cultural groups, to interact with them daily, and to view them as positive role models."[29]

Music Teacher Education

If these are the ideal requirements for the undergraduate music education curriculum, what about the requirements at the graduate level? What should be expected of doctoral students who will be the educators of the next generation of pre-service students?

Barbara Lundquist has suggested that collegiate music educators need even more training in the musics of various cultures, to the extent that they are competent in at least one other music culture, and knowledgeable in applying various musics in music education.[30]

To accomplish this goal, Lundquist suggested an ideal Ph.D. curriculum for the training of a multicultural teacher of teachers. This curriculum would combine courses in both ethnomusicology and music education. The ethnomusicology portion of such a program would include a survey of world music cultures, accompanied by performance experience in one or two music cultures. Several in-depth area-studies courses (such as Latin American musics, Asian musics) would follow. Additional work in cultural anthropology such as anthropological perspectives in music would be useful. Finally, courses in organology, transcription and analysis, and research design and field methods would round out the ethnomusicological portion of this program.

From the music education department, the primary course would be designed to focus on the teaching of the world's musics, including how to identify and select music appropriate for the classroom from the world repertoire, teaching methodologies from various cultures, and cultural context reflected in music and music reflecting cultural context. In conjunction with this course, a practicum for teacher educators would address instructional sequences, strategies, materials and resources, and the inclusion of guest performers to enhance the lesson.

Beyond this, a seminar dealing with the history, philosophy, and foundations of multicultural/world music education, and a course in learning theories would round out the music education portion of this course of studies. Lastly, Lundquist has recommended fluency in a second language, usually French, German, or Spanish.

Evaluation in this doctoral program would be ongoing: examinations in all courses should reflect the final product, a teacher who can synthesize the course work for use in the instructional setting. The culminating dissertation should examine some issue or theory related to multicultural/world music education.

SUMMARY

Students learn from what they experience more than from what they read about in classes; they teach as they have been taught. If schools of music wish to graduate music educators who are competent in multicultural music education, they need to model multicultural music education as well as they currently model the Western music program.[31] Performance, world musics survey courses, a balance of Western and world musics in all courses, and pre-service experience are all important aspects of multicultural music teacher education. It is best implemented by a faculty that is itself multicultural, multimusical, and knowledgeable in the various learning styles necessary to teach, and evaluate, a multicultural student population. Developing this kind of program is a slow process, but the progress over the last decade shows that it has begun.

There have already been many advancements in music teacher education; some programs are close to these ideal situations. Today, degree programs allow for more interface between ethnomusicology and music education than ever before. Some colleges offer separate courses in multicultural music education. Others are incorporating a multicultural perspective as much as possible within their existing methods courses. Teachers who are interested in teaching from a multicultural perspective now have opportunities to learn about other musics and how to teach them through in-service training provided by conferences and workshops, summer courses, and graduate classes. However, this multicultural approach is still often found only in "little pockets or an isolated model program here and there."[32] There is still much to be done.

Conclusions, Implications, and Questions

Across the century, the addition of each new genre of music to the music curriculum brought about no corresponding change in the music teacher curriculum, except in isolated instances. The Western music perspective lasted officially until 1967, but unofficially is still in effect in a great many schools across the country. This is the viewpoint that is challenged by the multicultural perspective.

Since 1967 collegiate music education curricula have tended to be a bit ahead of the general school of music offerings. Guitar classes and courses in jazz improvisation have often been incorporated first in music education departments as music educators found they needed a broader base in order to do their jobs. As a result, frequently "the level of curricular innovation is higher in music education."[33] Could music education's need to develop teachers able to teach world musics from a multicultural perspective prove the catalyst to cause the next changes in the music curriculum?

CHAPTER 11

Materials and Methodologies

What my students and I seek are materials and experiences that help us construct an idea of the potential of multicultural or world music education.

—MARY HOOKEY[1]

For every new development in multicultural music education, corresponding new research has helped implement it. By far, the greatest productivity has occurred in the area of methods and materials. Like most new ideas, they have had their good points and their shortcomings, and it is up to music educators to pick and choose among them to find the best combination for each class they teach.

METHODS AND MATERIALS ACROSS HISTORY

Folk Dancing and Folk Songs

At the turn of the nineteenth century, folk dancing in the schools came directly from the original sources. Elizabeth Burchenal learned most of the dances herself in Europe, and her transcriptions of both the steps and music are as accurate as she could make them. However, she gave no directions for how either physical education or music teachers were to teach these dances, other than following the steps she outlined. In addition, the dances were taken out of context with no real indication given other than the country of source. Granted, some of the contexts, especially the "occupation" dances, were easier for students to understand in the early twentieth century. For example, students dancing the Danish Shoemaker's Dance knew how their shoes were made or repaired by the cobbler down the street. For today's Reebok-shod students, handmade shoes are not the norm. The teacher needs to contextualize this dance not only in their culture but also for the occupation.

In the first quarter of this century folk songs were also totally out of context, though the melodies were often accurately transcribed. Their collectors sometimes credited the country of source, but more often not even that. No contextual information was offered in the texts, and the lyrics frequently were completely different from the original. In keeping with the philosophy of the day, music educators saw folk songs as "pretty tunes." They were more frequently taught through notation and solfège than by rote.

In spite of these inadequacies, folk songs and dancing found their place in the music curriculum. Francis Elliott Clark frequently expressed the opinion that folk songs and dances were the expressions of the people, and for the most part, it would seem the profession agreed with her. Music teachers, especially in urban centers, had opportunities to observe performances of the original songs and dances at folk festivals, but at the time, there was no way to access the contextual information. Satis Coleman's "creative music" program in New York City was the first to incorporate ethnomusicological information and social contexts.

African-American Spirituals

Spirituals first won the approval of the music education profession through demonstrations by culture bearers at MENC conferences. Although African-American music teachers taught this music in the segregated schools of the nation, once spirituals became acceptable to the profession, they became notated choral music, often with piano accompaniment. The oral tradition of the spirituals and their a cappella performance became lost in the classroom application as teachers expected it to conform to the existing Western music format. Rote teaching was primarily used in lower grades; the goal for the upper grade levels was music literacy. The oral/aural teaching metholodolgy had no place in such a program.

Latin American Musics

Latin American music materials were first produced in cooperation with the Pan American Union (PAU) for all segments of the music education program—general classroom, choral, and instrumental. They ranged from the original compositions of Latin American composers to arrangements of folk music and dances. These authentic school arrangements had the approval of the PAU and publishers made them available to music educators. As times changed, they gradually fell into disuse. Since publishers only print what will sell, it is possible they did not have enough demand for these materials. Today, some publishers have begun reprinting a few of these old standards. "Amparito Roca" by Jaime Texidor and Jose Padilla's "El Relicario" are examples of instrumental compositions that have currently found renewed interest.

Latin American folk songs in the music textbooks were so often reworked for school use that they lost both their authenticity and their validity as cultural representations. Both Domingo Santa Cruz and Louis Woodson Curtis pointed this out in the 1940s. Unfortunately, this is still somewhat true today,[2] although since the advent of knowledgeable consultants for publishing companies, considerably more care is taken to have authentic materials in the school texts.

Since the materials for band used to consist almost exclusively of marches and transcriptions of classical and popular music, instrumental concert performances often included at least one popular Latin selection in a concert performance. With the growth of composed pieces for school band and orchestra, transcriptions gradually fell out of favor. Of the original Latin American music materials, very little is available for band today. In fact, although there is some instrumental music that might be termed multicultural in its use of folk materials, there is little that is truly authentic in nature from any culture, although some inroads are being made.

Technology

From the beginning, sound recordings have been important in multicultural music education. Teachers were thrilled to be able to bring the sounds of actual performances into their classes. In particular, the folk dances so popular in music classes relied heavily on the use of recordings, although the RCA Victrola band or orchestra usually replaced the flute and fiddle accompaniments common to many of these dances. The result was melodically and rhythmically accurate for dancing, but totally lacking in timbre, often with an added "heaviness" as a result of instrumentation changes (for example, tubas playing bass lines originally performed by low strings). In some cases these orchestrations may have been second-generation transcriptions made from the piano arrangements of the original dance music supplied by Elizabeth Burchenal.

Music appreciation classes also benefited from these phonograph recordings. Although some of these old recordings were field recordings, many more of them were recordings of Western artists performing composed pieces inspired by folk materials. Gradually record companies added more selections of authentic performances to their catalogs, and since 1960, the availability of these musics has become so overwhelmingly accessible that discographies are available to help teachers choose world musics for classroom use.[3]

Besides the improvements in sound reproduction in terms of both quality and authenticity of product, the advent of films and videotapes opened new avenues for acquainting students with musics from many cultures. Ranging from documentary films to practical instruction videos, the addition of visual presentations brought the immediacy of contact with another culture into the classroom. Of all the videos that have been produced, the JVC Video Anthology of World Music and Dance is perhaps the most comprehensive collection currently available.

NEW MATERIALS

College Texts and Reference Books

Numerous materials provide general surveys of various music cultures for pre-service and in-service music educators. Some of these are texts; some are audio- or videotapes. They are most often used in world music courses, but they also provide excellent reference material and resource lists. Prior to 1967 materials such as these for music education were few to nonexistent. Only since music education and ethnomusicology have begun working together have these kinds of resources been developed. The following is a selected list of these materials:

> *Worlds of Music*, 3rd ed., Jeff Titon, ed. (New York: Schirmer, Inc., 1996). Text and accompanying tapes.
>
> *Excursions in World Music*, 2nd ed., Bruno Nettl et al. (Englewood Cliffs, NJ: Prentice-Hall, 1997). Text and accompanying tapes.
>
> *Musics of Many Cultures: An Introduction*, Elizabeth May, ed. (Berkeley: University of California Press, 1980).
>
> *Musical Instruments of the World: An Illustrated Encyclopedia*, Diagram Group (New York: Facts on File Publications, 1976).
>
> *World Music: A Source Book for Teaching*, Lynn Jessup (Danbury, CT: World Music Press, 1992).
>
> *The JVC Video Anthology of World Music · and Dance*, Folkways/ Smithsonian (Distributed through Multicultural Media, Barre, VT).
>
> *Our Musical Heritage Series: Discovering the Music of* . . . (Los Angeles: Horizon Entertainment). Introductory films.

General Music Materials

The music textbooks and their accompanying resource materials currently on the market have a great deal more to help educators incorporate a multicultural perspective in their classes. Besides performances of the printed songs, CDs also carry sound-bites demonstrating instruments from around the world. Videos show not only student groups but performing groups from various cultures demonstrating their songs, musical styles, and instruments. The texts include more contextual information. These are all added helps for the music educator as well as those general classroom teachers who teach music.

Besides the textbooks, a wealth of new materials is being published for implementing a multicultural approach in music education. Of these materials, their best feature is their acknowledgment of cultural integrity. For the most part, they have been written by music educators in collaboration with ethnomusicologists or culture bearers. Where this is not the case, the authors have devoted in-depth research to the culture before presenting it for classroom use. The best texts include contextual information sufficient for teaching the lessons, and often come with recordings of the original music. Those that do rely heavily on individual expertise may not be the wisest choice for a teacher just beginning to deal with a new music.

Excellent bibliographies and resource lists are also available. The most comprehensive is *Representative Resources for Teaching World Musics* compiled by Edward O'Connor for the Education Committee of the Society for Ethnomusicology, and published in the MENC compilation *Music in Cultural Context*.[4] This is an annotated bibliography, indicating availability, accuracy of authenticity and cultural representation, additional components such as audiotapes or slides, and a general description of the usefulness of the item. Other resource lists can be found in the October 1972, May 1983, and May 1992 special focus issues of the *MEJ*.

The following is a selected list of recommended current materials:

MENC resources

Multicultural Perspectives in Music, William M. Anderson and Patricia Shehan Campbell, eds. (1989, 2nd edition 1996). Accompanying cassettes for first edition also coordinate with the second; both editions include background information and lesson plans.

Multicultural Approaches to Music Education, William M. Anderson, ed. (1991). Text and accompanying videos.

Sounds of the World (1986–1990). Five sets of audio cassettes with lesson plans.

Strategies for Specialized Ensembles, Robert Cutietta, ed. (forthcoming).

Music in Cultural Context, Patricia Shehan Campbell, ed. (1996).

Books

Lessons from the World, Patricia Shehan Campbell (Schirmer, Inc., 1992). Gives examples of teaching/learning modalities and improvisatory practice from around the world with applications to music education.

Teaching the Music of Six Different Cultures, Luvenia George (World Music Press, 1987). Covers African, African-American, Native American, Jewish, Hawaiian, and Mexican and Puerto Rican musical traditions.

World Music Press Publications

Roots and Branches, Patricia Shehan Campbell and Ellen McColluch-Brabson (1994). Songs from a variety of cultures

Moving Within the Circle: Contemporary Native American Music and Dance, J. Bryan Burton (1993).

Let Your Voice Be Heard! Songs from Ghana and Zimbabwe, Abraham Kobena Adzinyah, Dumisani Maraire, and Judith Cook Tucker (1986).

Los Mariachis! An Introduction to Mexican Mariachi Music, Patricia W. Harpole (1989, rev. ed. 1991).

From Rice Paddies and Temple Yards: Traditional Music of Vietnam, Patricia Shehan Campbell and Phong Nuygen (1990).

Silent Temples, Songful Hearts: Traditional Music of Cambodia, Patricia Shehan Campbell and Sam-Ang-Sam (1991).

The Lion's Roar: Chinese Lou-Gu Music, Patricia Shehan Campbell and Han Kuo-Huang (1992).

All include contextual information, give classroom applications, songs and ideas for lessons, and come with an accompanying tape.

Warner Brothers Publications

Traditional Songs of Singing Cultures: A World Sampler, Patricia Shehan Campbell, Sue Williamson, and Pierre Perron (1996). Comes with accompanying CD.

Computer Resources

Classroom media have moved beyond simple audio or video recordings. Technological advances have given music educators a new tool for presenting the musics of the world. The entire world of sound is now available at the touch of a computer key. Resources for both teachers and students now include electronic keyboards, music writing programs with or without a MIDI, software programs, electronic mail and bulletin boards, and World Wide Web sites that offer encyclopedic information, contact with musicians around the world, and even virtual performance experiences.

Music educators wishing to introduce their classes to an unfamiliar musical culture may do so by having the students explore the sounds of the instruments and rhythms from that culture either directly on an electronic keyboard or with a MIDI interface to a computer music writing program, in which students can select instrumental sounds from a wide range of world musics. Software programs provide another access to world musics. Grolier's Multi-media Encyclopedia and Microsoft Encarta (both CD-ROMs) are two such programs. Musical Instruments by Microsoft (CD-ROM) provides even

more information about world musical instruments. With color photographs, sound examples of instruments, and accompanying historical information, this CD-ROM program is useful both for music class and for interdisciplinary work with social studies.

There are many Internet sites that can provide both resource information and personal contacts. The following is a selected list of World Wide
Web home pages that provide basic information and suggest links for further investigations into world musics:

> Music Educators National Conference (MENC): http://www.menc.org
>
> Society for Ethnomusicology (SEM): http://www.indiana.edu/~eth-
> music
>
> Indiana Music Library (IML): http://www.indiana.edu/musiclib.html
>
> Smithsonian Institution (Folkways) (SI): http://www.si.edu/folkways.
> This is a catalog of all the Folkways recordings by style of music. The
> catalog includes Folkways record number, artists' names, information
> about the contents of the record, and sound samples.
>
> J. W. Pepper. Inc.: http://www.jwpepper.com. This commercial music
> supply house provides a catalog of the multicultural compositions they
> carry. Ordering information included.
>
> Multicultural Media: http://www.multiculturalmedia.com. A catalog
> describing videos, CD, books, and CD-ROMs dealing with world music
> and dance. It is organized by geographic regions. Ordering information
> included.

In addition, numerous newsgroups can be found on Usenet and mail
lists on BITNET providing bulletin boards about any number of cultures, geographic regions, and music styles. These bulletin boards allow the posting
of questions and comments, and become interactive when another person
with a similar interest responds. Examples of Usenet newsgroups are:

> rec.music folk
>
> rec.music.Afro-Latin
>
> rec.music.reggae
>
> soc.culture.Arabic
>
> soc.culture.Australian[5]

There are also mail lists for just about any musical interest group. For
example, information on jazz literature and performance is accessible
through JAZZ@TEMPLEVM.BITNET. The ethnomusicology forum is found by
subscribing to ETHMUS-L@UMDD.BITNET. At a more personal level, there are
both individual home pages and e-mail access to many ethnomuscologists,
culture bearers, and music educators who will respond to queries directly.

These are only a sample of the Web possibilities available for teachers and students researching multicultural music education. Although Web addresses may change in the future, a key-word search (the name of the organization, "world musics," "music education," or "ethnomusicology") should produce the requested entry. Addresses for mailing lists of interest groups may be obtained through Internet publications available in book stores, or through linkages found on Web sites.

Choral Materials

Many authentic presentations of musics from various cultures for chorus are now available. Many are arrangements; some are transcriptions. Fewer piano parts are added out of context, original languages are increasingly used, often with pronunciation guides, and performance notes sometimes include dance movements, translations, and cultural/contextual information. Choral educators are increasingly aware of original timbres and styles (for example, gospel, or Appalachian folk).

Far more choral arrangements and transcriptions are available than can be mentioned here. Many more have been published since the selected list of multicultural choral materials found in the May 1992 issue of the *MEJ*.[6] Choral educators may wish to investigate the following:

Three Czech Folk Songs ("Above the Plain," "Zum-Ta-Di-Ya," "Walking at Night"), arr. Kirby Shaw (Hal Leonard)

Dance and Turn, Moravian folk song, arr. Jennings (Kjos)

Ahrirang, Korean folk song, arr. Robert DeCormier (Lawson Gould/ Alfred)

Sleep, My Little One (Duermete, Niño), Spanish/Mexican Lullaby, vocal arrangement by Judith Herington, accompaniment by Sara Glick (Pavane Publishing)

Minka, Russian Folk Song, arr. Jill Ann Jones (Shawnee Press)

Spanish Allelu, traditional, arr. Linda Steen Spevacek (Hal Leonard)

The Hannikkha Shalom, arr. Schwartz (Shawnee Press)

Dormi, Dormi (Sweetly Slumber), arr. Mary Goetz (Boosey and Hawkes)

O Sifuni Mungu, words and music by David Maddux, Marty McCall, Mmunga Mwenebulongo Mulongoy, and Asukulu Yunu Mukalay, arr. Roger Emerson. (Hal Leonard)

Niska Banja, Serbian Gypsy dance, arr. Nick Page (Boosey and Hawkes)

Three Spanish Christmas Carols, arr. Greenbury (Hal Leonard)

Riu, Riu, Riu, No. 3 of Three Spanish Christmas Carols, ed. Noah Greenberg (Hal Leonard)

Siyahamba (African song), edited by Doreen Rao, 3-part treble voices, *a cappella*. (Boosey and Hawkes)

South African Suite (I. *Tshotsholoza*; II. *Siyahamba*; III. *Gabi Gabi*), three-and four- part treble voices, a cappella, arr. Henry H. Leck (Plymouth Music)

Instrumental Materials

There is still a lack of multicultural materials for instrumental music, but some inroads have been made. Some composers are adding authentic elements such as scalar material (Chinese scales, Indian ragas) and traditional percussion such as Indian *tabla* (drums) or African *agogo* (double bell) to their compositions. And some good transcriptions of folk music pay attention to authenticity of timbres and performance styles. Some of these come with study helps along with warm-up materials and well written program notes giving cultural context for the music employed. Unfortunately, most do not, leaving it up to the teacher to seek out this information. The following are selected examples of currently available band and orchestra arrangements.[7] All of them make use of elements from folk or classical traditions, some more fully than others.

Band

Three Czech Folk Songs, Johnny Vinson (Hal Leonard)

Winter Fiesta (A La Media Noche), arr. Paul Jennings (MusicWorks)

Canadian Folk Song Rhapsody, James Curnow (Jenson)

Korean Folk Song (Arirang), arr. Ralph Gingery (William Allen Music)

Russian Folk Fantasy, James Curnow (Hal Leonard)

Cajun Folk Songs, Frank Ticheli (Manhattan Beach Music)

Arabian Suite, Paul Jennings (MusicWorks)

Yagi-Bushi, Naohiro Iwai (Ludwig)

Amparito Roca, Jaime Texidor, arr. Aubrey Winter (Boosey and Hawkes)

Norwegian Lullaby, Bjorn Morten (Carl Fisher)

Song of Krishna, Robert Washburn (Warner Brothers)

Theme and Variations on an African Hymn Song, Quincy Hilliard (Barnhouse)

Orchestra

Swedish Rhapsody (Opus 19), Hugo Alfven, arr. Merle Isaac (Wynn Music)

España Cañi (Spanish Folk Song), arr. Merle Isaac (Alfred)

String Orchestra

Folk Songs of Israel, Marsha Chusmir Shapiro (Concert Works Unlimited)

Ukrainian Folk Songs, arr. Sandra Dackow (Ludwig Music)

Mexican Hat Dance, arr. Steven Wieloszynski (Kendor)

Swing Low, Sweet Chariot, arr. Gruselle (Alfred)

Queen Noor Suite for Strings, Robert Washburn (Warner Brothers-Belwin)

The Question of Authenticity

In the past no one was particularly concerned about authenticity. Probably the general assumption was that if it was printed in the school music texts, it must be accurate. Many of the folk melodies were indeed accurately transcribed—but just as many were adjusted rhythmically, melodically, or textually for didactic purposes. Publishers frequently "Westernized" unfamiliar musics for school use.

Ethnomusicology and its acceptance of music in, and as, culture, raised the consciousness of music education in this regard. With the advent of music education's awareness of world musics combined with the general tenor of recent times regarding sensitivity for all peoples, authenticity suddenly became an issue. Music educators worried that inauthenticity would lead at best to inaccuracy and at worst to advancing stereotypical ideas.

Given the ever changing nature of music in living cultures, the easiest way to solve the authenticity problem is to rely on the culture itself. Whatever the culture bearers say is their music *is* their music.[8] While this may be so, the music teacher still must choose from materials that may or may not be authentic, by anybody's standard. School materials are often arrangements of transcriptions, and may in fact be three or four generations removed from the original source of the music.[9]

Judith Cook Tucker has written guidelines for evaluating unfamiliar materials for school use. She suggested checking to see if the musician or scholar who prepared the materials is actually from the culture, if cultural context is included (both about the cultural group and its attendant history and geography), if the materials contain adequate instructions, and how much adaptation have been done to the arrangements. She also recommended looking to see if the lyrics are in the original language (preferably transliterated for pronunciation) and how well it is translated for both meaning and singability. Last, and perhaps most important, the materials should include an audiotape for listening and performance.[10]

Another idea that may prove useful also uses the authenticity of performances by culture bearers as its frame of reference. The following categories are intended to provide a perspective for determining the degree of authenticity in school music materials.[11] They may prove especially helpful when selecting music for large performing organizations, but can be applied both to general music materials and to instrumental compositions at any level of difficulty. They are not intended to be strict codifications, since some compositions contain elements of more than one category. Neither are they intended to be a criticism of any specific piece or composer.

A careful reading of the composer/arranger's notes accompanying the selection is the first step in determining these categories. The clearer the explanation of the music in these notes, the better.

Category 1: Pieces whose only connection to the authentic music of another culture is in their titles. These are often very good compositions inspired by another place or time, but they may not even contain a melody from that culture. Instrumental selections in this category are often of the type "Impressions of . . ." Choral compositions in this category sometimes focus on brotherhood or world peace, or are contemporary compositions sung in another language.

Examples are:
Band: *Anasazi*, Edmundton (Queenswood Publications)

Chorus: *Sing/Canta la cancion*, Raposo/Huff (Hal Leonard). This is a *Sesame Street* song sung in Spanish.

Category 2: Pieces that essentially employ Western art music forms, but which incorporate melodies from other cultures. Often these melodies are credited in the score or in the composer's notes. These compositions sometimes carry titles with phrases like *Theme and Variations on a Folk Song from* (fill in country), *Rhapsody*, or *Folk Song Suite*. Choral compositions may also be folk melodies but with English translations without including the original language text, or newly composed texts designed to fit the melody.

Examples are:
Band: *Canadian Folk Song Rhapsody*, Curnow (Jenson Publications)

String Orchestra: *Folk Songs of Israel*, Shapiro (Concert Works Unlimited)

Category 3: Pieces that make a conscious effort to incorporate melodic and rhythmic elements from the music of another culture. These compositions often include the use of traditional percussion instruments or accurate instrumental substitutions, and sometimes include the harmonic structure and timbres from that culture. They are often arrangements of folk songs or dances. Choral works in this category use the original language.

Examples are:
Band: *Yagi-Bushi*, Naohiro Iwai (Ludwig)

Chorus: *The Hannikkha Shalom*, arr. Schwartz (Shawnee Press)

Category 4: Pieces that are either original compositions by composers from the culture, or arrangements that are a close approximation of the original music of the culture. These pieces include the use of authentic timbres, instrumentation, form (such as call and response as opposed to sonata allegro), harmony and accompaniment. Choral literature frequently presents transcriptions that are close to the original folk musics.

Examples are:
Orchestra: *El Relicario*, Padilla, arr. Isaac (Alfred)

Chorus: *South African Suite*, arr. Leck (Plymouth Music)
All these pieces can be taught effectively when paired with a recording of the original music of the place that provided the inspiration for the composition. Pairing the recording, or better yet a performance by a culture bearer from the community, along with the composition in concert would not only make a very interesting performance, but would also educate the audience.

Instrumental Substitutions

Replicating vocal timbres from various vocal styles may take time, careful listening, and practice, but the voice itself is the one instrument that is standard the world over. However, for centuries cultures have been developing musical instruments, and though there are many similarities from one culture to another, all instruments produce different sounds. It is these timbral differences that are challenging to the instrumental music educator and the general classroom teacher alike as they try to re-create the sounds of another culture as closely as possible.

This can be accomplished in two ways. The first and most obvious is to purchase copies of the original instruments.[12] There are many suppliers for world musical instruments ranging from Rhythm Band, Inc., to independent importers. The second solution is to substitute Western instruments that are already available, or "found sounds."

By matching timbres closely, cymbals, gongs, and drums are fairly interchangeable across cultures, as are maracas, shakers, and beaded gourd rattles. Cowbells can substitute for African double bells, triangles for small bells or cymbals, and flutes or recorders for wind instruments like the Chinese *dizi* or Thai *klui*. Orff instruments can come close to the timbre of many xylophone and metallophone sounds around the world. Some music cultures already consider violins authentic instruments (for example, Indian, Arabic, Mexican mariachi musics), and violins can also provide a fair approximation for the stringed instruments found in China and Southeast Asia.

Obviously, the closer the timbre the better; however, timbre is only one consideration. Intonation systems also vary from area to area, and most instruments' distinctive sounds are the results of intonation interwoven with timbre. Classroom teachers can change the intonation of Orff xylophones to replicate the tuning system of the Mandinka *balafon*[13] or the Thai *ranat ek* by placing nondrying modeling clay on the underside of the bars near the ends. Less than a gram of clay will lower an Orff alto xylophone bar nearly twenty cents. Recorders and tin whistles can also be adapted to other intonational systems by partially covering some of the fingerholes with masking tape. Covering a hole halfway changes the pitch by a quarter tone; covering it three-quarters changes the pitch by a half step.

One last form of substitution involves the performance practices of the instruments. Students should hold and play the substitute instruments as if they were the originals as much as possible. This will help produce the closest timbral approximations as well as giving the students the feel of the real instrument.

METHODOLOGIES

There are other ways to incorporate a variety of musics in the school music program. Using the aural/oral methodology can present students with interesting challenges. Although musical literacy remains high on the list of objectives for school music, employing the aural/oral methodology can not only provide an entry into the music of another culture, it can also improve aural skills and provide a way to teach stylistic elements such as ornamentation or characteristic rhythms, neither of which are frequently notated.

Like students in Africa, China, Egypt, India, and Thailand, our students can learn rhythms through mnemonic syllables. Unlike the rhythm syllables commonly used in American schools (*1 e and ah*, *du te ne tah*, or *ta ti ti*), the syllables employed in these countries are often onomatopoeic to the percussion sounds they represent.[14] The following is an example of a lesson plan for teaching Chinese percussion (*luogu*) to intermediate snare drum students. This lesson could easily be adapted for general music students. A similar idea could be employed in chorus when learning a song with accompanying percussion parts.

Example 1:   Chinese Percussion Ensemble for Drum Classes[15]

Content Standard: Performing on instruments, alone or with others, a varied repertoire of music.

Achievement Standard: Perform music representing diverse genres and cultures, with expression appropriate for the work being performed.

Objective: Students will learn to play *Shi Wu I* (Lion Dance 1) in the traditional Chinese manner through onomatopoeic chant and iconographic notation.

Materials: *Shi Wu I* from *The Lion's Roar: Chinese Luogu Percussion Ensembles*, Han Kuo-Huang and Patricia Shehan Campbell (Danbury, CT: World Music Press, 1992), and recording that accompanies the text. Chinese percussion instruments or their aural equivalents as suggested in this text.

Prior Knowledge and Experiences/Curricular Content: This ensemble is made up of middle school percussion students. They can play together on bass and snare drum parts in class or in band, and they are ready for a larger ensemble experience. This is their first lesson as a Chinese percussion ensemble.

Procedures

1. Explain that percussion music is very popular in China, and is often used as celebration music for festivals, as well as for accompanying Chinese opera. It is traditionally not notated but taught aurally. Note that to help memory a syllabic (iconographic) notation is sometimes used, and that the students will learn through both methods.
2. Have students listen to a recording of *Shi Wu I* from the tape that accompanies the text.
3. Ask students to identify what percussion sounds they hear playing this selection.
4. Introduce the instruments with their Chinese names, and demonstrate how they are played. Tell them that these instruments make up the traditional Chinese *luogu* (percussion) ensemble.
5. Explain how the onomatopoeic system works—for example, the word "chang" means that all instruments (gongs, cymbals, and drum) play together; the word "dong" means that the drum plays alone.
6. Teach the rhythmic onomatopoeic chant for *Shi Wu I*. Have students repeat it several times before they play it on their instruments. Students should speak the chant aloud while playing several more times before they "think" it as they play.
7. Point out to the students that traditionally there is no conductor for Chinese percussion and that the lead instrument is the drum. Students will therefore have to listen to the drum cues for starting and stopping. Demonstrate the drum cues. Have students listen to the tape again and identify these cues aurally. Drummer should practice these cues separately, then with the rest of the ensemble, working only on these cues.
8. Have the students practice the entire piece without conductor's aid, taking cues from the drum part.
9. Having learned *Shi Wu I* aurally, show the students the Chinese iconographic notation that symbolizes the chant (for example, K = chang; D = dong). Write chant notation for *Shi Wu I* on the blackboard or use an overhead projector.
10. Have students follow the chant notation as they perform.

Indicators of Success: The students will perform *Shi Wu I* in the Chinese manner, with accurate rhythms, from mnemonics and from iconographic notation.

Although band and string method books frequently include folk material from a variety of countries, at the beginning levels, these are often presented in a simplified form. A combined way of using both notation and orality is to use the music as written as a guideline for the melody, and to teach the culturally expressive elements orally. This method is in keeping with teaching methods in other parts of the world (China and Egypt, for example) where beginners are often instructed in the "bare bones" melody and shown improvisatory embellishments only after the basic mechanical skills of the instrument have been mastered. This combination method would be a good way to introduce string players to the fiddler's shuffle bow technique, beginning wind players to the syncopation in folk songs whose rhythms have been didactically simplified, or a choral group to swing rhythms for vocal jazz.

Improvisation can also be taught through the aural/oral methodology in instrumental lessons, ensemble rehearsals, or general music class. While jazz is the first idiom that many think of when discussing improvisation, other music cultures also have this personally expressive form of music making. In fact, for some cultures there is no such thing as a "wrong note" in music. Both Indian and Arabic classical music depends on improvising melodies from the pitches defined by the respective *raga* and *maqam*. Ornamentation is a second aspect of improvisation in many cultures. In Arabic countries a specific style of ornamentation is so characteristic of a certain performer that it is in effect a copyright. Students will not be taught the same ornaments as their teachers, and if they do perform using another person's style, they must credit the performance to that person. For Chinese musicians the art of improvised embellishment is the essence of the music. The simultaneous performance of a single melody by several people, each person contributing his or her own distinctive ornamentation to the total sound, is considered good music. Students can learn to improvise around a given melody using ornamentation in a similar manner. The following lesson plan introduces this type of improvisation to intermediate string players through a Chinese folk song. It can be adapted for wind players or for recorders or Orff instruments in a general music class. Using a similar format with a popular song, choral directors can adjust this plan for vocal jazz.

Example 2:   Chinese Folk Songs for Strings[16]

Content Standard: Performing on instruments, alone or with others, a varied repertoire of music. Improvising melodies, variations, and accompaniments.

Achievement Standard: Perform music representing diverse genres and cultures, with expression appropriate for the work being performed. Improvise melodic embellishments and simple rhythmic and melodic variations on given pentatonic melodies and melodies in major keys.

Objective: Students will play *Meng Chaing Nu—The Eldest Daughter of the Jiang Family* (a Chinese folk song) in a more authentic manner by adding improvised ornamentation (trills, turns, slides).

Materials: *Meng Chaing Nu—The Eldest Daughter of the Jiang Family*, from "Teaching the Music of Asian Americans," Han Kuo-Huang and Patricia Shehan Campbell, in *Teaching Music With a Multicultural Approach*, William

M. Anderson, ed. (Reston, VA: MENC, 1991). Recording of *er-hu* music (a good example is in *Hong Kong*, UNESCO/EMI recording, C 064-17068).

Prior Knowledge and Experiences/Curricular Content: This string ensemble is learning about ornamentation in Chinese music. They can play trills, turns, and slides (portamento), and can shift from first to third position, and have begun vibrato. They have played several Chinese folk songs without ornamentation and recognize that Chinese folk songs are frequently pentatonic. This is their first attempt at using these ornaments in context and improvising on the melody.

Procedures

1. Explain to the students that Chinese music requires the use of ornamentation to be what the Chinese consider "good music." Review techniques required to play trills, turns, slides (portamento), and point out that vibrato is used selectively as an ornament in Chinese music.
2. Play recording of the *er-hu* (Chinese two-stringed fiddle), or demonstrate the song, as an example of the style of ornamentation used in Chinese string music. Note how ornamentation embellishes the melody, and changes with the person performing. Explain that it is most often taught aurally, rather than notated.
3. Have the students experiment with each ornament, deciding for themselves which sounds best to them. Explain that Chinese music is heterophonic, and multiple ornamented variations when playing together are characteristic.
4. Have students play the folk song with each student including at least two ornaments of his or her choice.
5. Add Chinese percussion for more authenticity: a *xing* and a *bangzi* (a small bell and a double-tone wood block are good substitutes). The *xing* (bell) is struck on each downbeat; the *banzi* (wood block) alternates tones on each beat.

Indicators of Success: The students will perform *Meng Chaing Nu* with improvised ornamentation (melodic embellishment).

The methodology of movement, and in particular folk dancing, is more often associated with general music classes. However, dance and song are so intimately tied together that, just as the classroom teacher would present the song for dancing, it would not be amiss for a chorus to learn the accompanying dance before singing a folk song. In addition, with so many arrangements of folk dances available for instrumental ensembles, it would also seem appropriate to teach the dance to instrumental students. Movement through folk dancing, be it a Appalachian contradance, Polish polka, classical minuet, Native American round dance, or Argentine tango, gives students an entry into another music culture through a kinesthetic understanding of the rhythms and cultural context. The following is a lesson plan for teaching a

Native American round dance in general music class. The format of this lesson can be adapted for either chorus or instrumental ensemble.

Example 3:   Native American Music by Edwin Shupman[17]

Grade Level 3–6

Objectives   Students will:

1. Be able to demonstrate the pulse of a Plains Indians' Round Dance.
2. Be able to explain the function of the vocal trill found in the Round Dance.
3. Be able to discuss the significance of "round" and the circle in Plains Indian culture.
4. Be able to dance the Round Dance.

Materials

1. Recording: "Round Dance" on *Pow Wow Songs: Music of the Plains Indians.* New World Records NW 343. Or *Kiowa Round Dance Songs.* Indian Sounds Records IS-2501.
2. National Geographic Society, *The World of the American Indian* (Washington, D.C., 1974).
3. Kopper, Phillip. *The Smithsonian Book of North American Indians Before the Coming of the Europeans.* Washington, D.C.: Smithsonian Institution, 1986.

Procedures

1. Play a recording of "Round Dance." Ask students to listen for the basic pulse of the drum, and to tap lightly each time the drum sounds.
2. In a second listening, ask students to determine if the drum sounds precisely the same with each beat. Encourage the students to listen for the LOUD-soft tap. Suggest that they chant "ROUND dance" also in a LOUD-soft manner along with the drum. Introduce the term accent.
3. Listen again for the sound of a woman's vocal trill. Ask students to determine how the trill is produced (by fluttering the tongue against the roof of the mouth while singing) and to suggest reasons for its production (to express happiness, joy, pride, or to honor a veteran).
4. Encourage students to discover the symbolism of the name "Round Dance." Discuss the meaning of the circle in Plains Indian culture and its importance as a symbol of unity, equality, and the cycles of nature. Ask students to find examples of the circle in Native American art. Recommend as resources the books by the National Geographic Society and by Phillip Kopper and the Smithsonian Institution.
5. Perform a Round Dance. Ask students to form a circle and face inward. The foot movement is sideways, moving in a clockwise direction (to the

left). The basic step begins with feet parallel and spread slightly apart. The left foot takes the first step and the right foot follows in this repeated pattern:

♪.	♪ ♪.	♪ ♪.	♪ ♪.	♪
L	R L	R L	R L	R

Teachers can find more ideas of ways to bring a multicultural perspective into the general, choral, and instrumental programs in issues of the *MEJ*, at conferences and in-service classes, and in many of the published resources already mentioned.

SUMMARY

The methods and materials that worked most effectively in the past, and continue to do so today, have been those that addressed the principles of multicultural music education: acknowledging the validity of another music culture, contextualization, authenticity, and education that is reflective of the diversity both within music and the American population. Materials that have been discontinued over time did so primarily because they failed to consider these principles. Today's materials reflect these principles even more closely, especially with regard to the attention given to contextualization and authenticity both of the music and its presentation.

It will always be difficult to re-create the ensemble experience from one culture with an ensemble from another. Just as rock tunes translate only approximately when played by an orchestra, African melodies and rhythms can only begin to approach the original when played by a concert band. Choruses may come closer to many vocal ensembles, especially those in music cultures with a strong choral tradition such as Russia or South Africa.

Smaller ensembles and chamber-size groups might be a better way to introduce another music through performance, but for American students, large performing organizations are often the only performing experiences they will have with any music. Directors can ensure understanding by playing a recording of the original music before the students attempt the new material. Doing so helps them hear how the music "really goes," and to understand that they are only approximating that musical culture. It can also help them better approach the timbres and style needed for a more authentic performance.

Conclusions, Implications, and Questions

Performing the music of another culture is, after all, the best way to come to understand it. It is therefore incumbent upon the music educator to ensure performance experiences in the classroom, and upon departments of music education to prepare new teachers that have the ability to do so. The question of authenticity cannot be avoided in selecting materials, and teachers need to be able to choose materials wisely. With careful preparation, students of all levels can come close to authentic performance of an unfamiliar music culture.

Related to the issue of authenticity is that of cultural viability. Music cultures are dynamic, not static. This musical dynamism challenges teachers, composers and arrangers, authors of materials, and textbook consultants to an ongoing acquaintance with the music. How can music education meet this challenge?

CHAPTER 12

Final Considerations: Problems and Possibilities

In essence, a personal transformation needs to take place before we can teach music authentically from a world perspective.

—Marie McCarthy[1]

Difficulties still face music teachers, both nationally and internationally, who are trying to making the change to a multicultural perspective. Ensembles providing performance opportunities in the music of another culture are relatively scarce in academia, although they abound in the community. Method books are available for learning to play instruments from around the world, but they are culture-specific and do not yet have translations. A consistent pronunciation guide for all languages does not yet exist.[2] Even more important to classroom instruction, very little material deals with how to teach diverse musics to a diverse student population.

Resources for multicultural music education are readily available, but there are few up-to-date, annotated guides to assist teachers in choosing authentic and effective materials for their individual classes. *Music in Cultural Context* (MENC, 1996) contains an accurate bibliography of materials currently available. It is hoped that the as yet unpublished guidebook prepared by the International Society for Music Education (ISME) will be available soon.

Authenticity and accurate cultural representations are of prime importance. The critics of multicultural music education are right when they say presenting musics inauthentically does more harm than good. That is why in-service music educators must find out accurate information for themselves, and why pre-service teachers need to receive a rounded multicultural education. Teachers also should feel free to share their classrooms with community culture bearers, as resources, as teacher/demonstrators, and as mentors.

Presenting music in its cultural context cannot be stressed enough. Yet when music education takes the time to relate a culture's music to its cultural context (geography, history, religion, family structures, and social and political background), critics say it is making music secondary to social studies. This has indeed happened in the past. However, if students were learning this context through an interdisciplinary approach with a social studies class, the music teacher might be free to dwell only on the aspects of how music expresses and is expressed in that culture. Though it is a pleasant thought, that is probably not going to be the case, and it will be up to the music teacher to provide enough of the context to enable the students to understand the music as presented. While the interdisciplinary approach may be easier for the general classroom teacher who is also teaching music, these connections must still be indicated in the music series texts that they use. It is incumbent upon the music education profession to demand that music publishers include such information accurately in the music texts.

Unity and Diversity

For many music teachers, the issue of unity versus diversity is at the heart of discussions about multiculturalism today. The question often asked is "How do I reconcile the Western art tradition with world musics in the curriculum?" It might be helpful to consider that American music education has almost always taught from a point of balance—teaching both the Western heritage and opening the curriculum to other musics (see Figure 12.1).

At the turn of the nineteenth century, the diversity created by the arrival of great numbers of immigrants was not welcomed by many Americans. In their view, immigration had to be curbed and those immigrants al-

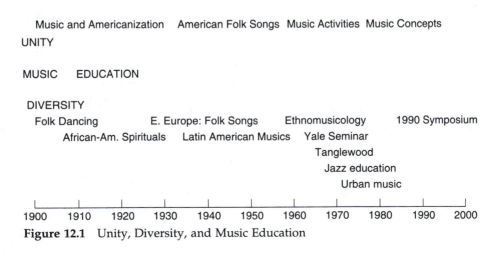

Figure 12.1 Unity, Diversity, and Music Education

ready in America absorbed into the mainstream majority society. "Unity" was the theme, and education's primary duty was to "Americanize" the immigrant population.

Working within this milieu, music educators taught both music and Americanization to students from diverse cultural backgrounds: music through the medium of European folk melodies with English texts, and love of country through patriotic music. At the same time, music education was forward thinking enough to recognize the folk musics as human expressions and taught them as as such. Viewed from today's perspective, these early presentations were noticeably limited and often stereotyped (for example, the sunny music of Italy), but they did enable students to appreciate a little bit of the culture of the immigrant populations. However little, it was a brave advancement in the face of a society determined to erase all traces of foreignness from its population.

By the 1930s, intercultural education fostered unity via the melting pot, while international relations encouraged diversity. Music education followed these movements in general education, teaching the traditional music curriculum and coordinating it with other subject areas. For these lessons, music educators employed folk songs from nearly all European cultures, along with a few African-American and Native American songs. These folk songs provided a rather imperfect representation of their respective musical cultures with frequent inaccuracies, but the fact of their inclusion in the music curriculum of the heavily segregated schools of those times is worthy of mention.

The developing idea of a "national identity," begun in the 1930s, reaffirmed itself as American folk music became popular in the schools of the 1940s. At the same time, the concept of hemispheric unity brought about the acceptance of the musics of Latin America. Unity modeled itself as the purpose for learning these musics, yet diversity in the music curriculum was the result.

The period from 1954 through the 1970s was one of great upheaval. Music education shifted from its post-World War II emphasis on peace and unity, with its exclusively Western perspective, to a position that would have once been thought impossible: acknowledging that all musics have their place in the curriculum. Following the social turmoil produced by desegregation and the civil rights movement, and the curricular changes recommended by the Yale Seminar and the Tanglewood Symposium, it seemed that music education had settled firmly on the side of diversity.

Since about 1980, there appears to be a return to the idea of balance. All musics are now acceptable for study, since the overriding concept of MUSIC as a human expression unifies them all. It is through the diversity of individual musics that teachers can provide access to universal musical concepts.

Today it is generally agreed that students should have both a solid grounding in the music of their own culture and a general knowledge of the musics of other cultures. But which musics? And once the choice is made, are one or two music cultures to be studied in depth? Should there be a broad survey covering a variety of musics across the year? Or should the curriculum somehow be a balance of both? How much consideration should be given to local cultures versus world cultures? There are no clearcut answers to these questions. These decisions are probably best made on an individual or district-wide basis taking into consideration the abilities of the teacher, the local school curriculum, the school population and cultural makeup of the area, and the accessibility of community involvement.

Rationales/Concepts Revisited

Historically, American music education, like general education, has moved through the several concepts of multiculturalism identified by Pratt and applied by Elliott.[3] The turn of the nineteenth century saw the greatest use of *assimilation*. In 1909, Zangwill coined the term "melting pot," and the concept of *amalgamation* that followed lasted until after World War II. In the 1950s, *insular cultural pluralism* began with the advent of ethnic studies. The civil rights movement of the 1960s and the ensuing Ethnic Heritage Act (1972) led to *modified multicultural education*. Elliott's last model, *dynamic multicultural education*, is possibly just beginning today. His *open society* appears to be a category all its own, although it may come to be sometime in the future. (see Figure 12.2).

All of these models are, in one way or another, still in evidence in today's classrooms, although most music education programs have moved beyond earlier assimilation and amalgamation models. Neither are there too

Dynamic
Multicultural
Education

Modified
Cultural
Pluralism

Insular Cultural Pluralism

Amalgamation ("Melting Pot")

Assimilation

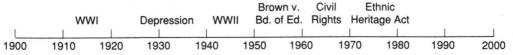

		WWI		Depression		WWII	Brown v. Bd. of Ed.	Civil Rights	Ethnic Heritage Act			
1900	1910	1920	1930	1940	1950	1960	1970	1980	1990	2000

Figure 12.2 Philosophical Concepts of Multiculturalism in Music Education History (after Pratt and Eliott)

many that are based on Elliott's "open society" model. For the most part, music education programs in the 1990s operate as insular or modified multicultural programs.

The music curriculum that allows for the study of African and African-American music only in February, and makes no other reference to it, or any other culture, all year long falls into the insular category—even if the teacher creates an excellent unit in February. Sometimes this is called an "added-on" or "tagged-on" approach.

The modified multicultural concept is probably more common. Under this concept, several musics are studied for their similarities and differences, and are often taught through the teaching modality for that culture. Teachers using this approach take advantage of community culture bearers by bringing them into the classroom both as performing artists and mentors. These programs also make use of both literate and aural methodologies, incorporate dance and drama, and employ various teacher-student relationships.

To move to full dynamic multiculturalism as Elliott sees it, teachers would have to broaden their curriculum even further, not just to include many musics, but also to employ the musical concepts from those cultures. This means that Western terms and concepts of music cannot necessarily be applied to other musics. For example, many cultures include song, poetry, and drama when they say "music," and we do them a disservice to limit our discussion of their music to sonic considerations of tone, time, and timbre. Beyond this, dynamic multicultural music educators will lead their students to a critical examination of such topics as the role of the performer, the functions of music, or gender issues in music.[4]

These concepts may also be considered stages in the development of a multicultural mind-set, just as they have been stages in the historical development of multiculturalism. They represent what many teachers experience individually as they first learn enough to be an "insular" educator, proceed to develop into the "modified" multicultural stage, and gradually grow to be a fully "dynamic" multicultural music educator.

Conclusions, Implications, and Questions

The greatest potential for multicultural music education remains the teacher. Regardless of methods or materials, the teacher is the factor that makes a difference in the classroom. Multicultural music education cannot happen unless the individual music educators in classrooms all around the country make it happen. It is a challenge to make the change from a Western-exclusive to a world-inclusive perspective. It requires a new mind-set, an openness to the new and different, "in essence, a personal transformation."[5]

How music educators go about working through this transformation will be as individual as the people themselves. Being open to new sounds, to another music culture, is the first step. There are many ways to take the second—a college course, a workshop at a conference, journal articles, help from a knowledgeable colleague or a culture bearer.

As colleges and universities work through their own transformation, there are still many problems to be resolved. The questions have come full circle. Can music education find a workable philosophy for multicultural music education? What about issues of aesthetics and praxis? What changes at the collegial level can best help new educators teach both multiple musics and the diverse populations they will face in their future?

Coda

Multicultural music education provides the power to perceive possibilities.

—Graham Welch[1]

The story of multicultural music education is not finished; perhaps it has only begun. The public school system and the society it reflects are now about twenty years apart.[2] Education in the classrooms of the nation is currently at just about the stage society reached during the 1970s with its heightened identification of ethnicity. If it is true that there is approximately a thirty-year cycle of events, then music education is at the beginning of a new and what could be a most exciting cycle.

Where will we be twenty years from now with regard to multicultural music education? There will undoubtedly be an enormous breadth of both repertoire and experiential resources from the personal to the electronic-interactive from which teachers can choose. Personal encounters with students teaching their own musics may well be the norm, and more music educators will have taken advanced study in ethnomusicology.

However, if Australia, where multicultural music education has already been officially in effect for thirteen years, can be taken as a case in point, there may be only slow growth in terms of a real redirection for music education. On the other hand, population changes in the United Kingdom are already redirecting the courses offered in some conservatories and school of music. So if the cycles of society and education run true to form in the United States, it is possible that multicultural music education will be so much a part of the curriculum in twenty years that it will cease to be a separate entity, and will merely be an accepted part of music education. That assumes,

193

of course, that teacher training and in-service education continue to make the changes necessary to provide a teaching staff for the future that is multimusically literate.

Our job as music educators remains the teaching of music. Multicultural music education is not a musical supermarket. If there is no growth in the understanding of *music*, then time spent in multicultural music education activities, chosen merely to provide a touch of this and a taste of that, is not time well spent.[3]

Multicultural music education presents both possibilities and the power to perceive them. Well taught, it gives students the ability to understand musical thought—their own and others. Multicultural music education is more than sonic choices in the classroom. It is also about providing options and opening doors. It may be the best medium to help break barriers and avoid close-mindedness. It is as much about people as it is about music. Multicultural music education offers the potential to counter the superficiality of the world; it has the capacity to be "the doorway to the spirit."[4]

APPENDIX **A**

Glossary

Antiracist education: A term found predominantly in European education. It goes beyond multicultural education to to combat racism and discrimination through teaching for equality and justice.

Bicultural: Describes the ability to function competently in two cultures.

Bimusical, multimusical: Describes the ability to function effectively in two or more music cultures.

Culture: "The learned ways of thinking, feeling, believing, and behaving of an individual in society";[1] a group's program for survival and adaptation in their environment.

Culture bearer: A person from a specific culture who practices the traditions of that culture.

Cultural diversity: The simultaneous existence of many separate cultural groups and subgroups.[2]

Cultural pluralism: The coexistence of diverse cultural groups with no one group favored over any other for the good of a larger society.[3]

Education: The formal transmission of the knowledge and skills needed to live in a culture.[4]

Ethnicity: The shared characteristics of a group of people, usually implying the commonality of a specific geographical location. Can also mean those characteristics retained by a group upon relocation within another group, such as Polish-American, Pakistani-British, Chinese-Malaysian.[5]

Ethnocentric: Describes the perspective of a single ethnicity.

Global education: Like *world education*, but with the addition of environmental concerns and issues of the way people interact with the earth itself.[6]

Global music education: Like *multicultural* and *world music education*, but with the addition of environmental concerns to the study of music cultures.[7]

Intercultural: Literally, "between cultures"; implies a sharing of experiences.

Intercultural education: Often used to describe an educational method that enables people from different cultures to understand each other. In Europe, it implies multicultural education that is more a sharing of, and exchanging between, cultures.

Monocentric: Describes a single perspective.

Multicultural: Literally, "of many cultures"; describes the ability to function competently in several cultures.

Multicultural education: Enables students to function competently within the myriad cultures of a society. Implies the study of diverse cultures for the purposes of understanding and tolerance. Can also be a process, strategy, or perspective that, in its fullest expression, implies a complete reformation of an educational system to give all students, regardless of background or ability, a full and complete education.[8]

Multicultural music education: Enables students to function musically within the multiple music cultures of a society. Tends to refer to the music of ethnicities and/or other cultures only. Can also imply the "intensive study of only a few musical cultures."[9] Can contain connotations and implications from *multicultural education*.

Music: A "human expression" exhibited through "patterned behvior" in sound, the value of which is "agreed upon by the members of the particular society involved."[10]

Music education: Formal transmission of that part of culture expressed through music.[11]

World education: Like *multicultural education*, but extended to cultures around the world.

World music education: Enables students to function musically within music cultures from around the world. Can contain connotations and implications from *world education*. Often uses topics such as concepts of rhythm and melody, or the role of the musician across cultures, as unifying elements. Frequently describes college survey courses devoted to musics outside the Western tradition.[12]

Recommendations of the Seventh International Conference*

The Seventh International Conference of ISME draws attention to the continuing importance of international co-operation in the field of music education, and the possibility of a more meaningful exchange of ideas concerning music education.

Such co-operation and exchange implies the use of art and folk music of one culture by all foreign nations with differing musical systems. Further it implies a broad interpretation of the word "foreign" to music that has, by virtue of its old age or youth, become strange or unfamiliar to its own culture. By the use of all such foreign and unfamiliar idioms music education can bridge both inter- and intracultural understanding and appreciation. One of the main prerequisites of such a co-operation would be the establishment of an International Center for Music Education, which has been one of the central concerns of ISME since its inception in 1953.

Plans are underway for the realization of a permanent International Center for Music Education, Study and Research, and ISME wishes to lend its enthusiastic support to such an effort. The Center could provide the following services:

a. Provide technical and professional assistance through individuals and materials to all countries.

b. Collect and disseminate significant contributions in the field of music and music education.

c. Publish special monographs on subjects of international interest in music education.

---

*Egon Kraus, "Recommendations of the Seventh International Conference," *International Music Educator* 14 (October 1966), 452–453. Used with permission.

d. Initiate and conduct special projects in music education on the international level.

General recommendations

1. A better and deeper mutual understanding between nations and the varied cultures is the main objective of UNESCO and its affiliated organizations. ISME serves this objective in the field of music education.
2. The most important objective of music education is to establish the prerequisites for a co-existence of musical cultures. This can only be achieved by means of a better understanding of the genuine values in art as they are manifested in the special context of each of the various cultures past and present.
3. Appreciation and understanding of the values of foreign musical cultures does not imply the devaluation of one's own musical culture. It is necessary to preserve all great musical traditions and the masterpieces which have been created in different times and countries and to avoid the production of unfortunate hybrid forms.
4. The superiority complex of Western civilization should be abolished through a deeper penetration into the significances which lie in the musical languages of other civilizations. Defense of occidental musical cultures is no longer necessary in light of the world-wide dissemination of Western music of both high and questionable value.
5. ISME should contribute to the task of communicating a most universal and objective concept of music to all countries and music educational systems.
6. In its manifold forms, in contrasts and similarities, and in continuous new possibilities the essence of music, and through this the essence of man, finds its expression. Music is not a universal language, but rather a universal medium of expression which finds many varied forms.

General educational objectives

A. Engagement with foreign cultures
   1. Develops a sense for the strange and unknown and leads to open-mindedness and non-prejudice;
   2. Destroys musical prejudices, national and racial resentments, and arouses a real understanding of the mentality of foreign nations;
   3. Leads to a better understanding of one's own position in the contemporary scene;

B. It is not sufficient that a few ethnomusicological experts interest themselves in the special idioms of foreign music cultures; every music educator should attempt to familiarize himself in the deepest possible way with at least one foreign music culture in order to make it accessible to his students.

C. In every musical tradition there are peculiarities of composition, performance, and appreciation. Introductory studies are necessary to clear away obstacles for listening and to prevent the judgment of foreign music by the criteria of one's own musical tradition.

Specific music educational objectives

1. Appropriate consideration of foreign music cultures in music teaching at all levels.

2. Methodological realizations of music of foreign cultures past and present.

3. Renewal of ear training, rhythmic training and music theory in view of the inclusion of music of foreign cultures.

4. Re-examination of school music text books and study materials in view of musical prejudices, as well as national and racial resentments.

5. Making available pedagogical materials concerning the music of foreign cultures, especially the publication and dissemination of authentic recordings with commentary and studies about the theory and history of different musical systems.

6. Organization of international seminars where musicians, music educators, musicologists, psychologists, and sociologists investigate the bases for a new orientation in music education in the above mentioned sense.

7. Co-operation with UNESCO, IMC, and the International Institute for Comparative Music Studies and Documentation, in their efforts to preserve and disseminate the great music traditions, whereby the important music of all cultures may retain the position which it deserves in the world of music.

8. There already exist considerable attempts to deal with foreign music cultures in the music education systems of some countries, such as the U.S.A., Israel, and Hungary, etc. It would be appropriate to recognize and exploit the pathfinding values of the experience gained by such experiments. Special study projects should make this information available and practical for music education in all countries.

9. It is recommended that ISME encourages co-operation between composers of all nations. As a result there might be a publication "Composers of the world to the Youth of our times."

Methodological recommendations

1. In order to include exotic music in the curricula of Western countries it seems necessary to solve the problems of notation and methodological presentation of such music independently from the concepts and tech-

niques of European music tradition, and to supply examples of exotic music which by their unpretentiousness and structural simplicity make it possible to exploit them in Western music education.

2. For the education exploitation of exotic music, some experiences of 20th century Western music may serve as models (suspended and expanded tonality, free structures of scales and modes—Bartók, Messiaen—asymmetrical chain structures, the nonmetrical music of Messiaen, new forms of monophonic, diaphonic, and heterophonic music, and free linearity).

3. An important stimulus in working with children and young people is the pleasure of tonal adventure. An approach to exotic music through improvisation is already possible in the elementary school. Melodic models of the type of Indian ragas and Japanese koto music would stimulate the creative approach through the musical elements even in children. Especially exotic rhythms would enrich the traditional and often uninteresting forms of improvisation.

4. The inclusion of exotic music in the curricula of higher education would broaden the listening capacity. Unique tonal and rhythmic structures could be recognized as new types, retained and recalled in the same way as stylistic differences in the Western system.

A last objective for higher music education might then be the task of developing ethnological tone profiles. Young musicians should learn to recognize from specific idiomatic tone structures the country and the people which are reflected in the sounds.

The Tanglewood Declaration*

The intensive evaluation of the role of music in American society and education provided by the Tanglewood Symposium of philosophers, educators, scientists, labor leaders, philanthropists, social scientists, theologians, industrialists, representatives of government and foundations, music educators and other musicians led to this declaration:

We believe that education must have as major goals the art of living, the building of personal identity, and nurturing creativity. Since the study of music can contribute much to these ends, *we now call for music to be placed in the core of the school curriculum.*

The arts afford a continuity with the aesthetic tradition in man's history. Music and other fine arts, largely nonverbal in nature, reach close to the social, psychological, and physiological roots of man in his search for identity and self-realization.

Educators must accept the responsibility for developing opportunities which meet man's individual needs and the needs of a society plagued by the consequences of changing values, alienation, hostility between generations, racial and international tensions, and the challenges of a new leisure.

Music educators at Tanglewood agreed that:

(1) Music serves best when its integrity as an art is maintained.

(2) Music of all periods, styles, forms, and cultures belongs in the curriculum. The musical repertory should be expanded to involve music of our time in its rich variety, including currently popular teenage music and avant-garde music, American folk music, and the music of other cultures.

---

*Allen Britton, Charles Gary, and Arnold Broido, "The Tanglewood Declaration," in *Documentary Report of the Tanglewood Symposium*, Robert Choate, ed. (Washington, D.C.: Music Educators National Conference, 1968), 139. Used with permission.

(3) Schools and colleges should provide adequate time for music in programs ranging from preschool through adult or continuing education.

(4) Instruction in the arts should be a general and important part of education in the senior high school.

(5) Developments in education technology, educational television, programmed instruction, and computer-assisted instruction should be applied to music study and research.

(6) Greater emphasis should be placed on helping the individual student to fulfill his needs, goals, and potentials.

(7) The music education profession must contribute its skills, proficiences, and insights toward assisting in the solution of urgent social problems as in the "inner city" or other areas with culturally deprived individuals.

(8) Programs of teacher education must be expanded and improved to provide music teachers who are specially equipped to teach high school courses in the history and literature of musics, courses in the humanities and related arts, as well as teachers equipped to work with the very young, with adults, with the disadvantaged, and with the emotionally disturbed.

Symposium Resolution for Future Directions and Actions*

The following resolution was adopted by the symposium attendees:

WHEREAS leaders in American education continue to call for all students to better understand different cultures both outside of and within the United States,

WHEREAS Americans are increasingly exposed to other world cultures through travel and a variety of electronic and print media,

WHEREAS demographic data continue to document the increasing multicultural nature of the United States,

WHEREAS in some states minority populations will soon become the majority population,

WHEREAS American schools now contain large percentages of students from various cultural backgrounds,

WHEREAS the field of ethnomusicology continues to document, through an array of printed material and aural and video recordings, an extraordinary array of world music traditions,

WHEREAS composers and popular musicians have increasingly drawn on a broad, worldwide "sound palette" for their creations,

WHEREAS organizations such as the Music Educators National Conference, the Society for Ethnomusicology, and the Smithsonian Institution have placed increasing emphasis on the importance of learning and teaching a broad array of musical traditions,

*William M. Anderson, "Symposium Resolution for Future Directions and Actions," in *Teaching Music with a Multicultural Approach,* William M. Anderson, ed. (Reston, VA: Music Educators National Conference, 1991), 89–91. Used with permission.

BE IT RESOLVED THAT we will seek to ensure that multicultural approaches to teaching music will be incorporated into every elementary and secondary school music curriculum. These should include experiences in singing, playing instruments, listening, and creative activity and movement/dance experiences with music.

BE IT RESOLVED THAT multicultural approaches to teaching music will be incorporated into music curricula in all education settings including general, instrumental, and choral music education. Such studies will involve both product and process.

BE IT RESOLVED THAT multicultural approaches to teaching music will be incorporated into musical experiences from the very earliest years of musical education.

BE IT RESOLVED THAT multicultural approaches to teaching music will be incorporated into all phases of teacher education in music: music education methods classes and clinical experiences, musics history/literature, theory, composition, performance.

BE IT RESOLVED THAT music teachers will seek to assist students in understanding that there are many different but equally valid forms of musical expression.

BE IT RESOLVED THAT instruction in multicultural approaches to teaching music will incorporate both intensive experiences in other music cultures and comparative experiences among music cultures.

BE IT RESOLVED THAT music instruction will include not only the study of other musics, but the relationship of those musics to their respective cultures: further that meaning of music within each culture be sought for its own value.

BE IT RESOLVED THAT music teachers will lay broad foundations for their students through developing appropriate concepts and using nomenclature which is supportive of the broadest manifestations of musical expression.

BE IT RESOLVED THAT MENC will establish strong national, regional, and state groups to promote multicultural approaches to music teaching and learning. These groups should seek the active participation of qualified professional minorities who are presently MENC members in the pre- and post-planning of symposia which represent the diversity of cultures being addressed or presented.

BE IT RESOLVED THAT MENC will continue to collaborate with other professional organizations to promote the development of instructional resources and in-service education sessions.

BE IT RESOLVED THAT MENC will encourage national and regional accrediting groups to *require* broad, multicultural perspectives for all educational programs, particularly those in music

Notes

CHAPTER 1

1. John Dewey, "Nationalizing Education," *Journal of Education* (2 November 1916): 116.
2. James Lynch, *Multicultural Education in a Global Society* (London and New York: Falmer Press, 1989), 14. Lynch identifies 15 name changes as the concept of multicultural education evolved in the twentieth century.
3. This conclusion is drawn primarily from Nicholas Montalto, *A History of the Intercultural Educational Movement 1924–1941* (New York: Garland Publishing, 1982); Geneva Gay, "Changing Conceptions of Multicultural Education," *Educational Perspectives* 16, no. 4 (1977): 4–9; and James A. Banks, *Multiethnic Education: Theory and Practice*, 2nd ed. (Boston: Allyn and Bacon, 1988).
4. See Geneva Gay, "Changing Conceptions of Multicultural Education," 6–7.
5. James A. Banks, *Multiethnic Education*; Carlos E. Cortés, "Multiethnic and Global Education: Partners for the Eighties?" *Phi Delta Kappan* 64, no. 8 (1983): 568–71.
6. Contemporary educational texts often have entire chapters devoted to these different aspects of multiculturalism. For example, see Donna M. Gollnick and Philip Chinn, *Multicultural Education in a Pluralistic Society*, 2nd ed. (Columbus, OH: Charles E. Merrill Publishing Co., 1986); James A. Banks, and Cherry A. McGee Banks, eds., *Multicultural Education: Issues and Perspectives* (Boston: Allyn and Bacon, 1989); Kenneth Cushner, Averil McClelland, and Philip Safford, *Human Diversity in Education: An Integrative Approach* (New York: McGraw-Hill, 1992).
7. William M. Anderson and Patricia Shehan Campbell, "Teaching Music from a Multicultural Perspective," in *Multicultural Perspectives in Music*, eds. William M. Anderson and Patricia Shehan Campbell (Reston, VA: Music Educators National Conference, 1996), 1.
8. Donna Gollnick, Frank H. Klassen, and Joost Yff, *Multicultural Education and Ethnic Studies in the United States: An Analysis and Annotated Bibliography of Selected ERIC Documents* (Washington, D.C.: AACTE and ERIC Clearinghouse for Teacher Education, 1976).

9. Carl A. Grant and Christine E. Sleeter, "The Literature on Multicultural Education: Review and Analysis," *Educational Review* 37, no. 2 (1985): 97–118; Carl A. Grant, Christine E. Sleeter, and James E. Anderson, "The Literature on Multicultural Education: Review and Analysis," *Educational Studies* 12, no. 1 (1986): 47–71; Christine E. Sleeter and Carl A. Grant, "An Analysis of Multicultural Education in the United States," *Harvard Educational Review* 57 (November 1987): 421–44.

10. James A. Banks, ed., "Multiethnic Education" [special issue], *Phi Delta Kappan* 64, no. 8 (1983); Richard Pratte, ed., "Multicultural Education" [special issue], *Theory Into Practice* 23 (Spring 1984); Joel Burdin, ed., "Symposium on Multicultural Education" [special issue], *The Journal of Teacher Education* 24 (Winter 1973); Tómas Arciniega, ed., "Multicultural Education and the Disciplines" [special section], *The Journal of Teacher Education* 28 (May/June 1977).

11. Examples include: Louis Ballard, "Put American Indian Music in the Classroom," *Music Educators Journal* 56, no. 7 (1969): 38–44; Carleton Inniss, "A Practical Introduction to African Music," *MEJ* 60, no. 6 (1974): 50–53; Malcom Tait, "World Musics: Balancing Our Attitudes and Strategies," *MEJ* 61, no. 8 (1975): 28–32; William Anderson, "Teaching Musics of the World: A Renewed Commitment," *MEJ* 67, no. 1 (1980): 38–41.

12. Patricia S. Campbell, "What's Wrong With This Picture? Cries for Research in Multicultural Music Education," (paper presented at the Orff-Schulwerk Association Conference, San Diego, CA, November 1991), 1. Campbell found thirty-seven curriculum-based research studies related to multicultural music education. See also the extensive reference list in Joyce Jordan, "Multicultural Music Education in a Pluralistic Society," in *Handbook of Research on Music Teaching and Learning*, ed. Richard Colwell (New York: Schirmer Books, 1992), 745–48.

13. Barbara Smith, ed., "Music in World Cultures" [special issue], *MEJ* 59, no. 2 (1972); Barbara Lundquist, ed., "The Multicultural Imperative" [special issue], *MEJ* 69, no. 9 (1983); William Anderson, ed., "Multicultural Music Education" [special issue], *MEJ* 78, no. 9 (1992).

14. Based on 1990 Census figures, predictions are that by the year 2020 over 50 percent of the American population will be nonwhite or Hispanic.

15. Carlos E.Cortés, "Multiethnic and Global Education: Partners for the Eighties?" *Phi Delta Kappan* 64, no. 8 (1983).

16. This conclusion is drawn primarily from Nicholas Montalto, *A History of the Intercultural Educational Movement 1924–1941*; Geneva Gay, "Changing Conceptions of Multicultural Education"; and James A. Banks, *Multiethnic Education: Theory and Practice*.

17. Jerrold Moore, "The Planetary Person" (paper presented at the College of the Redwoods, Eureka, CA, 1994), 8.

18. William A. Dorman, "The Not So Odd Couple: Critical Thinking and Global Education" (paper presented at the Annual International Conference for Critical Thinking and Moral Critique, Rohnert Park, CA, August 1992), CD-ROM, ERIC, ED 371980.

19. Bennett Reimer, "Music Education in Our Multimusical Culture," *MEJ* 79, no. 7 (1993): 22.

20. Estelle R. Jorgenson, "Music and International Relations," in *Culture and International Relations*, ed. J. Choy (New York: Praeger, 1990), 56–71.

21. For more information, see C. Victor Fung, "Rationales for Teaching World Musics," *MEJ* 82, no. 1 (1995), 36–40.

22. Alan Lomax, *Cantometrics: A Method in Musical Anthropology* (Berkeley: The University of California Extension Media Center, 1976); Alan Merriam, *The Anthropology of Music* (Evanston, IL: Northwestern University Press, 1964).

23. Alan Merriam, *The Anthropology of Music*, 219–26.

24. David J. Elliott, "Music as Culture: Toward a Multicultural Concept of Arts Education," *Journal of Aesthetic Education* 24, no. 1 (1990): 164; Jerrold Moore, 12–13.

25. Anthony J. Palmer, "World Musics in Elementary and Secondary Music Education: A Critical Analysis" (Ph.D. diss., University of California, Los Angeles, 1975); Patricia S. Campbell, "Multicultural Concerns in Music Teacher Education" (faculty forum presentation, Music Educators National Conference, New Orleans, LA, April 1992); Anderson, "Teaching Musics of the World: A Renewed Commitment," *MEJ* 67, no. 1 (1980): 40; Mantle Hood, "The Challenge of Bi-Musicality," *Ethnomusicology* 4 (May 1960): 55–59.

26. Michael Jenne, "Foreign Musics in Education—Needs and Problems," *The World of Music* 28 (No.1, 1986): 116.

27. Mantle Hood, *The Ethnomusicologist*, new ed. (Kent, OH: The Kent State University Press, 1982), 351.

28. Abraham Schwadron, "Comparative Music Aesthetics and Music Education," *Journal of Aesthetic Education* 9, no. 1 (January 1975): 105; Bennett Reimer, "Essential and Nonessential Characteristics of Aesthetic Education," *Journal of Aesthetic Education* 25, no. 3 (1991): 202–3; Lucy Green, *Music on Deaf Ears* (Manchester, England: Manchester University Press, 1988), 94, 137–41.

29. Reimer, "Essential and Nonessential Characteristics," 203; also "Music Education in Our Multimusical Culture," *MEJ* 79, no. 1 (1993): 25; Green, *Music on Deaf Ears*, 34; Elliott, "Music as Culture," 159; Hood, *The Ethnomusicologist*, passim.

30. For example: Joan Scott, "Liberal Historians: A Unitary Vision," *The Chronicle of Higher Education*, 11 September 1991, B(1–2); Richard J. Perry, "Why Do Multiculturalists Ignore Anthropologists?" *The Chronicle of Higher Education*, 4 March 1992, A(52); Margaret Hammersley, "Local Principal Helps to Revamp History Lessons, But More Emphasis on Role of Minorities Brings Criticism," *The Buffalo News*, 11 August 1991, A(1+); Robert W. Merry, "The Age of Separatism: Each Ethnic Bloc Wants Its Own Piece of Turf on Which to Do Its Own Thing," *The Congressional Quarterly*, reprinted in *The Buffalo News*, 18 August 1991, G(7+); Edward Rothstein, "Roll Over Beethoven," *The New Republic*, February 4, 1991, 29–34.

31. Raymond Boudon and Francois Bourricaud, "Culturalism and Culture," in *A Critical Dictionary of Sociology*, trans. P. Hamilton (University of Chicago Press, 1989), 95.

32. Ramon Santos, "Ideological and Conceptual Variations in the Understanding of World Musics: Implications on Music Education" (paper #4 for the Advisory Panel on World Musics, International Society for Music Education), 12–13.

33. Thomas Regelski, "A Critical Theory of Culturalism and Multiculturalism in Music and Education" (paper presented at the Border Crossings in Music Conference, Ottawa, Canada, March 1995), 10.

34. Dinesh D'Souza, *Illiberal Education* (New York: Free Press, 1991); Diane Ravitch, "Multiculturalism: E Pluribus Plures," *The American Scholar* (Summer 1990): 337–54; Arthur Schlesinger, Jr., *The Disuniting of America: Reflections on a Multicultural Society* (New York: Whittle Direct Books, 1991).

35. Carroll Gonzo, "Multicultural Issues in Music Education," *MEJ* 79, no. 6 (1993): 50.

36. Ibid.
37. Brian Bullivant, *The Pluralist Dilemma in Education* (Sydney: Allen and Urwin, 1981): 6. Cited in Gonzo, 50.
38. Christine E. Sleeter, "An Analysis of the Critiques of Multicultural Education," in *Handbook of Research on Multicultural Education*, ed. James A. Banks (New York: Macmillan Publishing, 1995), 81–84; William A. Dorman, "The Not So Odd Couple."
39. Peter Figueroa, "Multicultural Education in the United Kingdom: Historical Development and Current Status," in *Handbook of Research on Multicultural Education*, ed. James A. Banks (New York: Macmillan Publishing, 1995), 791–93.
40. Rod Allan and Bob Hill, "Multicultural Education in Australia: Historical Development and Current Status," in *Handbook of Research on Multicultural Education*, ed. James A. Banks (New York: Macmillan Publishing, 1995), 769; Mary Kalantzis, "The Cultural Deconstruction of Racism: Education and Multiculturalism" (paper presented at the Cultural Construction of Race conference, Sydney University, Sydney, Australia, August 1985), 9.
41. Kogila A. Moodley, "Multicultural Education in Canada: Historical Development and Current Status," in *Handbook of Research on Multicultural Education*, ed. James A. Banks (New York: Macmillan Publishing, 1995), 812–13.
42. Richard N. Pratte, "Multicultural Education: A Need for Philosophical Perspective" (*World Education* Monograph Series 3, 1981), 11, CD-ROM, ERIC, ED 216961.
43. Ibid., 8.
44. Carroll Gonzo, "Multicultural Issues in Music Education," *MEJ* 70, no. 6 (1993): 49–52; Jacqueline Chanda, "Multicultural Education and the Visual Arts," *Arts Education Policy Review* 94, no. 1 (1992): 12–16; Ralph Smith, "The Question of Multiculturalism," *Arts Education Policy Review* 94, no. 4 (1993): 2–18.
45. Gonzo, 49. This concern has been voiced for many years. See Edward O'Connor, "Discussion Groups," in *Becoming Human Through Music*, ed. David McAllester (Reston, VA: Music Educators National Conference, 1985), 132.
46. Patricia Shehan Campbell, "Multiculturalism and the Raising of Music Teachers for the Twenty-first Century," *The Journal of Music Teacher Education* 3, no. 2 (1994): 22 and 29, note 2.
47. Charles Gary, Professor of Music, Catholic University of America, letter to the author, 23 September 1995.
48. For a clearer picture of the various steps in this transmission process see Campbell, "Multiculturalism and the Raising of Teachers," 28.
49. This comparative approach to curricular concepts of multicultural education is drawn from a model in Thomas Regelski, "A Critical Theory of Culturalism and Multiculturalism in Music and Education" (paper presented at the Border Crossings in Music conference, Ottawa, Canada, March 1995), 25.
50. M. A. Gibson, "Approaches to Multicultural Education in the United States: Some Concepts and Assumptions," *Anthropology and Education Quarterly* 7, no. 4 (1976): 7–18.
51. James A. Banks, "The Multiethnic Curriculum: Goals and Characteristics," in *Education in the 80s: Multiethnic Education*, ed. James A. Banks (Washington, D.C.: NEA, 1981), 110–13.
52. Richard Pratte, *Pluralism in Education: Conflict, Clarity, and Commitment* (Springfield, IL: Charles C. Thomas, 1979), 79 and 151.

53. Carl A. Grant and Christine E. Sleeter, "Race, Class, Gender, Exceptionality, and Educational Reform," in *Multicultural Education, Issues and Perspectives*, eds. James A. Banks and Cherry A. McGee Banks (Boston: Allyn and Bacon, 1989), 46–65.

54. The terms "assimilation" and "amalgamation," used by Gibson, Gay Banks, and Pratte, are most often found in research on multiculturalism in education, and are derived from anthropological research into patterns of acculturation. Assimilation is acculturation through conformity to a dominant culture, and amalgamation is acculturation through a fusion of cultures. See Gibson's discussion in "Approaches to Multicultural Education," 12.

55. For a description of intercultural education in the schools, see Nicholas Montalto, *A History of the Intercultural Educational Movement 1924–1941*.

56. See Gibson, "Approaches to Multicultural Education," 18; Pratte, *Pluralism in Education*, 151; Grant and Sleeter, "Race, Class, Gender," 54; Banks, *Multiethnic Education*, 179.

57. Abraham Schwadron, "Philosophy in Music Education: State of the Research," *The Bulletin of the Council for Research in Music Education* No.34 (Fall 1973): 49; Abraham Schwadron, "Philosophy and Aesthetics in Music Education: A Critique of the Research," *The Bulletin for the Council for Research in Music Education* No. 79 (Summer 1984): 20.

58. Abraham Schwadron, "World Musics in Education," in *Music for a Small Planet* [ISME *Yearbook*, vol. 9], ed. Jack Dobbs (Nedlands, Western Australia: University of Western Australia Press, 1984), 92.

59. Abraham Schwadron, "Comparative Music Aesthetics and Music Education," *Journal of Aesthetic Education* 9, no. 1 (1975), passim.

60. David B. Williams, "SWRL Music Program: Ethnic Song Selection and Distribution," (SWRL Technical Note, TN-3–72–28, Sept. 6, 1972), CD-ROM, ERIC, ED 109040.

61. Ibid., abstract.

62. David J. Elliott, "Key Concepts in Multicultural Music Education," *International Journal of Music Education*, no. 13 (1989): 11–18.

63. Ibid., 15, 18.

64. David J. Elliott, *Music Matters: A New Philosophy of Music Education* (New York: Oxford University Press, 1995), 14.

65. Ibid., 43.

66. Ibid, 207. Elliott differentiates between MUSIC, Music, and music. He sees MUSIC as a diverse human practice containing many different individual practices (Musics), each comprised of sonic events, or works (music). See Elliott, *Music Matters*, 44–45.

67. Ibid., 209.

68. David J. Elliott, "Key Concepts," 17.

CHAPTER 2

1. Richard Current et al., *American History: A Survey, Vol. 11: Since 1865*, 7th ed. (New York: Alfred A. Knopf, 1987), 506–7 and 576–77; Roger Daniels, *Coming to America, A History of Immigration and Ethnicity in American Life* (New York:

Harper/Collins Publishers, 1990), 276; Arthur S. Link and Richard L. Mc-Cormick, *Progressivism* (Arlington Heights, IL: Harlan Davidson, 1983), 97.

2. For a description of the acceptance of Darwinism and other related factors on developing racism in the United States, see John Higham, *Strangers in the Land* (New Brunswick, NJ: Rutgers University Press, 1955), 131–57.

3. Samuel P. Hays, *The Response to Industrialism, 1885–1914* (Chicago: University of Chicago Press, 1957), 99.

4. *An Act to Regulate Immigration. United States Statutes at Large* 22 (1882): 214.

5. *An Act in Amendment to the various acts relative to immigration and the importation of aliens under contract or agreement to perform labor. United States Statutes at Large* 30 (1891): 1084.

6. *An Act to execute certain treaty stipulations relating to the Chinese. United States Statutes at Large* 22 (1882): 58–61.

7. For a description of the events surrounding this bill, see John Higham, *Strangers in the Land*, 101–5.

8. *An Act to provide for the allotment of lands in severalty to Indians on the various reservations, and to extend the protection of the laws of the United States and the Territories over the Indians, and for other purposes. United States Statutes at Large* 26 (1887): 388–91. Under this Act, large tracts of reservation lands were broken up and each Native American family was allotted 160 acres for independent farming, in effect destroying the tribal structure and nomadic existence the Native Americans had known for centuries. This law allowed those families who claimed the allotment to choose the land they wanted and granted them citizenship. It denied citizenship to those who did not, and allotted them whatever land the government deemed acceptable; the remaining unclaimed lands were sold to white settlers.

9. *United States Reports*, 163 U. S. 537 (1895). The lone dissenter on the Court, Justice Harlan, foresaw the grave consequences this ruling would produce, likening it to the Dred Scott decision in its long-term effects. The dissenting opinion may be found in *United States Reports*, 163 U.S. 553.

10. Higham contends that what white Americans feared was the evil of pollution or "defilement": politically through voting corruption; socially through "crime, disease, and immorality"; and racially through contamination of the "bloodstream of the nation." John Higham, *Send These to Me: Immigrants in Urban America*, rev. ed. (Baltimore: Johns Hopkins University Press, 1984), 195.

11. Daniel W. Bjork, *William James: The Center of His Vision* (New York: Columbia University Press, 1988), xiii.

12. William James, *A Pluralistic Universe*, excerpted in *William James: The Essential Writings*, ed. Bruce Wilshire (Albany: State University of New York Press, 1984), 362–69.

13. See the letters of James to Frances Morse and Mrs. Whitman in *The Letters of William James, Vol. I and II*, ed. Henry James (Boston: Little, Brown and Co., 1926), 102–6.

14. Booker T. Washington, *The Story of My Life and Work*, in *The Booker T. Washington Papers, Vol. I, The Autobiographical Writings*, eds. Louis R. Harlan and John W. Blassingame (Urbana: University of Illinois Press, 1972), 73–76.

15. David F. Burg, *Chicago's White City of 1893* (Lexington: The University Press of Kentucky, 1976), 259.

16. The large number of delegates from Latin America was not surprising. The first Pan American Congress (the forerunner of the Pan American Union, today

known as the Organization of American States) had met in Washington, D.C., in 1889.

17. David F. Burg, *Chicago's White City*, 168–69, 202, 214.
18. This was another manifestation of Social Darwinism, though this seems strange, even offensive, by today's standards.
19. David F. Burg, *Chicago's White City*, 238.
20. Selwyn K. Troen, "Education in the City," in *The Urban Experience: Themes in American History*, eds. Raymond A. Mohl and James F. Richardson (Belmont, CA: Wadsworth Publishing Co., 1973), 131–33.
21. Citywide music examinations were given in Buffalo, N.Y., in 1872. See Terese M. Volk, "The Growth and Development of Music Education in the Public Schools of Buffalo, New York, 1843–1988," *The Bulletin of Historical Research in Music Education* 9, no. 2 (1988): 100–101 and 132–33.
22. In the colleges and universities, a controversy raged over the place of the ancient (Latin and Greek) versus modern foreign languages as entrance and/or graduation requirements until the 1890s. The acceptance of the modern languages came partly though the advocacy of the Modern Language Association of America (founded 1883).
23. Ellwood Cubberley, *Changing Conceptions of Education* (Boston: Houghton Mifflin Co., 1909), 15.
24. One of the most famous of these schools, the United States Indian Industrial School at Carlisle, Pennsylvania, was established in 1879.
25. Oliver S. Ikenberry, *American Education Foundations, An Introduction* (Columbus, OH: Charles E. Merrill Publishing Co., 1974), 103–9 and 142.
26. James W. Noll and Sam P. Kelly, *Foundations of Education in America* (New York: Harper and Row, 1970), 184.
27. In commenting on the last four of these subjects (nature study, drawing, music, and physical education), Cubberley said that the "old conservative schoolmasters spoke sneeringly of these new 'fads and frills' " but that the schools in the cities were the leaders in adapting education to the changing conditions of American life. See Cubberley, *Changing Conceptions*, 40–41.
28. Sandford W. Reitman, *Foundations of Education for Prospective Teachers* (Boston: Allyn and Bacon, 1977), 108.
29. See for example: Joseph Krug, "The Recent Changes in Methods of Teaching Foreign Languages," *Journal of Proceedings and Addresses of the National Education Association* (1896), 575–86; Nellie S. Kedzie, "The Need of Manual Training for Girls," *Journal of Proceedings and Addresses of the NEA* (1896), 756–59; E. C. Branson, "What Kind of Normal Training Does the Common School Teacher of the South Need?" *Journal of Proceedings and Addresses of the NEA* (1898), 319–25; and Royal W. Bullock, "Some Observations on Children's Reading," *Journal of Proceedings and Addresses of the NEA* (1897), 1015–21.
30. The entire NEA meeting of 1893 was devoted to reports of the Congress on Education held in conjunction with the Chicago's World's Fair. See *Journal of Proceedings and Addresses of the NEA* (1893). Also Howard J. Rogers, "Education at the Paris Exhibition of 1900," *Journal of Proceedings and Addresses of the NEA* (1901), 201–9.
31. Cubberley, *Changing Conceptions*, 42.
32. Robert D. Oursler, "The Effect of Pestalozzian Theory and Practice on Music Education in the United States Between 1859 and 1900" (Ph.D. diss., Northwestern University, 1966), 173.

33. In music classes, Lowell Mason employed Pestalozzi's method of sound before sign, or rote singing before note reading. Mason's *Manual of the Boston Academy of Music* was based on the Pestalozzian system, though it is common knowledge today that the *Manual* was not original to Mason but was actually a translation of Kübler's *Anleitung zum Gesangunterrichte in Schulen*, a German text for teaching music with Pestalozzian methods.

34. How the German music model came to be accepted both in America and specifically in the schools can be found in Maria Navarro, "The Relationship Between Culture, Society, and Music Teacher Education in 1838 and 1988" (Ph.D. diss., Kent State University, 1989). See especially Chapter III, "An Application to Music Teacher Education of Bowers' Model of Foreign Impact," 32–137, for an explanation of the influences of the early German immigrants, the German artist/performers and the conservatory model, and the German conductors and the establishment of symphony orchestras.

35. Eleanor Smith, *Songs for Little Children* (Springfield, MA: Milton Bradley, 1887); Alice C. D. Riley and Jessie Gaynor, *Songs of the Child World, No. 1*, revised ed. (Cincinnati, OH: John Church Company, 1897).

36. An example of the tonic sol-fa method for American schools can be seen in Daniel Batchellor and Thomas Charmbury, *The Tonic Sol-fa Music Course* (Boston: Oliver Ditson and Co., 1894).

37. Lowell Mason, *The Song Garden, Second Book* (Oliver Ditson and Co., 1864).

38. Ibid., Preface.

39. See, for example, Lowell Mason, *Mason's Normal Singer: A Collection of Vocal Music for Singing Classes, Schools, and Social Circles* (New York: Mason Brothers, 1856); Lowell Mason and George J. Webb, *The Song Book of the School Room* (New York: Mason Brothers, 1856).

40. Lowell Mason and George J. Webb, *The Song Book of the School Room*.

41. Ibid., Preface, ii.

42. Lowell Mason, *The Moralist* (Boston, 1822), cited in Richard J. Colwell, "Program Evaluation in Music Teacher Education," *The Bulletin of the Council for Research in Music Education*, No. 81 (Winter 1985): 22.

43. Robert D. Oursler surveyed 268 music texts and songbooks published during the period from 1850 to 1870, and over 1000 books from 1850 to 1911. For the complete list see Robert D. Oursler, "The Effect of Pestalozzian Theory and Practice on Music Education in the United States Between 1859 and 1900" (Ph.D. diss., Northwestern University, 1966), 195 and Appendix.

44. Luther Whiting Mason, *The National Music Course* (Boston: Ginn and Co., 1870).

45. Since Germany did not become a unified country until 1871, the term "German" here refers to any of the German-speaking countries, duchies, kingdoms or regions in nineteenth-century Europe, for example, Austria, Switzerland, Bavaria, or Swabia.

46. Bonlyn G. Hall, "The Luther Whiting Mason–Osbourne McConathy Collection" (master's thesis, University of Maryland, 1983), 40. L. W. Mason owned imprints of books by many German authors, in particular, Christian Heinrich Hohmann (1811–1861), Georg Naegeli (1773–1836), Friederich Silcher (1789–1860) a collector and arranger of folk songs, Ludwig Erk (1807–1883) also a collector of German folk songs, and Joseph Mainzer (1801–1851). Hall traced the songs in Mason's *First Music Reader* to these sources.

47. In examining ninety school music textbooks from 1830 to 1900, Jones found this

to be true. See Walter R. Jones, "An Analysis of Public School Music Textbooks Before 1900" (Ed.D. diss., University of Pittsburgh, 1954), 134.

48. See, for example, Gertrude Walker and Harriet S. Jenks, *Songs and Games for Little Ones*, 5th ed. (Boston: Oliver Ditson Co., 1897); J. D. Luse, *Sovereign Wreath of Song*, third book (Columbus, OH: J. D. Luse, 1897); John Tufts, *The Euterpian* (Boston: Silver Burdett and Co., 1888); Frederick Ripley and Thomas Tapper, *Natural Music Series* (New York: American Book Co., 1898).

49. Jones's investigation confirms that the words and songs chosen for many of the school music texts were intended to be "inoffensive to the most sensitive minds." Jones, "An Analysis of Public School Music Textbooks," 135.

50. Walker and Jenks, *Songs and Games for Little Ones*, 86; J. P. McCasky, *Favorite Songs and Hymns for School and Home* (New York: American Book Co., 1899).

51. Lowell Mason and George James Webb, *The Song Book of the School Room*, Preface, ii.

52. Marie McCarthy, "American Music Education One Hundred Years Ago, as Reflected in the World's Columbian Exposition in Chicago, 1892–1893," *The Bulletin of Historical Research in Music Education* 15, no. 2 (1994), 141.

53. Ibid, 114–15. Dvořák made these statements soon after he came to the New York Conservatory of Music in 1892.

54. Leo R. Lewis, ed., *The National School Library of Song* (Boston: Ginn and Co., 1894), Preface, iii.

55. Ibid., iv. Lewis credited L. W. Mason for suggesting the format of the *School Library of Song*.

56. McCasky also reflected the attitudes of his day as he further commented that these folk songs were unique because they were "the utterances of wholly untutored minds, that the childlike, receptive minds of these unfortunates [African-Americans] were wrought upon with a true inspiration, and that this gift was bestowed upon them by an ever-watchful Father. The variety of forms presented in these songs is truly surprising, when their origin is considered." McCasky, *Favorite Songs and Hymns for School and Home*, 310.

57. Although some public school music educators still belong to the MTNA, since the growth of the Music Educators National Conference (MENC, founded 1907), the MTNA has become known more as an organization for private music instructors. Today there is a cooperative working relationship between the MTNA and the MENC.

58. Luther Whiting Mason, "Music in the Schools of Japan," *Addresses and Proceedings of the Music Teachers National Association, 1883*, 48–50.

59. Ibid., 48.

60. Sims Richards, "Canadian and American National Airs," *Journal of Proceedings and Addresses of the NEA* (1891), 810.

61. Francis Bellamy, "Americanization in the Public Schools," *Journal of Proceedings and Addresses of the NEA* (1892).

62. The topics discussed included methods of teaching musical notation, harmony, mechanical vocal exercises versus singing songs with feeling, the use of the piano in vocal class, care of the voice, the functions of the music specialist versus the classroom teacher, and various systems of musical notations. See the *Journal of Proceedings and Addresses of the NEA (1893)*, 507–98

63. For a concise discussion of the sessions at these congresses, see Marie McCarthy, "American Music Education One Hundred Years Ago," 129–38.

64. These were the topics most often presented at the meetings of the Music Department of the NEA in the 1890s.

CHAPTER 3

1. James Stuart Olson, *The Ethnic Dimension in American History* (New York: St. Martin's Press, 1979), 286–98. In addition, nonreservation boarding schools for Native American children continued to function, especially in the eastern United States.
2. George E. Mowry, *The Era of Theodore Roosevelt* (New York: Harper and Brothers, 1958), 92–93; George E. Mowry, *The Progressive Era, 1900–1920: The Reform Persuasion* (Washington, D.C.: American Historical Association, 1972), 11.
3. Arthur S. Link and Richard L. McCormick, *Progressivism* (Arlington Heights, IL: Harlan Davidson, 1983), 101–2. For a condensed description of the events surrounding the passage of this immigration bill, see Roger Daniels, *Coming to America* (New York: Harper/Collins Publishers, 1990), 276–79.
4. *An Act to limit the immigration of aliens into the United States. United States Statutes at Large* 42, Part I (1921): 5–7. A total number of 357,000 immigrants were allowed per year. The quota figures were established as 3 percent of the number of persons from any given nationality residing in the United States as of the 1910 Census.
5. *Immigration Act of 1924. United States Statutes at Large* 43, Part I (1924): 153–69. This law limited immigration to a total of 164,000 persons per year. The quota figures were established as 2 percent of the number of persons from any given nationality residing in the United States as of the 1890 Census. The minimum quota was 100 persons from any given nationality. For a brief description of the immigration laws of 1921 and 1924, see Sean Dennis Cashman, *America in the Twenties and Thirties* (New York: New York University Press, 1989), 46–48.
6. While this Americanization process was intended to be as painless as possible for the immigrants, unfortunately it was often accompanied by coercion. Editorial,"Making Aliens Into Citizens," *The Independent*, 28 February, 1916: 294.
7. Zangwill, *The Melting Pot*, new and rev. ed. (New York: Macmillan Co., 1930), 34.
8. Olson, *The Ethnic Dimension*, 305; Higham, *Send These to Me*, 211–13.
9. Olson, *The Ethnic Dimension*, 306–7.
10. Horace Kallen, *Americanism and Its Makers*, (Bureau of Jewish Education, 1944), 13–14, and *Culture and Democracy in the United States* (New York: Boni and Liveright, 1924), 124–25. See Milton M. Gordon, *Assimilation in American Life* (New York: Oxford University Press, 1964), 141–59, for a more complete analysis of Kallen's views.
11. Jane Addams, *Twenty Years at Hull House* (New York: Macmillan, 1910), chapters 11 and 16.
12. See Lissak, *Pluralism and Progressives*, 164–66; Krug, *The Melting of the Ethnics*, 71.
13. Jane Addams, "The House of Dreams," chapter 4 in *The Spirit of Youth and the City Streets* (New York: Macmillan, 1910), 101.
14. Robert F. Egan, "The History of the Music School of the Henry Street Settlement" (Ph.D. diss., New York University, 1967), 50–59.

15. Jane Addams, "Recreation as a Public Function in Urban Communities," American Sociological Society, *Proceedings* 6 (1911): 35–39. Excerpted in Ellen C. Lagemann, *Jane Addams on Education* (New York: Columbia University Teachers College, 1985), 187.

16. Robert A. Woods, and Albert J. Kennedy, eds., *Handbook of Settlements* (New York: Arno Press and *The New York Times*, 1970), 207.

17. John Dewey, "The School as Social Center," *Journal of Proceedings and Addresses of the National Education Association* (1902), 377.

18. Lissak, *Pluralism and Progressives*, 54–55; also Jane Addams, "Public School and the Immigrant Child," *Journal of Proceedings and Addresses of the NEA* (1908), 101–2.

19. John Dewey, "Nationalizing Education," *Journal of Proceedings and Addresses of the NEA* (1916), 185–86; also "Future Trends in the Development of Social Programs Through the Schools: The School as a Means of Developing a Social Consciousness and Social Ideals in Children," *Proceedings of the National Conference of Social Work, Washington, May 16–23, 1923* (Chicago: NCSW, 1923), 450, cited in J. Christopher Eisele, "John Dewey and the Immigrants," *History of Education Quarterly* 15, no. 1 (1975): 76–77.

20. Krug, *The Melting of the Ethnics*, 95.

21. Ellwood P. Cubberley, *Changing Conceptions of Education* (Boston: Houghton Mifflin, 1909), 15–16.

22. Lissak, *Pluralism and Progressives*, 52–55.

23. Jane Addams, "The Public School and the Immigrant Child," 101–102; see also Lissak, *Pluralism and Progressives*, 54–55.

24. John Dewey, "Nationalizing Education," 185–86; also "Future Trends."

25. The Staff of the Elementary Division of the Lincoln School, *Curriculum Making in an Elementary School* (Boston and New York: Ginn and Company, 1927); Frederick G. Bonser, *The Elementary School Curriculum* (New York: Macmillan, 1920), 85; Montalto, *A History of the International Educational Movement, 1924–1941*, 100.

26. The progressives advocated language courses in French, Spanish, German, Czech, Yiddish, Italian, and Polish.

27. Elizabeth Burchenal, "Folk Dancing," *Journal of Proceedings of the Music Supervisors National Conference* (1918), 39.

28. The New York City schools included folk dancing in its physical education and playground recreation programs in 1908. Elizabeth Burchenal and C. Ward Crampton, *Folk Dance Music* (New York: G. Schirmer, 1908), Preface.

29. Henry S. Curtis, *Practical Conduct of Play* (New York: Macmillan, 1925) 220–21.

30. "Folk Dancing in Americanization," in *The Victrola in Americanization* (Camden, NJ: Victor Talking Machine Company, 1920), 17–18. Frances Elliott Clark Collection, MENC Historical Center, Music Library, University of Maryland at College Park.

31. Elizabeth Burchenal and C. Ward Crampton, *Folk Dance Music*, Preface.

32. Luther H. Gulick, Preface, in Elizabeth Burchenal, *Folk-Dances and Singing Games* (New York: G. Schirmer, 1909).

33. Henry S. Curtis, *Practical Conduct of Play*, 220.

34. Elizabeth Burchenal, *Folk Dances from Old Homelands* (Boston: E. C. Schirmer Music Co., 1922), Preface, x.

35. Olson, *The Ethnic Dimension in American History*, 212–13; Richard N. Current et al., *American History: A Survey, Vol. II: Since 1865*, 7th ed. (New York: Alfred A. Knopf, 1979), 660. The anti-German sentiments were so strong that schools were

forbidden to teach the German language in many states, and the German conductor of the Boston Symphony, Dr. Karl Muck, was interned by the government for the duration of the war. In addition, the Big Red Scare of 1920–21 focused antiforeign feelings.

36. For good examples, see *Journal of Proceedings and Addresses of the NEA* (1919), especially sections "The New World and the Demand that It Will Make Upon Public Education," 47–63 and "Education for the Establishment of a Democracy in the World," 81–95.

37. "Resolutions of the World Federation of Education Associations," *Journal of Proceedings and Addresses of the NEA* (1925), 918.

38. Montalto, *History of Intercultural Education*, 85–95, 101.

39. Allen P. Britton, "Keokuk to San Antonio . . . 75 Years of Change," *MEJ* 68, no. 6 (1982): 43.

40. Constance Barlow-Smith, "The Educational Value of the Folk-Song," *Journal of the Addresses and Proceedings of the NEA* (1910), 818–22. Barlow-Smith cites many Western compositions that derived from folk sources.

41. Louis C. Elson, "Our Public Education in Music," *Atlantic Monthly* 92, no. 549 (1903): 254; also *The History of American Music* (New York: Macmillan, 1904), 349.

42. Louis C. Elson, *Folk Songs of Many Nations* (Cincinnati, OH: John Church Company, 1905), Preface.

43. Granville Bantock, ed., *One Hundred Folksongs of All Nations* (Boston: Oliver Ditson Co., 1911).

44. James D. Brown, ed., and Alfred Moffat, arr., *Characteristic Songs and Dances of All Nations* (London: Bayley and Ferguson, 1901).

45. These "music rack editions" often contained a disclaimer saying that the collections were not intended for "the scientific student of national music or folk song," but were arranged so as to be playable without impairing their authenticity. See Brown and Moffat, *Characteristic Songs and Dances*, Introduction.

46. I have checked several of the Chinese and Thai songs in these collections with master musicians from these cultures. They validated the accuracy of the melodic transcription. Personal conversations with Lu Guang, Assistant Professor, Central Institute for Nationalities, Beijing, China, 3 February 1993; Panya Roongruang, Professor of Thai Music, Department of Music, Faculty of Education, Chulalongkorn University, Bangkok, Thailand, 26 February 1993.

47. Many of those who attended the MSNC meetings were leaders in the school music section of the MTNA and the Music Department of the NEA. These "crossovers" included Ralph Baldwin, Edward B. Birge, Frances Elliott Clark, Julia Ettie Crane, Peter Dykema, Will Earhart, Karl Gehrkins, Thaddeus P. Giddings, Osbourne McConathy. See Michael L. Mark and Charles L. Gary, *A History of American Music Education* (New York: Schirmer Books, 1992), 209, 213–14, and 233.

48. Mme. Emilie LeJeune, "Creole Songs," *Papers and Proceedings of the MTNA, 1917* (Hartford, CT: Music Teachers National Association, 1918), 23–28; Fredrik Holmberg, "Swedish Folk Song," *Papers and Proceedings of the MTNA, 1917* (Hartford, CT: Music Teachers National Association, 1918), 145–61; Abraham Zvi Idelsohn, "The Distinctive Elements of Jewish Folk Music," *Papers and Proceedings of the MTNA, 1924* (Hartford, CT: Music Teachers National Association, 1925), 32–47; Percy Scholes, "Musical Education in the British Isles," *Papers and Proceedings of the MTNA, 1914* (Hartford, CT: Music Teachers National Association, 1915), 30–40.

49. "National Dance Festival," *MSNC Journal of Proceedings* (1913), 16; "Program of Folk Dances," *MSNC Journal of Proceedings* (1918), 20; "Negro Folk Music," *MSNC Journal of Proceedings* (1918), 21–22; "Fisk Jubilee Singers, *MSNC Journal of Proceedings* (1922), 16; Charles Griffith, Jr.,"Folk Music of the Philippine Islands," *MSNC Journal of Proceedings* (1924), 116–20; Harold Loring, "Music of the American Indian," *MSNC Journal of Proceedings* (1925), 94–97.

50. Constance Barlow-Smith, "The Educational Value of the Folk-Song;" Luise Haessler, "The Folk-Song," *Journal of Proceedings and Addresses of the NEA* (1916), 608–12; Elmer E. Brown "Our National Songs," *Journal of Proceedings and Addresses of the NEA* (1909), 695–96.

51. The long association between ethnomusicologist Charles Seeger and music educators began in 1916 with his membership in the United States Section of the IMS.

52. Because of the number of sessions which followed over the years, as examples, the reader is encouraged to peruse the entries in the *Papers and Proceedings of the MTNA*, the *MSNC Journal of Proceedings*, and the *Journal of Proceedings and Addresses of the NEA* for the decade 1917–1927.

53. Emma R. Knudson, "Folk Songs as a Tool for Intercultural Education" (Ph.D. diss., Northwestern University, 1946), appendices.

54. Editorial, "To Intern German Music," *Literary Digest* 57 (May 18, 1918): 31.

55. Robert Foresman, compiler, *Book of Songs* (New York: American Book Company, 1925–1928).

56. Knudson, "Folk Songs as a Tool for Intercultural Education," appendices.

57. Osbourne McConathy et al., *The Music Hour* (Boston: Silver Burdett and Co., 1927–1930); Margaret Diaz, "An Analysis of the Elementary School Music Series Published in the United States from 1926–1976" (Ed.D. diss., University of Illinois: Urbana-Champaign, 1980), 32; Janice James, "The Music of Afro-Americans in Elementary Music Series Books: An Investigation of Changing Textbook Content, 1864–1970" (Ph.D. diss., University of Southern Mississippi, 1976), 50, 55, and 91; Marvelene Moore, "Multicultural Music Education: An Analysis of Afro-American and Native American Folk Songs in Selected Elementary Music Textbooks of the Periods 1928–1955 and 1965–1975" (Ph.D. diss., University of Michigan, 1977), 47 and 50.

58. Frances Elliott Clark, "A World Brotherhood Through Music," *Journal of the NEA* 15, no. 5 (1926): 151.

59. From an annotation under editorial comment, "Democratization of Music," *Current Literature* 49 (September 1920), in Maude E. Glynn, "Music and Americanization: A Bibliography," *Music Supervisors Journal* 7, no. 1 (1920): 16.

60. Anne Shaw Faulkner, "We Need a Universal Language," *Ladies Home Journal* 36 (November 1919): 37; George Oscar Bowen, "How Flint, Michigan, Was Made a 'Singing City,' " *Musical America* 28, no. 15 (10 August, 1918): 4.

61. Faulkner, "We Need a Universal Language," 37. See also the quote by Ralph Radcliffe Whitehead in Luise Haessler, "The Folk-Song," *Journal of Proceedings and Addresses of the NEA* (1916), 612.

62. Lowell Mason, *The Song Garden*, Second Book (Boston: Oliver Ditson and Co., 1864). In the Preface Mason said the poetry of the songs "is pure in sentiment, and tasteful in expression." There is not much difference between his belief in the quality of these tunes and that of Harvey Worthington Loomis, who, in 1908, said each song was "selected for its own singing value and musical interest" in *The Lyric Song Book* (New York: Frank D. Beattys and Co., 1908), Preface.

63. Glynn's bibliography cites many articles on the Americanizing influence of community music.

64. Peter Dykema, Will Earhart, Osbourne McConathy, Hollis Dann, eds., *I Hear America Singing: 55 Community Songs* (Boston: C. C. Birchard and Co., 1917). The popularity of this edition resulted in the *Twice 55* series of songbooks under Dykema's editorship published by C. C. Birchard and Co. from 1919 through the 1950s.

65. Of the original eighteen songs, "The Ash Grove," "Auld Lang Syne," "Flow Gently, Sweet Afton," "O Tannenbaum" (in translation), and "Minstrel Boy" all have their origins in Germany or Great Britain. Frances Elliott Clark identified many more such assimilated folk songs in "A World Brotherhood Through Music," *Journal of the NEA* 15, no. 5 (1926): 151.

66. Elizabeth Casterton, "Correlation of Music with Other Branches of the School Curriculum," *Journal of Addresses and Proceedings of the NEA* (1905), 642.

67. Frances Elliott Clark, "Music in Education," *Music Supervisors Journal* 5, no. 1 (1918): 14–18; and no. 2 (1918): 12–18; Ernest Hesser, "Relation of Music Appreciation to Other Phases of Music Work, and Correlation with Other Subjects in the Curriculum," *MSNC Journal of Proceedings* (1920), 52–54; Thaddeus Giddings et al., *Music Appreciation in the Schoolroom* (Boston: Ginn and Co., 1926)), 42–47.

68. Mrs. Oberndorfer (Anne Shaw Faulkner), "Musical Geography," *MSNC Journal of Proceedings* (1924), 125–26.

69. Frances Elliott Clark, "Music in Education"; also "Music and Americans" (speech at the NEA meeting in San Francisco, July 1911), and "The Educational and Cultural Value of Music" (speech before the Ethical Society, 11 January 1932). Both typewritten manuscripts, the Frances Elliott Clark Papers (Box 1), MENC Historical Center, Music Library, University of Maryland at College Park.

70. Thaddeus Giddings, *Music Appreciation in the Schoolroom*, 46–47; see also "The Place of Special Teachers," chapter 8 in Staff of the Lincoln School, *Curriculum Making*, 304–17.

71. For a complete description of a third-grade unit on China with its accompanying assembly program, see Staff of the Lincoln School, *Curriculum Making*, 131–44. Some of the operettas published for school use during the 1920s had such titles as "Yanki San," "In India," "In the Gardens of the Shah," "The Belle of Barcelona," and "My Maid on the Bamboo Screen." See advertisements for operettas by the Willis Co., *Music Supervisors Journal* 9, no. 2 (1922): 5; 11, no. 5 (1925): 7; 10, no. 2 (1923): 5. This trend in publications is also found in the later part of the 1920s. See the H. T. FitzSimons Co., "The Tea-House of Sing Lo," advertisement in the *Music Supervisors Journal* 16, no. 1 (October 1929): 42. All are Western compositions.

72. Frances Elliott Clark, "Presenting Miss Elizabeth Burchenal" (speech at the Matinee Musical Club, 13 December 1932). Typewritten manuscript, Clark Papers (Box 1).

73. Frances Elliott Clark, "Festival of Nations with the Victor," *MSNC Journal of Proceedings* (1913), 72–74.

74. Ibid., 74.

75. Ibid., 72.

76. Frances Elliott Clark (speech before the Folk Dance Society, National Recreation Association, 1918). Clark Papers (Box 1), also "Music in Education," passim; "A World Brotherhood Through Music," 151.

77. Frances Elliott Clark, "Music and Americans" (speech at the NEA meeting, San Francisco, July 1911). Typewritten manuscript, p. 3. Clark Papers, Box 1.

78. *National Summer School of Music* (Ginn and Company, 1911), 15–19. Brochure, Clark Papers (Box 5).

79. David B. Poff, "The National Summer School of Music Sponsored by Ginn and Company, 1888–1919," *Contributions to Music Education* No. 4 (1976): 100.

80. American Book Co., "New School of Methods in Public School Music," advertisement in *Music Supervisors Journal* 2, no. 4 (1916): 15.

81. For examples, see A. S. Barnes Co., "Folk Dances and Games," advertisement in *Music Supervisors Journal* 3, no. 3 (1915): 31; Cecilia Van Cleve, *Folk Dances for Young People* (Springfield, MA: Milton Bradley Company, 1916).

82. "Music and Dancing by the Children at the Panama-Pacific Exposition," *Music Supervisors Journal* 1, no. 1 (1914): 28; "National Dance Festival," 16; "Program of Folk Dances," 26.

83. Frances Elliott Clark, "The Fruits of the Spirit of Keokuk 1907" (speech read at MENC conference, Seattle, 1947), 16. Typewritten manuscript, Clark Papers (Box 5).

84. Anne Shaw Faulkner, *What We Hear in Music* (Camden, NJ: Victor Talking Machine Company, 12 editions, 1913–1943).

85. Anne Shaw Faulkner, *What We Hear in Music*, 6th rev. ed. (Camden, NJ: Victor Talking Machine Company, 1928), Part I "Learning to Listen," 12–97, passim.

86. Arthur Farwell, "The Relation of Folk Song to American Musical Development," *Papers and Proceedings of the MTNA, 1907* (Hartford, CT: MTNA, 1908), 197–205; John Wesley Work, "The Development of the Music of the Negro from the Folk Song to the Art Song and the Art Chorus."

87. Helen Myers, "Ethnomusicology," in *Ethnomusicology: An Introduction*, ed. Helen Myers (New York: W. W. Norton and Co., 1992), 5–6.

88. An early pageant of this type was presented under the auspices of the Henry Street Settlement in 1913. A complete program of the pageant may be found in Egan, "The History of the Music School of the Henry Street Settlement," 57–59.

89. Marvelene Moore, "Multicultural Music Education," 183.

90. Janice James, "The Music of Afro-Americans in Elementary Music Series Books," 55.

91. Reginald T. Buckner, "A History of Music Education in the Black Community of Kansas City, Kansas, 1905–1954," *Journal of Research in Music Education* 30 (Summer 1982): 91–106; Edison H. Anderson, "The Historical Development of Music in the Negro Secondary Schools of Oklahoma and at Langston University" (Ph.D. diss., State University of Iowa, 1957). James Standifer, Professor of Music Education, University of Michigan, and Gerald Johnson, Professor and Chair of the Department of Fine Arts, University of Maryland, Eastern Shore Campus, attended segregated African-American schools. They confirm that African-American musics, especially spirituals, were taught in these segregated schools until court-ordered desegregation began in 1954. Gerald Johnson, conversation with author, 20 March 1993; James Standifer, telephone interview with author, 15 February 1993. Audiotape and transcript in the possession of the author.

92. "Monday Evening Program," *Journal of Proceedings of the MSNC* (1918), 21.

93. Ibid., 21.

94. Frances Elliott Clark, "The Fruits of the Spirit of Keokuk 1907" (speech read at the MENC convention, Seattle, WA, 1947), 16–23. Typewritten manuscript, Clark Papers (Box 1).

95. Knudson, "Folk Songs as a Tool for Intercultural Education," appendices; Moore, "Multicultural Music Education," 50.
96. Moore, "Multicultural Music Education," 183.
97. Anne Shaw Faulkner, "Does Jazz Put the Sin in Syncopation," *The Ladies Home Journal* 38 (August 1921): 16, 34. Faulkner cites jazz as responsible for brain dysfunctions, immoral dances, and worst of all, corset checkrooms.
98. Carl Engel, "Jazz, in the Proper Light," *MSNC Journal of Proceedings* (1922), 138.
99. The Staff of the Lincoln School, *Curriculum Making*, 304–18.
100. Satis Coleman, "The Progress of the Movement for Creative Music," *Progressive Education* 10 (December 1932/January 1933): 27–31. The name Creative Music was given to Coleman's work by a sixth-grade teacher at the Lincoln School. Coleman didn't particularly like the name, but, as she said, "it stuck," and she accepted it.
101. Satis Coleman, "The Progress of the Movement for Creative Music," 27.
102. Jan Southcott, "A Music Education Pioneer—Dr. Satis Naronna Barton Coleman," *British Journal of Music Education* 7, no. 2 (1990): 131.
103. Satis Coleman, *Creative Music for Children* (New York: G. P. Putnam's Sons, 1922), 29.
104. Ibid., 124.
105. Satis Coleman, *Creative Music for Children* and *Creative Music in the Home*, passim.
106. Satis Coleman, *Bells* (Chicago and New York: Rand McNally and Co., 1928); *The Drum Book* (New York: John Day Co., 1931); *The Marimba Book* (New York: John Day Co., 1926).
107. See Coleman, *The Drum Book*, 32–33.
108. Staff of the Lincoln School, *Curriculum Making*, 306–8.
109. Though inaccurate in the light of today's knowledge of music and cultures, this idea of music as an international "language" was generally believed in the decade following World War I, and has, to some extent, persisted to the present. This belief was fostered by the evidence found in the many accounts of immigrants who could join in group singing using a neutral syllable, well before they learned the words. For an example, see George Oscar Bowen, "How Flint, Michigan, Was Made a 'Singing' City," 4. Additional articles are listed in Glynn, "Music and Americanization: A Bibliography," 14–18.
110. Frances Elliott Clark, "A World Brotherhood Through Music," 151.

CHAPTER 4

1. Presidential Proclamation, *U.S. Statutes at Large* 46, Part II (1929): 2984.
2. Sean Dennis Cashman, *America in the Twenties and Thirties* (New York: New York University Press, 1989), 48.
3. Horace Kallen, "Americanism and Its Makers" (lecture given at the Adult School of Jewish Studies, November 20, 1944, Buffalo, New York), 13; also *Culture and Democracy in the United States* (New York: Boni and Liveright, 1924), 79–80, 114–55, 124–25.
4. See Mark M. Krug, "Cultural Pluralism—Its Origins and Aftermath," *Journal of Teacher Education* 28, no. 3 (1977): 6; Robert P. Swierenga, "Ethnicity in Historical Perspective," *Social Science* 52 (Winter 1977): 31–44.

5. Louis Adamic, "This Crisis Is an Opportunity," *Common Ground* 1, no. 1 (1940): 64–66.
6. Kenneth J. Bindas, "All of This Music Belongs to the Nation: The Federal Music Project of the WPA and American Cultural Nationalism, 1935–1939" (Ph.D. diss, University of Toledo, 1988), 101–2; William F. McDonald, *Federal Relief Administration and the Arts* (Columbus, OH: Ohio State University, 1969), 634–35.
7. Bindas, 233, 248.
8. Franklin D. Roosevelt, First Inaugural Address, in *Inaugural Addresses of the Presidents of the United States* (Washington, D.C.: U.S. Government Printing Office, 1989), 272.
9. *Department of State Appropriation Bill for 1942: Hearings Before the Subcommittee of the Committee on Appropriations, House of Representatives* (Washington, D.C.: U.S. Government Printing Office, 1941), 66.
10. *Department of State Appropriation Bill for 1941: Hearings Before the Subcommittee of the Committee on Appropriations, House of Representatives* (Washington, D.C.: U.S. Government Printing Office, 1940), 59; Edward O. Guerrant, *Roosevelt's Good Neighbor Policy* (Albuquerque, NM: University of New Mexico Press, 1950), 117.
11. *Department of State Appropriation Bill for 1941*, 61; Guerrant, 120.
12. Guerrant, 118, 125; *Department of State Appropriation Bill for 1942*, 62–64.
13. These laws eventually led to the "Mutual Educational and Cultural Exchange Act of 1961" [The Fulbright-Hays Act] (PL 87–256). See Stewart Fraser, ed., *Governmental Policy and International Education* (New York: John Wiley and Sons, 1965), 211.
14. Guy M. Whipple, ed., *Thirty-sixth Yearbook of the National Society for the Study of Education, Part II: International Understanding Through the Public-School Curriculum* (Bloomington, IL: Public School Publishing Company, 1937), Section III, "The School Curriculum," 45–258
15. The Junior Red Cross encouraged international correspondence. See John E. Harley, "Leading Organizations Promoting the Study of International Relations in the United States" and Margaret Kiely, "Teaching Aids and Materials," in *International Understanding Through the Public-School Curriculum*, 306 and 319.
16. American Council on Education, *Latin America in School and College Teaching Materials* (Washington, D.C.: American Council on Education, 1944), 38–43.
17. Nicholas Montalto, *A History of the Intercultural Educational Movement 1924–1941* (New York: Garland Publishing, 1982), 92.
18. Montalto, 84–85, 100; Lilla Belle Pitts, "Typical Music Activities of the School," in *Thirty-fifth Yearbook of the National Society for the Study of Education, Part II: Music Education*, ed. Guy M. Whipple (Bloomington, IL: Public School Publishing Company, 1936), 50. See also Kiely, 344–48.
19. See Section III, "The School Curriculum," in *International Understanding Through the Public-School Curriculum*, 45–258; Kiely, 311–64; NEA, "Where to Go for Help," *Journal of the NEA* 24 (March 1935), 94.
20. Kiely, 326, 340–41, 347, 350–51.
21. See, for examples, Frances Belcher, ed., "Learning World Goodwill in the Elementary School" [special issue] *National Elementary School Principal* 26 (September 1946); Howard E. Wilson, "Postwar Education for International Understanding," in National Society for the Study of Education, *American Education in the Postwar Period, Part I, Curriculum Reconstruction* (Chicago: University of Chicago Press, 1945), 246–66.

22. Percy Sholes, "Musical Education in the British Isles," *Papers and Proceedings of the MTNA* (1914), 30–40.
23. Frances E. Clark, "The British-American Field Day," *Proceedings of the Music Supervisors National Conference* (1929).
24. For a fuller description of these two conferences, see Marie McCarthy, "The Birth of Internationalism in Music Education, 1899–1938," *International Journal of Music Education* No. 21, 1993: 3–15. Also programs, photographs and lecture notes from the Second Anglo-American Music Education Conference, Lausanne, Switzerland, can be found in the scrapbook of Emma L. Kahrt, MENC Historical Center, Music Library, University of Maryland, College Park.
25. McCarthy, 22.
26. Mabelle Glenn, Helen S. Leavitt, Victor Rebman, and Earl L. Baker, eds., *The World of Music* (Boston: Ginn and Co., 1936). For statistics for Ginn and Co., the American Book Co., C. C. Birchard, and Silver Burdett and Co. through the 1930s and 1940s, see Margaret Diaz, "An Analysis of the Elementary School Music Series Published in the United States from 1926–1976" (Ed.D. diss., University of Illinois at Urbana-Champaign, 1980).
27. For comments on the lack of American folk songs, see Harold Spivacke, "The Archive of American Folk Song in the Library of Congress," in *Volume of Proceedings of the MTNA* (1940), 127.
28. John Beattie et al., *The American Singer* (New York: American Book Co., 1944); Osbourne McConathy et al., *New Music Horizons* (New York: Silver Burdett and Co., 1944); Theresa Armitage et al., *Singing School* (Boston: C. C. Birchard and Co., 1939–1943); Mabel Glenn et al., *The World of Music* (Boston: Ginn and Co., 1936).
29. For examples, see Peter W. Dykema, "Significant Relationships of Music to Other Subjects," in *Thirty-fifth Yearbook of the Society for the Study of Education, Part II: Music Education*, ed. Guy Whipple (Bloomington, IL: Public School Publishing Company, 1936), 23–33; Ida MacLean, "Experiences with Music in the Integrated Program," *MENC Yearbook 1935* (Chicago: MENC, 1935), 184–91; Karl W. Gehrkins, *Music in the Grade Schools* (Boston: C. C. Birchard and Co., 1934), 145–60.
30. Committee on Dancing of the American Physical Education Association for the Years 1931 and 1932, *Dancing in the Elementary Schools* (New York: A. S. Barnes and Co., 1933), 45–47.
31. Gehrkins, *Music in the Grade Schools*, 155.
32. Dykema, "Significant Relationships," 27.
33. Lilla Belle Pitts, *Music Integration in the Junior High School* (Boston: C. C. Birchard and Co., 1935), 67 and 75. For example, Pitts listed the *Danse Chinoise* from Tchaikovsky's *Nutcracker Suite* under Chinese music, and Grieg's *Anitra's Dance* from the *Peer Gynt Suite* under Arabic music.
34. Pitts, *Music Integration*, 60, 67, 75.
35. Gehrkins, *Music in the Grade Schools*, 163–65; James L. Mursell, *Music in American Schools* (New York: Silver Burdett and Co., 1943), 109–11.
36. Anne E. Pierce, "The Selection and Organization of Music Materials," in *Thirty-fifth Yearbook of the Society for the Study of Education, Part II: Music Education*, ed. Guy Whipple (Bloomington, IL: Public School Publishing Company, 1936), 159; Emma Knudson, "Folk Songs as a Tool for Intercultural Education) (Ph.D. diss, Northwestern University, 1946), 7; Paul Weaver, "Music," in *Thirty-sixth Yearbook of the Society for the Study of Education, Part II: International Understanding*

Through the Public-School Curriculum, ed. Guy Whipple (Bloomington, IL: Public School Publishing Company, 1937), 217.

37. Allen P. Britton, Dean Emeritus, School of Music, University of Michigan, Ann Arbor, interview by author, 13 November 1992, Ann Arbor. Audiotape and transcripts in possession of the author.

38. Domingo Santa Cruz, "On Hemispheric Unity," *MEJ* 28, no. 6 (1942): 13.

39. Louis Woodson Curtis, "School and College Music," in *American Council on Education, Latin America in School and College Teaching Materials* (Washington, D.C.: American Council on Education, 1944), 424–28; Marvalene Moore, "Multicultural Music Education: An Analysis of Afro-American and Native American Folk Songs in Selected Elementary Music Textbooks of the Periods 1928–1955 and 1965–1975" (Ph.D. diss., University of Michigan, 1977), 183.

40. Conference program, MENC biennial conference, Milwaukee, 1942. MENC Historical Center, Music Library, University of Maryland, College Park.

41. Ibid.

42. MENC Committee on Folk Music of the United States, "American Songs for American Children," *MEJ* 30, no. 3 (1944): 24; 30, no. 4 (1944): 39; 30, no. 5 (1944): 27; 31 no. 1 (1944): 39; 31, no. 3 (1945): 38; 31, no. 4 (1945): 36.

43. Ibid., *MEJ* 30, no. 3 (1944): 24.

44. Diaz, 99; George N. Heller, "From the Melting Pot to Cultural Pluralism: General Music in a Technological Age, 1892–1992," in *Ithaca Conference on American Music Education: Centennial Profiles*, ed. Mark Fonder (Ithaca, NY: Ithaca College, 1992), 105.

45. Moore, "Multicultural Music Education," 49–50, 182.

46. Pan American Union, "State Department Conferences on Inter-American Cultural Relations," *Bulletin of the Pan American Union* 74, no. 2 (1940): 80.

47. Vanett Lawler, "Music Education in the Americas," *Education* 69, no. 7 (1949): 392.

48. Charles Seeger, "Music for Uniting the Americas," *MEJ* 27, no. 6 (1941): 12; Vanett Lawler, "Latin Americans See Our Musical Life," *Bulletin of the Pan American Union* 76, no. 7 (1942): 369.

49. John Beattie and Louis Woodson Curtis, "South American Music Pilgrimage," *MEJ* 28, no. 2 (1941): 15.

50. John Beattie and Louis Woodson Curtis, "South American Music Pilgrimage, Part I: Columbia," *MEJ* 28, no. 2 (1941): 14–17; "South American Music Pilgrimage, Part II: Ecuador and Peru, *MEJ* 28, no. 3 (1942): 12–18; "South American Music Pilgrimage, Part III: Chile," *MEJ* 28, no. 4 (1942): 16–19; "South American Music Pilgrimage, Part IV: Argentina and Uruguay," *MEJ* 28, no. 5 (1942): 22–27; "South American Music Pilgrimage, Part V: Brazil," *MEJ* 28, no. 6 (1942): 22–27.

51. Ibid., 369–370. For example, the MENC scheduled Olga Coelho, a noted Brazilian folk singer, to appear in concert, and asked Francisco Mignone, a well-known composer and Professor of Conducting at the National School of Music, University of Brazil, Rio de Janiero, to conduct one of his compositions performed by the Lane Technical High School Orchestra. See "Brazilian Who Interprets Folk Songs of the World Is Coming to Milwaukee," *Milwaukee Journal*, 20 March 1942; MENC, "Hands Across the Air," *MEJ* 28, no. 6 (1942): 14.

52. Resolutions: MENC, Milwaukee, April 2, 1942. MENC Historical Center, Music Library, University of Maryland, College Park.

53. Lawler, "Latin Americans See Our Musical Life," 371.

54. See program listing for the MENC biennial conference (Cleveland, 1946), in *MEJ* 32, no. 6 (1946): 30; also Conference Program of the MENC biennial conference (Detroit, 1948). MENC Historical Center, Music Library, University of Maryland, College Park. Because of the logistics of travel between their various countries, it was actually easier for them to discuss the problems of Latin American music education while in the United States. See Domingo Santa Cruz, "On Hemispherical Unity," 14.

55. See, for example, Luis Sandi, "Music Activities in Mexico," *MEJ* 30, no. 2 (1943): 15–16; Margarita Menendez, "Public School Music in Cuba," *MEJ* 30, no. 3 (1944): 27–28; Mary Santos, "Music in Columbia," *MEJ* 31, no. 1 (1944): 24–25; Elizabeth S. Lamb, "Music Education in Puerto Rico," *MEJ* 34, no. 4 (1948): 65–66.

56. For an early article on comparative music education, see Charles Griffith, "School Music in an Oriental Setting," *MEJ* 18, no. 4 (1932): 32–35.

57. Soviet Embassy, Mary Milovitch, transl., "Music Education in the U.S.S.R.,"*MEJ* 32, no. 5 (1946): 28–31; Stella Marie Graves, "Music Education in China," *MEJ* 33, no. 1 (1946): 26–27+; Yngve Haren, "Music and Music Education in Sweden," *MEJ* 35, no. 2 (1948): 28–30.

58. Among the first such articles are: Max Krone, "Music in Iran," *MEJ* 39, no. 1 (1952): 24–25, and "Music in Turkey," *MEJ* 39, no. 2 (1952): 28–30; Maria Luisa Munoz, "Puerto Rico and Its Music," *MEJ* 39, no. 3 (1953): 51.

59. Charles Seeger, "Music Education in the Americas," *MEJ* 30, no. 6 (1944): 15.

60. Vanett Lawler, "Music Education in Fourteen Latin-American Republics," *MEJ Journal* 31, no. 3 (1945): 16–22; 31, no. 4 (1945): 20–23+; 31, no. 5 (1945): 16–19.

61. Gilbert Chase, *Bibliography of Latin American Folk Music* (Washington, D.C.: Library of Congress, Division of Music, 1942), Introduction, i. MENC, "Latin-American Music," *MEJ* 31, no. 6 (1945): 50.

62. Gustavo Duran, *Recordings of Latin American Songs and Dances* (Washington, D.C.: Pan American Union, 1942).

63. Chase, *Bibliography.*

64. Gilbert Chase, compiler, *Partial List of Latin American Music Obtainable in the United States* (Washington, D.C.: Pan American Union, 1942).

65. Vanett Lawler, "Music Education in the Americas," *Education* 69 (March 1949): 393.

66. Examples are *Canciones Panamericas* (NY: Silver Burdett Co, 1942, published in collaboration with the Pan American Union, Washington, D.C.); David Stevens, *Latin American Songs* (C.C. Birchard and Co., 1941); Beatrice and Max Krone, *Spanish and Latin American Songs* (Chicago: Neil A. Kjos Music Co., 1942).

67. Letter from Fowler Smith, President of MENC to music educators, January 16, 1942; also letter from C. V. Buttleman, to instrumental music educators, 1945. MENC Historical Center, Music Library, University of Maryland, College Park.

68. For example, see MENC, "Books and Music Related to the American Unity Theme," *MEJ* 27, no. 5 (1941): 40, and "Books and Music" columns in succeeding issues. Advertisements for folk song and folk dance collections, *MEJ* 30, no. 4 (1944): 13; anthems of the United Nations, *MEJ* 30, no. 1 (1943): 60; "Music of the New World Handbook," *MEJ* 29, no. 2 (1942): 44.

69. Lilla Belle Pitts, "Music Education in International Relations: Information Sources and References," mimeographed copy of bulletin to MENC Committee on Music Education in International Relations. Vanett Lawler Collection, ISME Archives (III-2-1/2), Music Library, University of Maryland, College Park.

70. Curtis, "School and College Music," 416–17; Elizabeth Dominy, "Music Textbooks in Elementary Education: The Appropriateness of Current Textbook Materials in Elementary School Music in Relation to the Aims and Purposes of Modern Elementary Education" (Ed. D., New York University, 1958), 78–79; Diaz, "An Analysis of the Elementary School Music Series," 79, 99, 109, 122.

71. Gladys Evelyn Moorhead and Donald Pond, *Music of Young Children* (Santa Barbara, CA: Pillsbury Foundation for Advancement of Music Education, Book I: *Chant*, 1941; Book II: *General Observations*, 1942; Book III: *Musical Notations*, 1944; Book IV: *Free Use of Instruments*, 1951; reprint, Santa Barbara, CA: Pillsbury Foundation for Advancement of Music Education, 1978, 5th printing).

72. Ibid., 47, 50.

73. Ibid., 46.

74. Ibid., 47.

75. "Young Musicians Intrigued by the Tinkle of Temple Bell," *Santa Barbara [CA] News Press*, 26 February 1937.

76. Ibid., 7.

77. B. Marian Brooks and Harry A. Brown, *Music Education in the Elementary School* (New York: American Book Co., 1946), 326.

78. John Kendel, President of MENC, "Proposed participation in the Inter-American and International Programs in the field of music exchange," mimeographed copy, 1944. MENC Historical Center, Music Library, University of Maryland, College Park.

79. Henry and Sidney Cowell, "Whither Music in America? Barriers Down!" *Frontiers of Democracy* 10 (October 1943): 30–31.

80. David McAllester, Professor Emeritus of Anthropology and Music, Wesleyan University, Middletown, CT, telephone interview by author, 8 December 1992. The influence of returning service people is also confirmed by William P. Malm, Professor Emeritus of Ethnomusicology, University of Michigan, Ann Arbor, interview by author, 13 November 1992. Original audiotapes and transcripts in possession of the author.

81. McAllester and Malm interviews.

82. MENC, "A Declaration of Faith, Purpose and Action," in Hazel Nohavec Morgan, ed., *Music Education Source Book* (Chicago: MENC, 1947), xii.

83. MENC, "UNESCO and Music," *MEJ* 33, no. 2 (1946): 28.

84. MENC, "International Music Council," *MEJ* 35, no. 5 (1949): 40.

85. Ibid., 40.

86. Eastern Division conference program, Buffalo, NY, 1953. MENC Historical Center, Music Library, University of Maryland, College Park. It is likely that the Eastern Division was not alone in anticipating the International Conference. Nearly all the other divisional conferences that year had a special focus on international relations. Paul Lehman, Senior Associate Dean, School of Music, University of Michigan, Ann Abor, interview by author, 13 November 1992; and Charles Gary, Professor of Music Education, Catholic University of America, Washington, D.C., interview by author, 13 January 1993. Original audio tapes and transcripts in possession of the author.

87. *Music in Education* (Paris: UNESCO, 1955). See Domingo Santa Cruz, "Music and International Understanding," 38; Sir Steuart Wilson, "The Role of Folk Music in Education," 47; Maud Karpeles, "Folk Music as a Social Binding Force," 190.

88. Charles Seeger, "A Proposal to Found an International Society for Music Education," in *Music in Education*, 325–31.

89. "UNESCO and Music Education," Appendix A to the meeting report of the Third IMC roundtable meeting, Oslo, 1953. Vanett Lawler Collection, ISME Archives, (I-1–1/1), Music Library, University of Maryland, College Park.

CHAPTER 5

1. Daniel Steele, "An Investigation into the Background and Implications of the Yale Seminar on Music Education" (D.M.E. diss., University of Cincinnati, 1988), 21–22.

2. *National Defense Education Act of 1958*. *U.S. Statutes at Large* 72, Part I (1958): 1580–1605.

3. Henry Steele Commager, ed., *Documents of American History, Vol. II Since 1898* (New York: Appleton-Century-Crofts, 1968), 608.

4. *Civil Rights Act of 1964*. *U.S. Statutes at Large* 78 (1964): 247.

5. *Elementary and Secondary Education Act of 1965*. *U.S. Statutes at Large* 79 (1965): 39.

6. *National Foundation on the Arts and Humanities Act of 1965*. *U.S. Statutes at Large* 79 (1965): 855.

7. *International Education Act of 1966*. *U.S. Statutes at Large* 80 (1966): 1070.

8. Michael Mark, *Contemporary Music Education*, 2nd ed. (New York: Schirmer Books, 1986), 90.

9. Karen J. Winkler, "After Years in Academic Limbo, the Study of Religion Undergoes a Revival of Interest Among Scholars," *Chronicle of Higher Education* 34, no. 21 (1988): 4–5; Patricia M. Lines, "Prayer, the Bible, and the Public Schools," (Issuegram #3, Education Commission of the States, Denver, CO, 1983), CD-ROM, ERIC, ED 234514.

10. *An Act to Amend the Immigration and Nationality Act*. *U.S. Statutes at Large* 79 (1965): 911–922.

11. George M. Marsden, "The Soul of the American University: A Historical Overview," in *The Secularization of the Academy*, eds. George M. Marsden and Bradley J. Longfield (New York: Oxford University Press, 1992), 9–45. See especially 25–32.

12. Harry J. Asmus, *The Polite Escape: On the Myth of Secularization* (Athens: Ohio University Press, 1982), 44.

13. Jerome Bruner, *The Process of Education* (Cambridge: Harvard University Press, 1960), 12.

14. John F. Usher, Jr., "Music Education in an Age of Ferment," *MEJ* 54 (1967): 89–91.

15. Gordon W. Allport, "Basic Principles in Improving Human Relations," in Gordon W. Allport et al., *Cultural Groups and Human Relations* (New York: Teachers College, Columbia University, 1951), 2–28. In this presentation, Allport summarized his hypothesis for improving human relations: "Maximize situations in which the individuals can participate fully and on terms of equal status in projects of joint concern." (p. 27) For a more complete explanation, see Gordon W. Allport, *The Nature of Prejudice* (Cambridge, MA: Addison-Wesley, 1954).

16. John D. Redden and Francis A. Ryan, *Intercultural Education* (Milwaukee, WI: Bruce Publishing Company, 1951), 6–7.

17. Hilda Taba, Elizabeth Hall Brady, and John T. Robinson, *Intergroup Education in Public Schools* (Washington, D.C.: American Council on Education, 1952), 35–52.

18. A case study of how desegregation was implemented can be found in Robert J. Dwyer, "A Study of Desegregation and Integration in Selected School Districts of Central Missouri" (Ph.D. diss., University of Missouri, 1957).
19. An example of the type of criticism that was leveled against the textbooks of the period can be found in *Prejudice in Textbooks*, Public Affairs Pamphlet No.160 (New York: National Conference of Christians and Jews, c. 1950).
20. Geneva Gay, "Multiethnic Education: Historical Developments and Future Prospects," *Phi Delta Kappan* 64 (April 1983): 560; Marvelene C. Moore, "Multicultural Music Education: An Analysis of Afro-American and Native American Folk Songs in Selected Elementary Music Textbooks of the Periods 1928–1955 and 1965–1975" (Ph.D. diss., University of Michigan, 1977), 78.
21. James G. Rice, ed., *General Education: Current Issues and Concerns* (Washington, D.C.: Association for Higher Education/National Education Association, 1964), 52.
22. Ibid., 53–60.
23. Thorsten Sellin, ed. "The Non-Western World in Higher Education" [special issue], *Annals of the American Academy of Political and Social Science* (Philadelphia: American Academy of Political and Social Science, 1964).
24. Myer Domnitz, *Educational Techniques for Combating Prejudice and Discrimination and for Promoting Better Intergroup Understanding* (Hamburg, Germany: UNESCO Institute for Education, 1965); Betty Atwell Wright, *Educating for Diversity* (New York: John Day Co., 1965).
25. Domnitz, *Educational Techniques*, 20; Wright, *Education for Diversity*, 153–55. Wright suggested several lessons on jazz, including a study of the origins of jazz, famous jazz artists, and society's gradual acceptance of various jazz styles.
26. Mark, *Contemporary Music Education*, 228; Paul Lehman, "The Stage Band: A Critical Evaluation," in *Perspectives in Music Education: Source Book III*, ed. Bonnie C. Kowall (Washington, D.C.: Music Educators National Conference, 1966), 526–32.
27. George N. Heller, "From the Melting Pot to Cultural Pluralism: General Music in a Technological Age, 1892–1992," in *Ithaca Conference on American Music Education: Centennial Profiles*, ed. Mark Fonder (Ithaca, NY: Ithaca College, 1992), 106.
28. Music educators had objected to jazz in the classroom for many years. Examples of this attitude can be found in Warrick L. Carter, "Indigenous American Music: Its Fight for Educational Acceptance," *NAJE Educator* 4, no. 3 (1972): 6–8+, and Harry Allen Feldman, "Jazz: A Place in Music Education?" *MEJ* 50, no. 6 (1964): 60–64.
29. Feldman, "Jazz: A Place in Music Education?" 62.
30. William Tallmadge, "Afro-American Music," *MEJ* 33, no. 1 (1957): 37.
31. Bryce Luty, "Jazz Education's Struggle for Acceptance," *MEJ* 69, no. 3 (1982): 39 and 53; David A. Herfort, "A History of the National Association of Jazz Educators and a Description of Its Role in American Music Education, 1968–1978" (D.E. diss., University of Houston, 1979), 17–18.
32. Mark, *Contemporary Music Education*, 229.
33. Edmund Souchon, "Jazz in New Orleans," *MEJ* 43, no. 6 (1957): 42–45.; Tallmadge, "Afro-American Music," 37–39; Max Krone, "Jazz and the General Music Class," *MEJ* 45, no. 6 (1959): 23–25.
34. Conference programs, MENC National Biennial Convention, Atlantic City, 1960, and Chicago, 1962. MENC Historical Center, Music Library, University of Maryland at College Park; Allen P. Britton, Dean Emeritus, School of Music, Univer-

sity of Michigan, Ann Arbor, interview by author, 12 November 1992. Original audiotape and transcript in the possession of the author.

35. Vanett Lawler, "Trends in Music Education in the United States," in *The Present State of Music Education in the World*, ed. Egon Kraus (Cologne, Germany: The International Society for Music Education, 1960), 181–82.

36. Britton interview; Conference program, MENC biennial convention, Seattle, WA, 1968. MENC Historical Center, Music Library, University of Maryland at College Park.

37. Editorial, *Ethno-Musicology* Newsletter No. 1 (1953): 1.

38. "Notes and News," *Ethno-Musicology* Newsletter No. 6 (1956): 1–3.

39. Ibid., 3–4.

40. Conference programs, MENC National Biennial Convention, (Chicago, 1954), 86; (St. Louis, 1956), 82; (Los Angeles, 1958), 77–78; (Atlantic City, 1960), 23. MENC Historical Center, Music Library, University of Maryland at College Park.

41. Conference program, MENC National Biennial Convention, (Los Angeles, 1958), 77. The performers at this concert included two student ethnomusicologists from UCLA, William Malm and Robert Garfias, who continued over the years to work closely with music education to bring the musics of many cultures to the classroom. See conference programs, MENC National Biennial Conventions, (Chicago, 1962), 68; (Philadelphia, 1964), 78; (Kansas City, 1966), 86. MENC Historical Center, Music Library, University of Maryland at College Park.

42. Elizabeth May and Mantle Hood, "Javanese Music for American Children," *MEJ* 48, no. 5 (1962): 38–41. Conference programs, MENC Southwestern Division Conference (Albuquerque, 1961) and MENC Eastern Division Conference (Atlantic City, 1953). MENC Historical Center, Music Library, University of Maryland at College Park. A photograph of the visitors at the 1953 Eastern Division Conference is in the Vanett Lawler Collection (Scrapbook III-4-3–Leaf 24), Music Library, University of Maryland at College Park.

43. Gerald Abraham, "Music in the World Today," in *Comparative Music Education*, ed. Egon Kraus (Mainz, Germany: International Society for Music Education, 1962), 26.

44. Ibid., 264.

45. Frank Calloway, "Seventh International Conference of ISME," *International Music Educator (IME)* No. 14 (October 1966): 447–448.

46. Karl D. Ernst, "An International Scope for Music Education," *IME* No. 14: 458 and 460.

47. Egon Kraus, "Recommendations of the Seventh International Conference," *IME* No. 14: 452.

48. Vanett Lawler, "Report on the Vienna Conference," *IME* No. 4 (October 1961): 136–37.

49. Conference program, MENC National Biennial Convention, Chicago, 1954.

50. Margaret Diaz, "An Analysis of the Elementary School Music Series Published in the United States from 1926–1976" (Ed.D. diss., University of Illinois: Urbana-Champaign, 1980), 143, 183–84, 239–40.

51. Janice James, "The Music of Afro-Americans in Elementary Music Series Books: An Investigation of Changing Textbook Contents, 1864–1970" (Ph.D. diss., University of Southern Mississippi, 1976), 68, 82–83, 91; Moore, "Multicultural Music Education," 103.

52. Heller, "From the Melting Pot," 107; Anderson, "World Music in American Education," *Contributions to Music Education* No. 3 (Autumn 1974): 36. *Together We*

Sing also contained units on music from the Near East, Africa, Asia, Australia, islands of the Pacific, and many Western countries with explanations of the types of music and musical instruments in each area.

53. Louise K. Meyers, *Teaching Children Music in Elementary Schools* (Englewood Cliffs, NJ: Prentice-Hall, 1950), 271–92.
54. Vernice Nye, Robert Nye, and H. Virginia Nye, *Toward World Understanding with Song in the Elementary School* (Belmont, CA: Wadworth Publishing Co., 1967).
55. Ibid., 39.
56. Allen Sapp, Professor of Composition, College Conservatory of Music, University of Cincinnati, interview by author, 20 November 1992. Original audiotape and transcript in the possession of the author.
57. Elizabeth May and Mantle Hood, "Javanese Music for American Children," 41.
58. Moore, "Multicultural Music Education," 183. There were also instances in the 1960s when teachers were forbidden to use songs with African-American dialect because they were considered degrading. Joy E. Lawrence, Professor Emeritus of Music Education, Kent State University, personal coversation with author, February 18, 1993.
59. Moore, 183. Moore's conclusion is accurate for the musics of other minorities as well. Ricardo Trimillos found this to be true for Hispanic-American and Asian-American children. Ricardo Trimillos, Professor of Ethnomusicology, University of Hawaii at Manoa, telephone interview by author, 7 February 1993. Original audiotape and transcript in possession of the author.
60. Siegfried Borris, "The Importance of Exotic Music for Music Education," *International Music Educator* Number 14 (October 1966): 466; Ernst, "An International Scope for Music Education," 460.
61. Nye, Nye and Nye, *Toward World Understanding with Song*, Preface, vi.
62. A. L. Lloyd, ed., *Folk Songs of the Americas* (London: Novello and Co. for IMC/UNESCO, 1965).
63. The entire Folkways record collection is now housed at the Smithsonian Institution, Washington, D.C., and is available through the Smithsonian Office of Folklife Programs.
64. Moore, "Multicultural Music Education," 103.
65. Heller, "From the Melting Pot," 107; Anderson, "World Music in American Education," 41.
66. *Innovation and Experiment in Education: A Progress Report of the Panel on Educational Research and Development* (Washington, D.C.: U.S. Government Printing Office, 1964), 49–55.
67. Ibid., 15.
68. Ibid.
69. Claude Palisca, *Music in Our Schools: A Search for Improvement* (Washington, D.C.: U.S. Government Printing Office, 1964), 1.
70. Charles Gary, Professor of Music Education, Catholic University of America, Washington, D.C., interview by author, 13 January 1993. Original audiotape and transcript in possession of the author.
71. Ibid.
72. Palisca, *Music in Our Schools*, Foreword.
73. Ibid., 11.
74. Ibid., 12–13.
75. Ibid., 3.
76. Ibid., 3–4.

77. Allen Sapp, secretary for the panel, confirmed the influence of Hood and Ellington. Sapp, interview.
78. Sapp, interview.
79. Palisca, *Music in Our Schools*, 11.
80. Ibid., 12 and 13.
81. Ibid., 13.
82. Ibid., 18–20. Quote on 20.
83. Ibid., 25. The report of Section II, as submitted at the end of the Yale Seminar, reads even more strongly than Palisca's final report. It states, "An undergraduate program of which internship and methodology comprises the major segment and a sampling of instruments another, with a semester devoted to 'music of the world' is simply not going to be enough." (Report of Section II: Repertory in Its Historical and Geographical Contexts, Seminar on Music Education, p. 11). Allen P. Britton Papers, (Box 28, #20), MENC Historical Center Music Library, University of Maryland at College Park.
84. Ibid., 32–34.
85. *Innovation and Experiment in Education*, 15–16.
86. Sapp, interview.
87. Judith Murphy and Lonna Jones, *Research in Arts Education* (Washington, D.C.: U.S. Government Printing Office, 1978), 27; Jerrold Ross, "Since Yale," *Bulletin of the Council for Research in Music Education* Number 60 (Fall 1979): 46.
88. Sapp, interview; Murphy and Jones, *Research in Arts Education*, 27; Robert John, "The Yale Seminar—Fifteen Years Later," *Bulletin of the Council for Research in Music Education* Number 60 (Fall 1979): 38.
89. Gary, interview.
90. Murphy and Jones, *Research in Arts Education*, 29.
91. Irving Lowens, "Music: Juilliard Repertory Project and the Schools," *Sunday Star* (Washington, D.C.), 30 May 1971.
92. *Juilliard Repertory Project*, Reference/Library edition (Cincinnati: Canyon Press, 1970), Preface.
93. Joseph Michalak, "Juilliard's Task—Music Curriculum," *New York Herald Tribune*, 4 August 1964.
94. Peter Mennin, "Development of an Enlarged Music Repertory from Kindergarten through Grade Six," *MEJ* 51, no. 2 (1964): 79. Research consultants Nicholas England of Columbia University (foreign folk musics) and John Jacob Niles (American folk musics) guided the selection of these songs.
95. *Juilliard Repertory Project*, 192–232.
96. Ibid., 76.
97. Elizabeth May and Mantle Hood, "Javanese Music," 38–41.
98. Paul Larson and William Anderson, "Sources for Teaching Non-Western Music," *School Music News* 30 (December 1966): 27–31.
99. Elizabeth May, "An Experiment with Australian Aboriginal Music," *MEJ* 54, no. 4 (1967): 47–50.
100. Charlotte M. Hartwig, "An Intercultural Approach to Music Education in Underdeveloped Areas" (master's thesis, Indiana University, 1967).
101. For examples see William Larson, ed., "Bibliography of Research Studies in Music Education, 1949–1956" [special issue], *Journal for Research in Music Education* 5 (Fall 1957): 182.
102. See Hazel Morgan, ed., *Music in American Education* (Chicago: MENC, 1955), 55–56.
103. *Teaching General Music: A Resource Handbook for Grades 7 and 8* (Albany, NY:

State Education Department Bureau of Secondary Curriculum Development, 1966), 45–64, 103–14. Units included music from Latin America, sub-Saharan Africa, Asia, and American folk musics: African-American, Appalachian, and cowboy and sailor songs.

104. Mark, *Contemporary Music Education*, 229.

105. Following the precedent set by the Yale Seminar for government funding, this seminar was funded by the Arts and Humanities Division of the U.S. Office of Education. See Charles Leonhard,"Was the Yale Seminar Worthwhile?" *Bulletin of the Council for Research in Music Education* No. 60 (Fall 1979): 61.

106. David McAllester, "Teaching the Music Teacher to Use the Music of His Own Culture," in *International Seminar on Teacher Education (ISTE)* (Ann Arbor: University of Michigan Press, 1967), 210.

107. Kwabena Nketia, "Music Education in African Schools: A Review of the Position of Ghana," in *ISTE*, 239–40, 243.

108. William P. Malm, "Preparing the Teacher for Handling the Music of Non-Western Traditions," in *ISTE*, 251–52.

109. Ibid., 255. The generic use of the masculine pronoun, though inappropriate by today's standards, was acceptable in 1966.

110. Elizabeth May, "Teaching a Music Teacher to Use the Music of Other Cultures Than His Own," in *ISTE*, 258–60.

111. Donald Shetler, chair, "Group #2 Recommendations," in *ISTE*, 392.

112. David McAllester, Chair, "Group #4 Recommendations," in *ISTE*, 399.

113. Mark, *Contemporary Music Education*, 228.

114. Robert A. Choate and Max Kaplan, "The Tanglewood Symposium Project," *MEJ* 53, no. 8 (1967): 77.

115. Robert A. Choate, ed., *Documentary Report of the Tanglewood Symposium* (Washington, D.C.: MENC, 1968), 122.

116. David McAllester, "The Substance of Things Hoped For," in *Documentary Report*, 96.

117. Ibid., 97.

118. See "Pop Music Panel," in *Documentary Report*, 104–8.

119. David McAllester, Professor Emeritus of Anthropology and Music, Wesleyan University, Middletown, CT, telephone interview by author, 8 December 1992. Original audiotape and transcript in the possession of the author.

120. "Implications for the Music Curriculum," in *Documentary Report*, 136.

121. "Implications for Music in Higher Education and the Community," in *Documentary Report*, 134–35.

122. Letter from Allen P. Britton to Hilda Humphreys, August 9, 1967, pp. 2–3. Pencil manuscript, Allen P. Britton Papers (Box 16, #138), MENC Historical Center, Music Library, University of Maryland at College Park.

123. Allen Britton, Arnold Broido, and Charles Gary, "The Tanglewood Declaration," in *Documentary Report*, 139.

124. Charles Fowler, "Joining the Mainstream," *MEJ* 54, no. 3 (1967): 69.

125. Vanett Lawler, "50 Years 1907–1957: Look to the Future," *MEJ* 43, no. 5 (1957): 38.

CHAPTER 6

1. J. H. Kwabena Nketia, "Exploring Intercultural Dimensions of Music Education," in *A World View of Music Education* [ISME Yearbook vol. 15], ed. Jack Dobbs (Austria: ISME, 1988), 106.

2. Examples include: Michael Novak, *The Rise of the Unmeltable Ethnics* (New York: Macmillan, 1971); James Stuart Olson, *The Ethnic Dimension in American History* (New York: St. Martin's Press, 1979); Roger Daniels, *Coming to America: A History of Immigration and Ethnicity in American Life* (New York: Harper/Collins Publishers, 1990); and scholarly journals such as *Ethnicity*, *Ethnic Groups*, *Ethnic Forum*, and the *Journal of American Ethnic History* were founded in 1974, 1976, 1980, and 1981, respectively.

3. U.S. Department of Commerce, Bureau of Census, *1980 Census of Population: Supplementary Report, Ancestry of the Population by State* (Washington, D.C.: U.S. Government Printing Office, 1983).

4. For example, Arthur Schlesinger, Jr., *The Disuniting of America: Reflections on a Multicultural Society* (New York: Whittle Direct Books, 1991); Diane Ravitch, "Multiculturalism, E Pluribus Plures," *American Scholar* (Summer 1990): 337–54; see also Section 4, "Criticism of the New Ethnicity," in *America and the New Ethnicity*, eds. David Coleburn and George Poizzetta, 185–226 (Port Washington, NY: Kennikat Press, 1979).

5. The seminal report of this period was *A Nation at Risk*, which recommended a "New Basics" curriculum of reading, mathematics, science, social studies, and computer science complemented by foreign language study and the arts. See the National Commission on Excellence in Education, *A Nation at Risk: The Imperative for Educational Reform*, (Washington, D.C.: U. S. Government Printing Office, 1983).

6. These illegal aliens were given a one-year amnesty period to apply for legal status.

7. *Bilingual Education Act. U.S. Statutes at Large* (1968): 816.

8. *Indian Elementary and Secondary School Assistance Act. U.S. Statutes at Large* 86 (1972): 335.

9. *Ethnic Heritage Program. U.S. Statutes at Large* 86, part I (1972): 346–347.

10. Ibid., 347.

11. While gender and handicapping conditions have been acknowledged to be part of the diversity within the population of the United States, there have been some questions about whether these differences should be considered "cultures."

12. Douglas Lamont, *Winning Worldwide: Strategies for Dominating Global Markets* (Homewood, IL: Business One Irwin, 1991), 252.

13. *International Trade Education: Issues and Programs*, eds. James R. Mahoney and Clyde Sakamoto (Washington, D.C.: American Association of Community and Junior Colleges, 1985), 37–52.

14. A comprehensive view of the busing issue in Boston can be found in Ronald P. Formisano, *Boston Against Busing* (Chapel Hill: University of North Carolina Press, 1991).

15. *Bibliography of Resources in Bilingual Education: Curricular Materials* (Rosslyn, VA: National Clearinghouse for Bilingual Education, 1980). Of the 926 resources cited, there is only one for music education. It gives directions for organizing an *estudiantina* (traditional group of serenading musicians found in Spain and Latin America) in a Spanish-English class.

16. *Compendium of Papers on the Topic of Bilingual Education of the Committee on Education and Labor, House of Representatives, 99th Congress, 2nd Session* (Washington, D.C.: U.S. Government Printing Office, June 1986).

17. This is not so different from the way music was employed in the standard modern foreign language classes (French, German, Spanish). In the 1940s, musical "realia" or audiovisual aids (e.g., songbooks and recordings) were considered a

regular part of modern language instruction in order to bring the foreign culture closer to the students. In the 1970s modern language teachers, like the bilingual teachers, began to use music as an aid to teaching grammar. See chapter 8, "Teaching the Foreign Civilization: Realia and Audio-Visual Aids," and Appendix B, "Realia Lists" in *Twentieth Century Modern Language Teaching, Sources and Readings*, ed. Maxim Newmark (New York: The Philosophical Library, 1948), 430–62 and 690–715; Yukiko S. Jolly, "The Use of Songs in Teaching Foreign Languages," *Modern Language Journal* 59, no. 1 (1975): 11–14.

18. Carlos J. Ovando and Virginia P. Collier, *Bilingual and ESL Classrooms, Teaching in Multicultural Contexts* (New York: McGraw-Hill, 1985), 177–78.

19. Ibid., 178.

20. Geneva Gay, "Changing Conceptions of Multicultural Education," *Educational Perspectives* 16, no. 4 (1977): 6–7; Donna M. Gollnick and Philip C. Chinn, *Multicultural Education in a Pluralistic Society*, 2nd ed. (Columbus, OH: Charles E. Merrill Publishing Co., 1986), 24. Some of the collegiate ethnic studies programs which were established in the 1970s included the Afro-American Studies programs at Yale University, Boston University, and Atlanta University; Mexican-American Studies at California State University; the Center for Puerto Rican Studies at City University of New York; and a Multiethnic program at the University of California at Los Angeles. These programs were all funded to some extent by the Ford Foundation. See Jack Bass, *Widening the Mainstream of American Culture, A Ford Foundation Report on Ethnic Studies* (New York: Ford Foundation, 1978), CD-ROM, ERIC, ED 167649.

21. In the early 1970s, the terms "multiethnic" and "multicultural" were interchangeable; however, by the mid-1970s, "multicultural education" became the accepted term.

22. *Multicultural/Bilingual Division, Multicultural Planning Conferences* (Washington, D.C.: U.S. Department of Health, Education, and Welfare, February 1976), Introduction.

23. See, for examples, Christian Skjervold and Bruce Tipple, *Minneapolis Multi-Ethnic Curriculum Project: Unit Overviews* (Minneapolis: Minneapolis Public Schools, 1975), CD-ROM, ERIC, ED 183476; *Multi Ethnic Handbook, Vol. I. Later Elementary and Middle Schools. Lesson Plans for Teaching Concepts Dealing with Racism, Contributions of Blacks, Latinos, Native Americans* (East Lansing: Michigan Education Association, 1973); *Roots of America: A Multiethnic Resource Guide for the 7th, 8th, and 9th Grade Social Studies Teachers* (Washington, D.C.: NEA, 1975), CD-ROM, ERIC, ED 115639.

24. Examples include: Zola J. Sullivan, "Teaching Multicultural Awareness and Understanding through the Language Arts—'Creative Writing,' " CD-ROM, ERIC, ED 198554; Gretchen Klopfer, "A Multicultural Approach to High School History Teaching," *Social Studies* 78, no. 6 (1987): 273–77.; Sally Botzler et al., *A Cross-Cultural and Interdisciplinary Multicultural Education Curriculum for Grades 4–8* (Eureka, CA: Humboldt County Office of Education, 1980), CD-ROM, ERIC, ED 202784; *Ethnic Heritage Curriculum Guide, Grades 7–12* (Marion City, AL: Marion City Board of Education, 1978), CD-ROM, ERIC, ED 170447. These curriculum guides offered units for English, math, music, social studies and vocational education.

25. Examples include: *A Curriculum of Inclusion: Report of the Commissioner's Task Force on Minorities: Equity and Excellence* (Albany: NYS Special Task Force on Equity and Excellence in Education, 1989), CD-ROM, ERIC, ED 338535; Jon Reyh-

ner, ed., *Teaching the Indian Child, A Bilingual/Multicultural Approach*, 2nd ed. (Billings: Eastern Montana College, 1988). See also the women's studies units developed for the grade schools by the National Women's History Project of Santa Rosa, CA. One example is their third-grade social studies unit which may be found in CD-ROM, ERIC, ED 260998.

26. Examples include: Harold J. Sylwester, ed., *Teaching Global Perspectives: Syllabi and Modules for University Courses* (Warrensburg: Central Missouri State University, 1983), CD-ROM, ERIC, ED 233957; George Arakapadavil, "Introducing Multicultural/Global Education into the Schools" (paper presented at the National Multicultural Conference, Oshkosh, WI, Oct. 24–25, 1985), CD-ROM, ERIC, ED 289805; Merry Merryfield, *Teaching about the World: Teacher Education Programs with a Global Perspective* (Columbus: Ohio State University, 1990), CD-ROM, ERIC, ED 339623.

27. Grant and Sleeter identify these topic areas in their research reviews of over 200 articles and 68 books from 1973 to 1987. See Carl A. Grant and Christine E. Sleeter, "The Literature on Multicultural Education: Review and Analysis," *Educational Review* 37, no. 2 (1985): 97–118; and Carl A. Grant, Christine E. Sleeter, and James E. Anderson, "The Literature on Multicultural Education: Review and Analysis," *Educational Studies* 12, no. 1 (1987): 47–71. An ERIC system search of over 300 entries under "multicultural education and social studies" for the period from 1968 to 1990 produced similar results.

28. This is the descriptive term used by Gollnick et al., *Multicultural Education and Ethnic Studies in the United States: An Analysis and Annotated Bibliography of Selected ERIC Documents* (Washington, D.C.: AACTE and ERIC Clearinghouse for Teacher Education, 1976), 136.

29. See Grant and Sleeter, "The Literature on Multicultural Education: Review and Analysis," 110.

30. See, for example, Ollye L. B. Shirley, "The Impact of Multicultural Education on the Self-Concept, Racial Attitude, and Student Achievement of Black and White Fifth and Sixth Graders" (Ph.D. diss., University of Mississippi, 1988); C. Bennett, A. Okinaka, and X. Wu, "The Effects of a Multicultural Education on Preservice Teachers' Attitudes, Knowledge, and Behavior" (paper presented at the American Educational Research Association, New Orleans, April 1988), CD-ROM, ERIC, ED 308161.

31. Richard K. Mastain, ed., *Manual on Certification and Preparation of Educational Personnel in the United States* (Dubuque, IA: Kendall/Hunt Publishing Co., for the National Association of State Directors of Teacher Education and Certification, 1991), C-4, C-21 through C-38.

32. For an example of the teacher competencies expected for multicultural education, see William A. Hunter, ed., *Multicultural Education Through Competency-Based Teacher Education* (Washington, D.C.: American Association of Colleges for Teacher Education, 1974.)

33. Nancy Siefert, "Education and the New Pluralism: A Preliminary Survey of Recent Progress in the 50 States" (paper presented at the 1973 Annual Meeting of the National Coordinating Assembly on Ethnic Studies, Detroit, May 19, 1973), 4–5, CD-ROM, ERIC, ED 081885.

34. The National Association of State Boards of Education (NASBE), *The American Tapestry: Educating a Nation* (Alexandria, VA: NASBE, 1991), 10. A backlash of negative reaction greeted the Iowa legislation as fears surfaced that somehow a global perspective would impinge on job security.

35. N.Y. State Education Department, *New Part 100 of the Commissioner's Regulations* (Albany: NYS Education Department, 1984), Sections 100.3 and 100.4 parts "b" and "c." Also N.Y. State Education Department, *Statement of Regents' Goals for Elementary and Secondary School Students—1984* (Albany: NYS Education Department, 1984), Points 1.6, 2.5, 3.1, 4.2, 5.2, 6.0, and 9.1; Delaware Statewide Multicultural Education Committee, *Guidelines for Infusing Multicultural Education into School Curricular and Co-Curricular Programs* (Dover, DE: Department of Public Instruction, 1989); NASBE, *The American Tapestry*, 11.

36. AACTE Commission on Multicultural Education, "No One Model American," *Journal of Teacher Education* 24, no. 4 (1973): 264–65.

37. *NCATE Standards, Procedures, and Policies for the Accreditation of Professional Education Units* (Washington, D.C.: NCATE, 1990).

38. Minutes of the MENC National Executive Board, 1969. The Charles Moody Papers, manuscript copy, MENC Historical Center, Music Library, University of Maryland at College Park.

39. Final Report, MENC Committee 18. GO Project (C3–2–2), MENC Historical Center, Music Library, University of Maryland at College Park.

40. Committee 18 Assignment Sheet. GO Project, MENC Historical Center, Music Library, University of Maryland at College Park.

41. Final Report, Committee #18.

42. MENC *Goals and Objectives*, MENC publication, 1970. MENC Historical Center, Music Library, University of Maryland at College Park.

43. For a review of how well these goals were accomplished during the first decade following the GO project see Michael Mark, "The GO Project: Retrospective of a Decade," *MEJ* 67, no. 4 (1980): 42–47.

44. James Standifer, Professor of Music Education, University of Michigan. Telephone interview by author, 12 February 1993. Original audiotape and transcript in possession of the author.

45. James Standifer, "Project Report One: Music in Urban Eduction, Philadelphia," September 1969. CMP Files (Box 48–6), MENC Historical Center, Music Library, University of Maryland at College Park.

46. Allen Britton, personal notes taken at the Tanglewood Symposium. Manuscript margin notes in Tanglewood program. Allen Britton Papers (Box 16 #140), MENC Historical Center, Music Library, University of Maryland at College Park.

47. Standifer, interview.

48. See MENC, "Teacher Education: Stop Sending Innocents into Battle Unarmed," and "Recommendations for Teacher Education Programs," *MEJ* 56, no. 5 (1970): 102–11.

49. For a broader view of music in urban education, see Michael Mark, *Contemporary Music Education*, 2nd ed. (New York: Schirmer Books, 1986), 221–32.

50. Standifer, interview.

51. Charles Fowler, ed., "Facing the Music in Urban Education" [special issue] *MEJ* 56, no. 5 (1970).

52. Max Kaplan, "We Have Much to *Learn* from the Inner City," *MEJ* 56, no. 5 (1970): 39–42; Stuart Smith, "Rock—Swim in It or Sink," *MEJ* 56, no. 5 (1970): 86–87; Barbara Reeder, "Afro Music: As Tough as a Mozart Quartet," *MEJ* 56, no. 5 (1970): 88–91; James Standifer, "Listening Is an Equal Opportunity Art," *MEJ* 56, no. 5 (1970): 97–99+.

53. Otis D. Simmons, "Research, the Bedrock of Student Interest," *MEJ* 58, no. 3 (1971): 38–41; Harry Morgan, "Music—A Life Force in the Black Community,"

MEJ 58, no. 3 (1971): 34–47; Beverely Blondell, "Drums Talk at Howard," *MEJ* 58, no. 3 (1971): 45–48.

54. MENC, "Selected Resources in Black Studies in Music," *MEJ* 58, no. 3 (1971): 56+.

55. Barbara Reeder and James Standifer, *Source Book of African and Afro-American Materials for Music Educators* (n.p.: Contemporary Music Project, MENC, 1972).

56. Letter from Robert Werner, CMP, to Barbara Reeder, June 4, 1969. CMP Collection (Box 48, file 1), MENC Historical Center, Music Library, University of Maryland at College Park; notification of CMP grant to James Standifer. CMP Collection (Box 48, file 6), MENC Historical Center, Music Library, University of Maryland at College Park.

57. Letter from David Willoughby, assistant director of the *Source Book* project, to Professor Klaus Wachsman, Northwestern University, 4 February 1972. CMP Collection (Box 64, file 1), MENC Historical Center, Music Library, University of Maryland at College Park.

58. Standifer, interview.

59. See the several articles under "Youth Music—A Special Report," *MEJ* 56, no. 3 (1969): 43–74; MENC, "National Association of Jazz Educators," *MEJ* 54, no. 8 (1968): 57.

60. "Jazz" [special issue], *MEJ* 62, no. 3 (1975); Duke Johns, ed., "Improvisation, [special issue], *MEJ* 66, no. 4 (1980).

61. See the various comments in "An Assessment of Jazz Education, 1968–1978," *NAJE Educator* 10, no. 3 (1978): 10–13+.

62. Arlynn Nellhaus, "School Jazz—A Disaster Area," *NAJE Educator* 10, no. 3 (1978): 12.

63. Robert Werner, "The United States and International Music Education," *Design for Arts in Education* 92, no. 1 (1990): 27.

64. See the several articles under "Youth Music—A Special Report," *MEJ*; Peter Winkler, "Pop Music's Middle Years," *MEJ* 66, no.4 (1979): 26–33; Dick Thompson, "Plugging Into Pop at the Junior High Level," *MEJ* 66, no. 4 (1979): 54–59; "Point of View: Does Popular Music Have Educational Value?" *MEJ* 66, no. 4 (1979): 60–65.

65. This is evidenced in Eunice Boardman and Beth Landis, *Exploring Music* (New York: Holt, Rinehart and Winston, 1975); Eunice Boardman and Barbara Endress, *The Music Book* (New York: Holt, Rinehart and Winston, 1984); Bennett Reimer, Elizabeth Crook, and David Walker, *Music* (Morristown, NJ: Silver Burdett Co., 1974); Carmen E. Culp, Mary E. Hoffman, and Lawrence Eisman, *World of Music* (Morristown, NJ: Silver Burdett Ginn, 1988).

66. Terence O'Grady, "A Rock Retrospective," *MEJ* 66, no. 4 (1979): 34–45; Robert Cutietta, "Using Rock Videos to Your Advantage," *MEJ* 71, no. 6 (1985): 47–49; Robert Cutietta, ed., "Pop Music and Music Education" [special issue], *MEJ* 77, no. 8 (1991).

67. Many of the arguments against rock music sound very like those voiced against jazz during the 1930s and 1940s.

68. These percentages are confirmed by Margaret Diaz, "An Analysis of the Elementary School Music Series Published in the United States From 1926–1976" (Ed.D. diss., University of Illinois: Urbana-Champaign, 1980), 342, 373, 393, 411, and 432; Janice James, "The Music of Afro-Americans in Elementary Music Series Books: An Investigation of Changing Textbook Contents, 1864–1970" (Ph.D. diss., Uni-

versity of Southern Mississippi, 1976), 83; Marvelene C. Moore, "Multicultural Music Education: An Analysis of Afro-American and Native American Folk Songs in Selected Elementary Music Textbooks of the Periods 1928–1955 and 1965–1975" (Ph.D. diss., University of Michigan, 1977), 100–102, also table 4.

69. *World of Music—Master Index* (Morristown, NJ: Silver Burdett Ginn, 1991), 53–61. In 1995 this had increased to 77 cultures in *The Music Connection—Master Index* (Morristown, NJ: Sillver Burdett Ginn, 1995), 76–82.

70. Robert Choate, Richard Berg, Eugene Troth, eds., *New Dimensions in Music* (New York: American Book Co., 1970); also William Anderson, interview; Eunice Boardman and Beth Landis, *Exploring Music.*

71. Bennett Reimer, Mary E. Hoffman, and Albert McNeil, *Music* (Morristown, NJ: Silver Burdett Co., 1978).

72. Janice James, "The Musics of Afro-Americans in Elementary Music Series Books," 92–93; Patricia K. Shehan, "The Effect of Didactic and Heuristic Instruction on the Preference, Achievement, and Attentiveness of Sixth Grade Students for Indonesian Gamelan Music" (Ph.D. diss., Kent State University, 1981), 26.

73. Janice James, "The Musics of Afro-Americans in Elementary Music Series Books," 92–93; Charles Leonhard, Beatrice Krone, Irving Wolfe, and Margaret Fullerton, eds., *Discovering Music Together* (New York: Follett Educational Corp., 1970); Robert Choate, Richard Berg, and Eugene Troth, eds., *New Dimensions in Music.*

74. Jill Trinka, "The Performance Style of American Folksongs on School Music Series and Non-School Music Series Recordings: A Comparative Analysis of Selected Factors" (Ph.D. diss., University of Texas at Austin, 1987).

75. Ricardo Trimillos, Professor of Ethnomusicology, Chair of Asian Studies Program, University of Hawaii, Manoa, telephone interview by author, 7 February 1993. Original audiotape and transcript in possession of the author.

76. Anthony Palmer, Associate Professor of Music Education, University of Hawaii, Manoa, interview by author, 23 October 1993, Seattle, Washington. Original audiotape and transcript in possession of the author.

77. "Conference Here Criticized by Negro Music Educators," *Atlanta Constitution* 13 March 1972 (6–B).

78. Ibid.

79. Letter from T. J. Anderson, Chair, Black Music Caucus, to Robert Klotman, Chair, Minority Concerns Commission, 17 September 1973. Minority Concerns Commission Files (A61.1), MENC Historical Center, Music Library, University of Maryland at College Park.

80. See, for example, Camille C. Taylor, compiler, *A Comprehensive Source Book on Black Derived Music, Books, and Related Materials: Submitted by Music Companies and Individuals* (New York: National Black Music Caucus, 1982).

81. For a detailed account of the first decade of the NBMC, see Camille C. Taylor, "The First Decade of the Black Music Caucus of the Music Educators National Conference" (Ed.D. diss., Teachers College, Columbia University, 1984).

82. MENC National Executive Board Minutes, July 5–7, 1972. MENC Historical Center, Music Library, University of Maryland at College Park.

83. Euana Gangware, "Minority Concerns Concern Us All," *MEJ* 62, no. 1 (1975): 50. However, there is no doubt that the NBMC influenced the actions of the MCC since its members often served on the commission.

84. Letter from Jack E. Schaeffer, president, MENC, to Euana Gangware, University
    of Illinois. Minority Concerns Commission Files (A61.1), MENC Historical Cen-
    ter, Music Library, University of Maryland at College Park.

85. Minority Concerns Commission Policy Statement. Minority Concerns Commis-
    sion Files (A61.1), MENC Historical Center, Music Library, University of Mary-
    land at College Park.

86. Arnold K. Williams, "Minority Concerns," *Indiana Musicator*, n.d.: 13–14. Mi-
    norities Concerns Commission Files (A61.1, box 1), MENC Historical Center,
    Music Library, University of Maryland at College Park; minutes from the Mi-
    norities Concerns Commission Open Forum, Anaheim, 1974, and Denver, 1975.
    Minorities Concerns Commission Files, MENC Historical Center, Hornbake Mu-
    sic Library, University of Maryland at College Park. I was struck by the urgency
    and intensity with which speakers addressed these issues at the open forums of
    the MCC. It is impossible to record this emotion in a few quotations. Readers
    who wish to experience their full impact are encouraged to read the complete
    minutes of these meetings.

87. "Goals and Objectives." Minority Concerns Commission Files, MENC Histori-
    cal Center, Music Library, University of Maryland at College Park.

88. National Executive Board Minutes, June 8–10, 1977. MENC Historical Center,
    Music Library, University of Maryland at College Park. See also Minority Con-
    cerns Commission Files (A61.1), MENC Historical Center, Music Library, Uni-
    versity of Maryland at College Park.

89. Ella J. Washington, "Multi-Cultural Awareness Committee: New Directions,"
    MEJ 69, no.9 (1983): 67.

90. Ibid.

91. Because of the quantity of research in the field of multicultural music education,
    it is impossible to do a complete review of literature in this chpater. For a more
    detailed analysis of the research during this period, see Milagros Agostini Que-
    sada and Terese M. Volk, "World Musics and Music Education: A Review of
    Research, 1973–1993," *Bulletin for the Council of Research in Music Education*,
    (Spring 1997) no. 131:46–68. Also Joyce Jordan, "Multicultural Music Education
    in a Pluralistic Society," in *Handbook of Research on Music Teaching and Learning*,
    ed. Richard Colwell (New York: Schirmer Books, 1992), 735–48.

92. See, for example, Ruth De Cesare, "An Experimental Study of Selected Ethno-
    centric Attitudinal Change Among American Elementary School Children To-
    ward the Culture of Japan" (Ph.D. diss., New York University, 1972); James E.
    Mumford, "The Effect on the Attitudes of Music Education Majors of Direct Ex-
    periences with Afro-American Popular Music Ensembles—A Case Study" (Ph.D.
    diss., Indiana University, Bloomington, 1984); Patricia K. Shehan, "The Effect of
    Didactic and Heuristic Instruction on the Preference, Achievement, and Atten-
    tiveness of Sixth Grade Students for Indonesian Gamelan Music"; Robert W.
    Stevens, "The Effects of a Course of Study on Afro-American Popular Music in
    the Undergraduate Curriculum" (Ph.D. diss., Indiana University, Bloomington,
    1984).

93. Examples include: Brenda A. Ellis, "Strategies for Teaching African-American
    Music in the Elementary Music Class" (Ed.D. diss., Teachers College, Colum-
    bia University, 1990); Arthur L. Evans, "The Development of the Negro Spiri-
    tual as Choral Art Music by Afro-American Composers with an Annotated
    Guide to the Performance of Selected Spirituals" (Ph.D. diss., University of Mi-
    ami, 1972); Charles V. Burnsed, "The Development and Evaluation of an In-

troductory Jazz Improvisation Sequence for Intermediate Band Students" (Ph.D. diss., University of Miami, 1978); Joseph Hurwitz, "Plan for the Implementation of Traditional Instrumental Ghanaian Ensemble in Secondary Schools" (master's thesis, University of California, Los Angeles, 1971); Vada E. Butcher, "Development of Materials for a One-Year Course in African Music for the General Undergraduate Student," CD-ROM, ERIC, ED 04504.

94. Examples include: Mary Jane Montague, "An Investigation of Teacher Training;" Willie L. Sullivan, Jr., "Preparing Prospective Music Teachers to Teach Effectively in Urban Schools" (Ed.D. diss., University of Cincinnati, 1982); Russel Thomas, Jr., "A Survey of Jazz Education Courses in Colleges and Universities in the State of Mississippi for the Preparation of Music Educators" (Ph.D. diss., University of Mississippi, 1980); Charles H. Gilchrist, "An Assessment of the Preparation of North Carolina Public School Music Teachers in Performance Practices of Black Gospel Music: Implication for Curriculum Revisions in Higher Education" (Ed.D. diss., University of North Carolina, Greensboro, 1980).

95. Anthony J. Palmer, "World Musics in Elementary and Secondary Music Education: A Critical Analysis" (Ph.D. diss. , University of California, Los Angeles, 1975); Abraham A Schwadron, "Comparative Music Aesthetics, Toward a Universality of Musicality," *Music and Man* 1, no. 1 (1973): 17–31, and "Comparative Music Aesthetics and Education: Observations in Speculation," in *Music Education for Tomorrow's Society: Selected Topics*, ed. Arthur Motycka (Jamestown, RI: GAMT Music Press, 1976), 21–29. Schwadron's search for musical truth through comparative aesthetics was also confirmed by Anthony Palmer. Palmer, interview.

96. Paul Burgett, "Aesthetics of the Music of Afro-Americans: A Critical Analysis of the Writings of Selected Black Scholars with Implication for Black Music Studies and for Music Education" (Ph.D. diss., University of Rochester, Eastman School of Music, 1976); Marvin V. Curtis, "Understanding the Black Aesthetic Experience," *MEJ* 77, no. 2 (October 1988): 23–26.

97. David J. Elliott, "Key Concepts in Multicultural Music Education," *International Journal of Music Education* No. 13 (1989): 18.

98. See, for example, J. J. Yudkin, "An Investigation and Analysis of World Music Education in California's Public Schools, K–6" (Ph.D. diss., University of California, Los Angeles, 1990); Mary Jane Montague, "An Investigation of Teacher Training"; Maria Navarro, "The Relationship Between Culture, Society, and Music Teacher Education" (Ph.D. diss., Kent State University, 1988).

99. Examples include: Margaret Diaz, "An Analysis of the Elementary School Music Series Published in the United States from 1926–1976," (Ed.D. diss., University of Illinois, Urbana-Champaign, 1980); Janice James," The Music of Afro-Americans in Elementary Music Series Books: An Investigation of Changing Textbook Content, 1864–1970;" B. A. B. Curry, "An Evaluation of African and Afro-American Music in Selected Elementary Music Textbooks Series and Recommendations for Supplementary Song Material" (ED.D. diss., University of Houston, 1982); Jill Trinka, "The Performance Style of American Folksongs on School Music Series and Non-School Music Series Recordings."

100. Werner first broached this topic at the ISME meeting in Tunis, Tunisia, in 1972. He explained it more fully at the meeting at Montreux, Switzerland. See Robert J. Werner, "A Proposed International Curriculum for the Education of the Music Teacher," *International Music Educator* No. 2 (1972): 15–17; and "The Development of Music Curricula for International Education in Schools and Col-

leges," *Challenges in Music Education* [ISME Yearbook vol. 3], ed. Egon Kraus (Perth: Department of Music, University of Western Australia, 1976), 86–90.

101. J. H. Kwabena Nketia, "New Perspectives in Music Education," *International Music Education* [ISME Yearbook, vol. 5], ed. Egon Kraus (Mainz: B. Schott's Söhne, 1978), 110.

102. Leon H. Burton, "Commonalities in the Musics of Diverse Cultures," in *International Music Education* [ISME Yearbook, vol. 13], ed. Jack Dobbs, (Nedlands: University of Western Australia Press, 1986), 111–18.

103. Jack Dobbs, "Music as Multi-Cultural Education," in *Tradition and Change in Music and Music Education* [ISME Yearbook, vol. 9], ed. Jack Dobbs (Mainz: B. Schott's Söhne, 1982), 145; William M. Anderson, "Music of the Americas, Its Influence on a Multicultural Society," in *Music for a Small Planet* [ISME Yearbook vol. 11], ed. Jack Dobbs (Nedlands: University of Western Australia Press, 1986), 40.

104. J. H. Kwabena Nketia, "Exploring Intercultural Dimensions of Music Education," in *A World View of Music Education* [ISME Yearbook, vol. 15], ed. Jack Dobbs (Austria: ISME, 1988), 104 and 106.

105. Ibid., 105–6.

106. David Elliott, "The Role of Music and Musical Experience in Modern Society: Toward a Global Philosophy of Music Education," in *Music for a Small Planet* [ISME Yearbook, vol. 11], ed. Jack Dobbs (Nedlands: University of Western Australia Press, 1984), 81.

107. Charles H. Benner, "Implication of Social Change for Music Education," in *Challenges in Music Education* [ISME Yearbook, vol. 3], ed. Egon Kraus (Mainz: B. Schott's Söhne, 1976), 37.

108. Abraham Schwadron, "World Music in Education," in *Music for a Small Planet* [ISME Yearbook, vol. 11], ed. Jack Dobbs (Nedlands: University of Western Australia Press, 1984), 96.

109. Ibid., 93–94.

110. National Association of Schools of Music, *1972 Handbook* (Washington, D.C.: NASM, 1972), 23–24.

111. National Association of Schools of Music, *1974 Handbook* (Reston, VA: NASM, 1974), 24.

112. Ibid., 32.

113. Chuck Ball et al., "Report of the MENC Commission on Graduate Music Teacher Education," *MEJ* 67, no. 2 (1980): 48.

114. In 1992, Colorado, New Hampshire, Vermont, and Virginia had this type of requirement. See Robert L. Erbes, *Certification Practice and Trends in Music Teacher Education*, 4th ed. (Reston, VA: MENC, 1992).

115. Advertisements for these courses were found primarily in the *MEJ*. Examples include: New York University, advertisement, *MEJ* 55, no. 8 (1969): 114; Indiana University and Wesleyan University, advertisements, *MEJ* 58, no. 8 (1972): 116–18; Northwestern University, advertisement, *MEJ* 64, no. 8 (1978): 92 and 71, no. 8 (1985): 58; Central Connecticut State University, advertisement, *MEJ* 74, no. 8 (1988): 58.

116. Montague, "An Investigation of Teacher Training in Multicultural Music Education in Selected Universities and Colleges."

117. Navarro, "The Relationship Between Culture, Society, and Music Teacher Education in 1838 and 1988."

118. Charles Gary, letter to author, 23 September 1995.

119. Conference Program, MENC National Biennial Convention, Seattle, 1968. MENC Historical Center, Music Library, University of Maryland at College Park.

120. Charles Gary, Professor of Music, Catholic University, Washington, D.C., interview by author, 13 January 1993. Original audiotape and transcript in the possession of the author.

121. For a description of this first MENC "jazz night," see *NAJE Newsletter* 1, no. 1 (n.d.): 1. Allen Britton, Dean Emeritus, University of Michigan, and Charles Gary, Professor of Music Education, Catholic University, also described the excitement of this evening. Interviews by author, 12 November 1992, and 13 January 1993, respectively. Original audiotapes and transcripts in possession of the author.

122. Allen Scott, "The Past Ten Years in Retrospect," *NAJE Educator*, 10, no. 3 (1978): 9; Willson is quoted in Matthew Bretton, "Jazz Night in Seattle—March 1968," *NAJE Newsletter* 1, no. 1 (n.d.): 1; his statement was also confirmed by Allen Britton, conversation with author, 5 November 1992.

123. William M. Anderson, Associate Dean for Academic Affairs, College and Graduate School of Education, Kent State University, interview by author, 24 February 1993. Original audiotape and transcript in possession of the author.

124. O. M. Hartsell, Professor Emeritus of Music, School of Music, University of Arizona, Tucson, telephone interview with author, 10 February 1993. Original audiotape and transcript in possession of the author.

125. Conference Program, MENC National Biennial Convention (Chicago, 1970). MENC Historical Center, Music Library, University of Maryland at College Park.

126. Conference Program, MENC National Biennial Convention (Atlanta, 1972). MENC Historical Center, Music Library, University of Maryland at College Park.

127. Conference Program, MENC National Biennial Convention (Anaheim, 1974). MENC Historical Center, Music Library, University of Maryland at College Park.

128. Conference Program, MENC National Biennial Convention (Miami Beach, 1980). MENC Historical Center, Music Library, University of Maryland at College Park.

129. MENC, program listing of biennial conference, San Antonio, *MEJ* 68, no. 4 (1981): 58–62.

130. Conference Programs, MENC National Biennial Conventions (Anaheim, 1986, and Indianapolis, 1988). MENC Historical Center, Music Library, University of Maryland at College Park.

131. Conference Program, MENC National Biennial Convention (Washington, D.C. 1990). MENC Historical Center, Music Library, University of Maryland at College Park.

132. MENC, "Call for papers for the 1989 Eastern Division Conference in Boston," *MEJ* 73, no 5 (1988): 52; 1989 Eastern Division Conference Program. MENC Historical Center, Music Library, University of Maryland at College Park.

133. See, for examples, Barbara Reeder, "Afro-music: As Tough as a Mozart Quartet"; "Getting Involved in Shaping the Sounds of Black Music," *MEJ* 59, no. 2 (1972): 80–84; Dominique de Lerma, "Black Music Now!" *MEJ* 57, no. 3 (1970): 25–29; Kwabene Nketia, "Music Education in Africa and the West: We Can Learn From Each Other," *MEJ* 57, no. 3 (1970): 48–55.

134. Marie Joy Curtiss, "Essays in Retribalization: India," *MEJ* 56, no. 1 (1969): 60–62; Don DeNevi, "Essays in Retribalization: Hudson Bay," *MEJ* 56, no. 1 (1969): 66–68; Louis Ballard, "Put American Indian Music in the Classroom," *MEJ* 56, no. 7 (1969): 38–44.

135. Thomas F. Johnston, Matthew Nocolai, and Karen Nagozruk, "Illeagosuik! Eskimo String-Figure Games," *MEJ* 65, no. 7 (1978): 54–61.

136. John C. Laughter, "Bagpipes, Bands and Bearskin Hats," *MEJ* 63, no. 3 (1976): 66–69; Thomas F. Johnston, "How to Make a Tsonga Xylophone," *MEJ* 63, no. 3 (1976): 38–49.

137. Randall Armstrong, "The Adaptable Appalachian Dulcimer," *MEJ* 66, no. 6 (1980): 38–41; Horace Boyer, "Gospel Music," *MEJ* 64, no. 9 (1978): 34–43; Samuel D. Miller, "Lessons in the Blues," *MEJ* 70, no. 6 (1985): 39–40; Michael Stevens, "The Training of Indian Musicians," *MEJ* 61, no. 8 (1975): 33–39.

138. Nick Rossi, "The Music of Argentina," *MEJ* 59, no. 5 (1973): 51–53; Fred Fisher, "The Yellow Bell of China and the Endless Search," *MEJ* 59, no. 8 (1973): 30–33+; Ivan Vandor, "Cymbals and Trumpets from the 'Roof of the World,' " *MEJ* 61, no. 1 (1974): 106–9+; Paul Parthun, "Tribal Music in North America," *MEJ* 63, no. 5 (1976): 32–45.

139. Malcom Tait, "World Musics: Balancing Our Attitudes and Strategies," *MEJ* 61, no. 6 (1975): 28–32; Albert J. McNeil, "The Social Foundations of the Music of Black America," *MEJ* 60, no. 6 (1974): 47–49.

140. Paul Berliner, "Soda Bottles, Whale Bones, Sitars, and Shells—a World Music Perspective," *MEJ* 59, no. 7 (1973): 50–52+; Elsie Buck, "Mom, Pack My Bags for Music Class," *MEJ* 70, no. 6 (1985): 33–35; Jerry and Bev Praver, "Barb'ra Allen, Tom Dooley, and Sweet Betsy from PS 42," *MEJ* 70, no. 5 (1984): 56–69; Patricia Shehan, "Teaching Music Through Balkan Folk Dance," *MEJ* 71, no. 3 (1984): 47–51; Martha Holmes, "Israeli Folk Dance: A Resource for Music Educators," *MEJ* 67, no. 2 (1980): 36–39.

141. See "Improvisation in World Musics," *MEJ* 66, no. 5 (1980): 118–47, and "Improvisation at the High School and College Levels," *MEJ* 66, no. 5 (1980): 86–104.

142. Patricia S. Campbell, "Cross-Cultural Views of Musical Creativity," *MEJ* 76, no. 9 (1990): 43–46.

143. David G. Klocko, "Multicultural Music in the College Curriculum," *MEJ* 75, no. 5 (1989): 39–40+; Marvin V. Curtis, "Understanding the Black Aesthetic Experience"; Patricia K. Shehan, "World Musics: Windows to Cross-Cultural Understanding," *MEJ* 75, no. 3 (1988): 22–26.

144. O. M. Hartsell, telephone interview.

145. Barbara Smith, Professor Emeritus of Ethnomusicology, University of Hawaii, audiotape communication with the author, 20 February 1993. Original audiotape and transcript in possession of the author.

146. Margaret Mead, "Music Is a Human Need," *MEJ* 59, no. 2 (1972): 24–27.

147. See *MEJ* 59, no. 2 (1972): 30–64.

148. Malcom Tait, "Increasing Awareness and Sensitivity though World Musics," *MEJ* 59, no. 2 (1972): 85–89; Ricardo Trimillos, "Expanding Music Experience to Fit Today's world," *MEJ* 59, no. 2 (1972): 90–94; Charles Seeger, "World Musics in American Schools: A Challenge to be Met," *MEJ* 59, no. 2 (1972): 107–11.

149. MENC, bibliographies and photography sections, *MEJ* 59, no. 2 (1972): 65–72 and 112–41. Information for the bibliography section was supplied by members of the Society for Ethnomusicology Education Committee. Anderson, interview.

150. MENC, Book Reviews section, *MEJ* 59, no. 2 (1972): 145–61.

151. See, for example, David Reck, review of *Teaching the Music of Six Different Cultures in the Modern Secondary School*, by Luvenia George, in *MEJ* 64, no. 9 (1977): 15–16. The Book Browsing and Study Shelf columns, especially in the 1983 special issue, contained content descriptions. Examples of video reviews include: Jo Ann Baird, review of "Arabic Musical Instruments" in Video Views, *MEJ*

76, no. 3 (1989): 11–14; William Anderson, review of "The JVC Video Anthology of World Music and Dance" in Video Views, *MEJ* 77, no. 7 (1991): 51–52.

152. Anderson, "Teaching Musics of the World: A Renewed Commitment," *MEJ* 67, no. 1 (1980): 40–41; Jack P. B. Dobbs, "Music as a Multicultural Education," *MEJ* 69, no. 9 (1983): 33–36; Robert Garfias, "Music in the United States: Community of Cultures," *MEJ* 69, no. 9 (1983): 30–31; Bess Lomax Hawes, "Our Cultural Mosaic," *MEJ* 69, no. 9 (1983): 26–27.

153. See "Educational Tactics" and "Tools for Teaching World Musics," *MEJ* 69, no. 9 (1983): 39–51, 58–61.

154. Emma S. Brooks-Baham, "Collecting Materials in Your Community," *MEJ* 69 (1983): 52–55; Barbara Smith, "Musics of Hawaii and Samoa: Exemplar of Annotated Resources," *MEJ* 69, no. 9 (1983): 62–65; MENC, Book Browsing and Study Shelf, *MEJ* 69, no. 9 (1983): 22–25.

155. MENC, Resource Listing, *MEJ* 69, no. 9 (1983): 66–70.

156. Advertisement for Wesleyan Symposium, *MEJ* 70, no. 8 (1984): 57–58.

157. David McAllester, Professor Emeritus of Anthropology and Music, Wesleyan University, telephone interview by author, 8 December 1992. Audiotape and transcript in possession of the author.

158. Advertisement for Wesleyan Symposium. For the texts of the papers presented at the Symposium, see David P. McAllester, project director, *Becoming Human Through Music* (Reston, VA: MENC, 1985).

159. David P. McAllester, project director, *Becoming Human Through Music*, 2.

160. Barbara Smith, "Variability, Change, and the Learning of Music," *Ethnomusicology* 31, no. 2 (1987): 204; McAllester, interview.

161. Examples include: Elizabeth May, ed., *Music of Many Cultures* (Berkeley: University of California Press, 1980); Kazadi wa Mukuna, *African Children's Songs for American Elementary Children* (Lansing: Michigan State University Press, 1979); Patricia Campbell and Phong Nguyen, *From Rice Paddies and Temple Yards: Traditional Music of Vietnam* (Danbury, CT: World Music Press, 1990). Also MENC, *Sounds of the World* audiotape cassette series, (Reston, VA: MENC, 1986–1990). Five sets of tapes, each recorded by ethnomusicologist Karl Signell and accompanied by a teacher's guide. *Music of East Asia: Chinese, Korean, and Japanese*, guide by William M. Anderson, with Terry Liu and Ann Prescott; *Music of Eastern Europe: Albanian, Greek, and South Slavic*, guide by Patricia Shehan Campbell; *Music of the Middle East: Arab, Persian/Iranian, and Turkish*, guide by Sally Monsour with Pamela Dorn; *Music of Latin America: Mexico, Ecuador, Brazil*, guide by Dale Olsen, Charles Perrone, and Daniel Sheehy; *Music of Southeast Asia: Lao, Hmong, Vietnamese*, guide by Patricia K. Shehan.

162. William Anderson and Patricia Campbell, eds., *Multicultural Perspectives in Music Education* (Reston, VA: MENC, 1989).

163. Patricia Shehan Campbell, Professor of Music Education, University of Washington, Seattle, interview by author, 22 October 1992. Original audiotape and transcript in possession of the author.

164. Though MENC was originally a bit reluctant to undertake a publication of this magnitude, the book has since become a "bestseller." Anderson, interview.

165. William M. Anderson, compiler and ed., *Teaching Music with a Multicultural Approach* (Reston, VA: MENC, 1991); set of four videos: *Teaching the Music of African Americans, Teaching the Music of Hispanic Americans, Teaching the Music of Asian Americans, Teaching the Music of the American Indian.*

166. William M. Anderson, compiler and ed., *Teaching Music with a Multicultural Approach*, Preface, vii; Anderson, personal interview. The advisory committee for the symposium was composed of William M. Anderson, Kent State University, Kent, OH; Patricia Brown, Supervisor of Music, Knoxville, TN; Olivia Cadaval, Office of Folklife Programs, Smithsonian Institution; Patricia Shehan Campbell, University of Washington, Seattle; Lise DeLorenzo, Montclair State College, Upper Montclair, NJ; John E. Hasse, National Museum of American History, Smithsonian Institution; Barbara Reeder Lundquist, University of Washington, Seattle; Hunter March, University of Texas, Austin; Nancy L. Marsters, Lyon High School, Tallahassee, FL; William T. McDaniel, Ohio State University, Columbus; Frank Prochan, Office of Folklife Programs, Smithsonian Institution; Bernice Johnson Reagon, National Museum of American History, Smithsonian Institution; Timothy Rice, University of California, Los Angeles; Anthony Seeger, Office of Folklife Programs, Smithsonian Institution; Caroline Wendt, Chair, Education Committee, Society for Ethnomusicology. Cited in William M. Anderson, compiler and ed., *Teaching Music with a Multicultural Approach*, ix.
167. Advertisement for Multicultural Symposium, *MEJ* 76, no. 3 (1989): 15.
168. For a more detailed account of the Multicultural Symposium, the reader is referred to William M. Anderson, compiler and ed., *Teaching Music with a Multicultural Approach* and the set of four videos produced from the symposium: *Teaching the Music of African Americans, Teaching the Music of Hispanic Americans, Teaching the Music of Asian Americans, Teaching the Music of the American Indian.*
169. Reagon is quoted in William M. Anderson, "Toward a Multicultural Future," *MEJ* 77, no. 9 (1991): 30.
170. McAllester is quoted in William M. Anderson, "Toward a Multicultural Future," 31.
171. Edwin Schupman, "Understanding American Indian Music and Selecting Resources," in *Teaching Music with a Multicultural Approach*, compiler and ed. William M. Anderson (Reston, VA: MENC, 1991), 34; Anderson, "Toward a Multicultural Future," 31. ORBIS Associates is an educational consulting firm in Washington, D.C.
172. William Anderson, "Toward a Multicultural Future," 29–39; Bernice Johnson Reagon, "African-American Congregational Songs and Singing Traditions," 5.
173. Ibid., 33.
174. Allen Sapp, Professor of Composition, College Conservatory of Music, University of Cincinnati, interview by author, 20 November 1992. Original audiotape and transcript in possession of the author.

CHAPTER 7

1. Edwin Shupman, "Understanding American Indian Music and Selecting Resources," in *Teaching Music with a Multicultural Approach*, compiler and editor William M. Anderson (Reston, VA: Music Educators National Conference, 1991), 34.
2. The National Council for Standards and Testing, *Raising Standards for American Education* (Washington, DC: The Council, 1992).
3. U.S. Department of Labor: Secretary's Commission on Achieving Necessary Skills, *Skills and Tasks for Jobs: A SCANS Report for America 2000* (Washington,

D.C.: The Commission, 1992); National Commission on Time and Learning, *Prisoners of Time* (Washington, D.C.: The Commission, 1994).

4. Goals 2000: *Educate America Act, U.S. Statutes at Large* 108, 131.
5. Ibid.
6. *Supreme Court Reporter*, 115B Interim edition (1995): 2041.
7. "Appeals Court Bars Racial Preferences in College Admissions," *Chronicle of Higher Education*, 29 March 1996, A26; "Text of the Appeals Court's Opinion on Affirmative Action in Admissions," *Chronicle of Higher Education*, 29 March 1996, A37.
8. *Goals 2000: A Progress Preport* (Washington, D.C.: U.S. Government Printing Office, Spring 1995), 2.
9. National Council of Teachers of Mathematics, *Curriculum and Evaluation Standards for School Mathematics* (Reston, VA: The Council, 1989); Charles N. Quigley, ed., *Civitas: A Framework for Civic Education* (Calabasas, CA: Center for Civic Education, 1991); National Geographic Society, *Geography for Life: National Geography Standards* (Washington, D.C.: National Geographic Research and Exploration, 1994).
10. The content in the history standards as originally presented created a furor in both academic circles and in the press. The controversy centered on the role of minority peoples in American history and the Western perspective from which some historical events were portrayed.
11. *National Standards for Arts Education* (Reston, VA: MENC, 1994); *National Science Education Standards* (Washington, D.C.: National Academy Press, 1996); *Standards for the English language arts* (Urbana, IL: National Council of Teachers of English, 1996).
12. *Goals 2000: A Progress Report*, 2
13. Ibid., 1
14. *National Standards for Arts Education*, 24, 41, 57.
15. Ibid., 29, 45, 63.
16. Ibid., 35, 50, 71.
17. Ibid., 66.
18. Ibid., 13–14.
19. *Learning Standards for the Arts*, rev. ed. (Albany: NYS Education Department, 1996), 1.
20. Ibid., 26–33.
21. American Music Conference, *AMC News* (Fall 1996): 1. Four states had no plans to adopt the national standards for statewide implementation: Georgia, Montana, New Hampshire, and Virginia.
22. Anthony Seeger, "Celebrating the American Music Mosaic," *MEJ* 78, no. 9 (1992): 26–29.
23. See *MEJ* 78, no. 9 (1992): 33–36; Patricia Campbell, "Cultural Consciousness in Teaching General Music," *MEJ* 78, no. 9 (1992): 30–33.
24. Judith Tucker, "Circling the Globe: Multicultural Resources," *MEJ* 78, no. 9 1992): 37–41.
25. Will Schmid, "World Music in the Instrumental Music Program," *MEJ* 78, no. 9 (1992): 41–44; Joan C. Conlon, "Explore the World in Song," *MEJ* 78, no. 9 (1992): 46–48; *MEJ* 78 (May 1992): 44–45 and 49–51.
26. William M. Anderson, "Rethinking Teacher Education: The Multicultural Imperative," *MEJ* 78, no. 9 (1992): 52–55.

27. Patricia Shehan Campbell, "David P. McAllester on Navaho Music," *MEJ* 81, no. 1 (1994): 17–23; "Terry E. Miller on Thai Music," *MEJ* 81, no.2 (1994): 19–25; "Bruno Nettl on Music of Iran," *MEJ* 81, no. 3 (1994): 19–25; "Anthony Seeger on Music of Amazonian Indians," *MEJ* 81, no. 4 (1995): 17–23; "Bell Yung on Music of China," *MEJ* 81, no. 5 (1995): 39–46; "Christopher Waterman on Yoruba Music of Africa," *MEJ* 81, no.6 (1995): 35–41; "Mellonee Burnim on African American Music," *MEJ* 82, no.1 (1995): 41–48; "Steven Loza on Latino Music," *MEJ* 82, no. 2 (1995): 45–52. These interviews were collected and published together with introductory remarks and an annotated bibliography of resources in the MENC publication *Music in Cultural Context*, ed. Patricia Shehan Campbell (Reston, VA: MENC, 1996).
28. For examples, see Ramona Holmes, "An Overture to Africa for Beginning String Class," *Teaching Music* 3, no. 4 (1996): 32–35; Natalie Sarrazin, "Exploring Aesthetics: Focus on Native Americans, *MEJ* 81, no. 4 (1995): 33–35; Pamela Hopton-Jones, "Introducing the Music of East Africa," *MEJ* 82, no. 3 (1995): 26–30.
29. *Strategies for Teaching: Specialized Ensembles*, Robert A. Cutietta, ed. (Reston, VA: MENC, forthcoming); *Multicultural Perspectives in Music*, 2nd ed., William M. Anderson and Patricia Shehan Campbell, eds. (Reston, VA: MENC, 1996).
30. MENC, "1992 Conference Performing Groups and Education Sessions," *MEJ* 78 (1992): 39–43.
31. MENC, National Biennial Conference Program, Cincinnati (1994), 59, 72, 89, 132, 135, 147, 154.
32. These key sessions focused on four music cultures: African-American (both secular and sacred), Asian (Balinese), Mexican-American (mariachi) and Native American musics.
33. MENC, "Preliminary Conference Program," *Teaching Music* 3, no. 3 (1995): special supplement, 13, 20–32; MENC National Biennial Conference Program, Kansas City, MO (1996), 45, 53, 116–17, 201–2.
34. For a more complete picture of ISME's involvement with multicultural music education see Marie McCarthy, "The Role of ISME in the Promotion of Multicultural Music Education, 1953 to Present" (paper presented at the ISME conference, Amsterdam, July 1996).
35. For example, see Pieter Roos, " A Changing Curriculum for Multicultural Music Education in Namibia: A Contemporary Approach," and Lee Yong II, "A Study of Korean Music Education and Its Development," in *Music Education: Facing the Future*, ed. Jack P. B. Dobbs, (Christchurch, New Zealand: ISME, 1990), 251–54 and 260–66, respectively.
36. Bruno Nettl, "Ethnomusicology and the Teaching of World Music," in *Music Education: Sharing Musics of the World*, ed. Heath Lees (Christchurch, New Zealand: ISME, 1992), 7.
37. See "Shared Horizons: The Multicultural Environment," in *Music Education: Sharing Musics of the World*, ed. Heath Lees (Christchurch, New Zealand: ISME, 1992), 153–266.
38. See Mary Hookey, "Culturally Responsive Music Education: Implications for Curriculum Development and Implementation," 84–90; Rita Klinger, "Multiculturalism in Music Education: Authenticity versus Practicality," 91–103; and Robert Engle, "Singing Translations and Cultural Loss," 104–10, in *Musical Connections: Tradition and Change*, ed. Heath Lees (Auckland, New Zealand: ISME, 1994).
39. See, for example, Huib Schippers (Netherlands), "Approaches to Cultural Diversity in Music Education"; Krystyna Henke, "Attempts at Multicultural Mu-

sic Education in Toronto, Canada"; Sarita Hauptfliesch, "Transforming South Africa Music Education"; and Tatsuko Takizawa (Japan), "Music Beyond Cultural Boundaries," ISME Conference program, Amsterdam (1996), 47, 52, 61, 63.

40. Frans de Ruiter, "Nothing Is as It Was Before," and Kazadi wa Mukuna, "The Universals of Music versus the Universality of Music" (plenary speeches, ISME Conference, Amsterdam, July 1996), ISME Conference program, 30–32.

41. Summary of Proposed Revisions of the [ISME] Constitution and Bylaws, 1.

42. Bruno Nettl, "ISME Panel on Musics of the World's Cultures," *International Journal of Music Education* No. 24 (1994): 66.

43. Ibid., 67–68.

44. Ibid., 66.

45. Patricia Shehan Campbell, e-mail correspondence with author, 8 August 1996.

CHAPTER 8

1. Patricia Shehan Campbell, *Lessons from the World* (New York: Schirmer Books, 1991), 77.

2. Michael Mark, "Unique Aspects of Historical Research in Music Education," *Bulletin of Historical Research in Music Education* 6, no. 1 (1985): 22.

3. Maude E. Glynn, "Music and Americanization: A Bibliography," *Music Supervisors Journal* 7, no. 1 (1920): 14–20. See also Michael L. Mark and Charles L. Gary, *A History of American Music Education* (New York: Schirmer Books, 1992), 240–41.

4. Charles L. Gary, Professor of Music Education, Catholic University, interview by author, 13 January 1993. Original audiotape and transcript in possession of the author.

5. Allen P. Britton, Dean Emeritus, School of Music, University of Michigan, Ann Arbor, interview by author, 12 November 1992. Original audiotape and transcript in possession of the author.

6. Patricia Shehan Campbell, Professor of Music Education, University of Washington, Seattle, interview by author, 22 October 1992. Original audiotape and transcript in possession of the author.

7. Anthony Palmer, Associate Professor of Music Education, University of Hawaii, Manoa, interview by author, 23 October 1992. Original audiotape and transcript in possession of the author.

CHAPTER 9

1. Laurence Lepherd, "Comparative Music Education: Viewing the Forest as well as the Trees," *International Journal of Music Education* No. 5, May 1985: 48.

2. *British Nationality Act* (London: Her Majesty's Stationery Office [HMSO], 1981).

3. *Immigration Act* (London: Her Majesty's Stationery Office, 1988).

4. Lucy Green, Institute of Education, University of London, letter to author, 14 May 1996.

5. Peter Figueroa, "Multicultural Education in the United Kingdom: Historical Development and Current Status," in *Handbook of Research on Multicultural Education*, ed. James A. Banks (New York: Macmillan, 1995), 784–85.

6. Peter Figueroa, 794–795; George Male, "England," *Education and Urban Society* 18, no. 4 (1986): 485.
7. Sandra Davies,"Multicultural Education in Britain," *Canadian Music Educator* 34, no. 3 (1993): 12.
8. *Music in the National Curriculum* (London: Department for Education, 1995), Foreword; Gerald Unks, "Three Nations' Curricula: What Can We Learn from Them?" *National Association of Secondary School Principals Bulletin* 76, no. 548 (1992): 34.
9. J. K. P. Watson, "From Assimilation to Anti-Racism: Changing Educational Policies in England and Wales," *Journal of Multilingual and Multicultural Development* 9, no. 6 (1988): 541.
10. Figueroa, 786.
11. Department of Education and Science, *West Indian Children in Our Schools* (London, Her Majesty's Stationery Office, 1981); Department of Education and Science, *Education for All* (London, Her Majesty's Stationery Office [HMSO], 1985).
12. Watson, 543.
13. Figueroa, 793.
14. *Education Act* (London, HMSO, 1994); Figueroa, 794.
15. Ibid., 7.
16. Figueroa, 796.
17. Davies, 14; H. Eugene Karjala, "Thinking Globally, Teaching in England," *MEJ* 81, no. 6 (1995): 32.
18. Lucy Green, letter to author.
19. Keith Swanwick, *Music Education and the National Curriculum* (London: Tufnell Press, 1992), 2.
20. Swanwick, 7.
21. Many of the schools in East Sussex have gamelans and students regularly perform in gamelan orchestras. Janet Mills, Her Majesty's Inspector, Oxford, conversation with author 15 July 1996. Also, David Ruffer, "Out of Africa . . . into Hasting—Reflections on African Week at William Parker school, April 1991," *British Journal of Music Education* 9, no. 2: 163–69.
22. Department of Education and Science, *National Curriculum: Music in the National Curriculum (England)* (London: HMSO, 1992), cited in Swanwick, 25–26.
23. Department of Education and Science, *National Curriculum: Music in the National Curriculum (England)* (London: HMSO, 1992), cited in Robert Kwami, "Music Education in Britain and the School Curriculum: A Point of View," *International Journal of Music Education* vol. 21, 1993: 29.
24. Davies, 7–8.
25. Ibid. See also Kwami, 30.
26. Swanwick, 30.
27. *Music in the National Curriculum (England)* (London: Department for Education, 1995), 2.
28. Ibid., 4, 6.
29. Ibid., 3, 5, 7.
30. Ibid., 9.
31. Ibid., 10.
32. Janet Mills, "A Comparison of the Quality of Class Music Teaching in Primary and Secondary Schools in England" (paper presented at the ISME Research Commission Seminar, Frascati, Italy, July 1996).
33. Lucy Green, letter to author.

34. Dr. June Boyce-Tillman, King Alfred's College, letter to author 9 November 1995.
35. Davies, 9–10.
36. Figueroa, 788.
37. Watson, 547.
38. Rod Allan and Bob Hill, "Multicultural Education in Australia: Historical Development and Current Status," in *Handbook of Research on Multicultural Education*, ed. James A. Banks (New York: Macmillan, 1995), 766.
39. Peter Dunbar-Hall, Sydney Conservatorium of Music, University of Sydney, e-mail to author, 6 March 1996.
40. Allan and Hill, 767–768.
41. Lois Foster and David Stockley, *Australian Multiculturalism: A Documentary History and Critique* (Clevedon and Philadelphia: Multilingual Matters, 1988), 56.
42. Allan and Hill, 768.
43. New South Wales Department of Education, *Multicultural Education Policy Statement 1983*, 2.
44. New South Wales Department of School Education, *Multicultural Education Plan, 1993–1997* (October 1992), 1.
45. Ibid., 3.
46. Gary E. McPherson, "Integrating the Arts into the General Curriculum: An Australian Perspective," *Arts Education Policy Review* 97, no. 1 (1995): 25.
47. Martin Comte, "The Arts in Australian Schools: The Past Fifty Years, *Australian Journal of Music Education*, vol. 1 (1988): 112.
48. Gillian Weiss, "Fundamental or Frill?: Music Education in Australian Schools Since the 1880s," *Research Studies in Music Education* no. 5 (December 1995): 62. These folk songs were always in English translation. Kathryn Marsh, University of Western Sydney, e-mail to author, 18 February 1996.
49. Graham Bartle, *Music in Australian Schools* (Melbourne: Australian Council for Educational Research, 1968), cited in Frank Murphy, "Ethnomusicology and Australian Schools: Part I, the Present Situation," *Australian Journal of Music Education* No. 19 (October 1976): 33–34.
50. Ibid., 35; *Curriculum for Primary Schools: Music* (New South Wales [NSW]: Department of Education, 1963).
51. James Lynch, "Community Relations and Multicultural Education in Australia," *Comparative Education* 18, no. 1 (1982): 22.
52. NSW Department of Education, *Music (K–6) Syllabus and Support Statements 1984*, 10.
53. McPherson, 25.
54. Ibid., 28.
55. Ibid., 25–26, 30
56. Kathryn Marsh, University of Western Sydney, e-mail to author, 13 February 1996.
57. NSW Department of Education, *Music Years 7–10, 1994*, 5.
58. Ibid., 16.
59. Ibid., 17. This emphasis on Australian music is a reflection of the "New Federalism" and its corresponding redefinition of "Australianism."
60. Board of Studies NSW, *Music 2 Unit Course 1, Preliminary and HSC Courses Syllabus* (North Sydney: Board of Studies NSW, 1994), 15–16.
61. Board of Studies NSW, *Music 2/3 Unit Preliminary Course 1 and HSC Course* (North Sydney: Board of Studies NSW, 1994), 30–32.
62. Peter Dunbar-Hall, e-mail to author.

63. Kathryn Marsh, e-mail to author, 28 April 1996.

64. House of Commons, *Debates* (Ottawa: Government Printer, 1971), 8546.

65. Secretary of State, *Multiculturalism* [news release] (Ottawa: Ministry of Multiculturalism, May 30, 1988), cited in Kogilia A. Moodley, "Multicultural Education in Canada: Historical Development and Current Status," in *Handbook of Research in Multicultural Education*, ed. James A. Banks (New York: Macmillan, 1995), 803.

66. Spicer Commission, *The Citizen's Forum on Canada's Future: Report to the People and Government of Canada* (Ottawa: Canadian Government Publication Center, 1991).

67. Aminur Rahim, "Multiculturalism or Ethnic Hegemony: A Critique of Multicultural Education in Toronto," *Journal of Ethnic Studies* 18, no. 3 (1990): 35.

68. Kogila A. Moodley, "Multicultural Education in Canada: Historical Development and Current Status," in *Handbook of Research in Multicultural Education*, ed. James A. Banks (New York: Macmillan, 1995), 803.

69. Moodley, 805.

70. Ibid., 805–6.

71. Lawson, p. 454, 458.

72. J. Paul Green and Nancy F. Vogan, *Music Education in Canada* (Toronto: University of Toronto Press, 1991), 34, 59.

73. Ibid., 110.

74. Green and Vogan, 212, 247.

75. Ibid., 204, 209, 235, 303.

76. Ibid., 251, 397.

77. Mary Hookey, Nipissing University, North Bay, Canada, e-mail to author, 10 April 1996.

78. Green and Vogan, 326.

79. June Countryman, "An Analysis of Selected Song Series Textbooks Used in Ontario Schools, 1946–1965," (master's thesis, University of Western Ontario, 1981), 153. Cited in Green and Vogan, 326.

80. Green and Vogan, 416.

81. Ibid., 328.

82. Examples include: Patricia Sand, "In Search of Our Own Music," *Canadian Music Educator* 17, No. 2 (1976): 7–14; Barbara Cass-Beggs and Kieth Bissell, "Canadian Folk Songs for Schools," *Canadian Music Educator* 18, no. 4 (1977): 15–16.

83. Mary Hookey, "Reflections on Other Voices: Music Education Curriculum and Multiculturalism," *Canadian Music Educator* 34, no. 3 (1993): 37–42. See also David Roe, *The Canadian Mosaic: Teaching Native and Multicultural Music in the Classroom* (Scarborough, Ontario: Board of Education, 1992).

84. Green and Vogan, 441.

85. Mary Hookey, e-mail to author.

86. For examples, see David Roe, *The Canadian Mosaic: Teaching Native and Multicultural Music in the Classroom*; Timothy Rice and Patricia Martin Schand, eds., *Multicultural Music Education: The "Music Means Harmony" Workshop* (Toronto: Institute for Canadian Music, University of Toronto, 1989).

87. Elizabeth Miller, "The Problems Involved in Implementing Multicultural Music in the Elementary Classroom," *Canadian Music Educator* 33, no. 1 (1991): 17.

88. Bernard Andrews, "Music Instruction in a Multi-cultural Context: Conflict in Patterns of Socialization," *Canadian Music Educator* 34, no. 5 (1993): 14.

89. Robert Walker, "The Education of Music Teachers in Today's Educational Milieu," *Canadian Music Educator* 34, no. 1 (1992): 9.

90. Mary Hookey, e-mail to author.
91. Siegmund Helms, "Interkultureller Musikunterricht in Deutschland" [Intercultural Music Education in Germany] (paper presented at the European Association of Music Educators Conference, University of Presov, Slovakia, May 1996), 1–2.
92. Gerd R. Hoff, "Multicultural Education in Germany: Historical Development and Current Status," in *Handbook of Research on Multicultural Education*, ed. James A. Banks (New York: Macmillan, 1995), 829–30.
93. Ibid., 835.
94. Ibid., 825.
95. Ibid., 824.
96. Wolfgang Mitter, "Germany," *Education and Urban Society* 18, no. 4 (1986): 440.
97. Hoff, 826.
98. Ibid., 828.
99. Wilfried Gruhn, Hochschule für Musik, Freiberg, Germany, conversation with author, 14 July 1996.
100. Ü. Akpinar and J. Zimmer, eds., *Von wo kommst'n du? Interkulturelle Erziehung im Kindergarten*, 4 vols. (Munich: Kösel, 1984).
101. Hoff, 836.
102. Egon Kraus, ed., *Studying Music in Germany* (Mainz: B. Schott's Söhne, 1962), 20–21.
103. See, for examples, Irmgard Merkt, "Interkulturelle Musikerziehung," *Musik und Unterricht* 4, no. 22 (1993): 4–7; Dorrit Klebe-Wontroba, "Aus fremden Ländern. Beispiele bi- und multicultureller Erziehung im Musikunterricht der Primarstufe," *Musik und Bildung* 22, no. 9–10 (1990): 550–53.
104. Friedhelm Brusniak, University of Erlangen-Nürnberg, Germany, letter to author, 6 February 1996. The video was a class project of students in the 7th class of the Hauptschule, Saarbrückener Strasse 26, Nürnberg, under the direction of their teacher, Harald Stoltmann.
105. Wilfried Gruhn, conversation with author.
106. Siegmund Helms, 7.
107. Wilfried Gruhn, conversation with author.
108. Amtsblatt des Bayerischen Staatsministeriums für Unterricht und Kultur, KMBI 1 So.Nr. 18/1976; Nr. 4/1977; Nr. 9/1977.
109. Amtsblatt des Bayerischen Staatsministeriums für Unterricht und Kultur, KMBI 1 So.Nr. 20/1981; Nr. 5/1982; Nr. 13/1985.
110. Amtsblatt des Bayerischen Staatsministeriums für Unterricht und Kultur, KMBI 1 So.Nr. 1/1993.
111. Friedhelm Brusniak, University of Erlangen-Nürnberg, and Ludwig Striegel, Staatsinstitut für Schulpädagogik und Bildungsforschung, Munich, members of the Arbeitskreis der Musikdidaktiker an den bayerischen Musikhochschulen und Universitäten, and co-authors of the new music curriculum for Bavaria, conversation with author, 29 July 1996; Friedhelm Brusniak, Telephone conversation with author, 26 February 1997.
112. Elizabeth Oehrle, "An African Network for Intercultural Education through Music," in *Music Education: Sharing Musics of the World*, ed. Heath Lees (1992 Yearbook for the International Society for Music Education), 259.
113. Ana Lucia Frega, "Argentina," in *Music Education in International Perspective: National Systems*, ed. Laurence Lepherd (Toowoomba, Australia: University of Queensland Press, 1995), 37–39.

114. Ibid., 39.

115. Ana Lucia Frega, e-mail to author, 18 May 1996; conversation with author 14 July 1996.

116. Thomas W. Goolsby, "Music Education in the Republic of Indonesia: A Model of Cultural Pluralism," CD-ROM, ERIC document ED 382491. See especially pages 8, 32.

117. Ibid., 32.

118. Ramon P. Santos, University of the Philippines, "Ideological and Conceptual Variations in the Understanding of World Musics: Implications on Music Education" (unpublished material for the Advisory Panel on World Musics #4, International Society for Music Education), 9.

119. Goolsby, 18–19.

120. Ibid., 32.

121. Johami Abdullah, "Music Education in Malaysia: An Overview," *The Quarterly* 1, no. 4 (1990): 45–46.

122. Ibid., 46.

123. Ibid., 47.

124. Ibid., 50–52.

125. Minette E. Mans, "Namibia," in *Music Education in International Perspective: National Systems*, ed. Laurence Lepherd (Toowoomba, Australia: University of Queensland Press, 1995), 27.

126. Oehrle, "An African Network," 261–64.

127. Philomen O. Anosike, "The Extension of Indigenous Culture: A Proposed Model for Teaching Music to Nigerian Children" (paper presented at the MENC Biennial Convention, Kansas City, 1996), 4.

128. Joy Nwosu Lo-Bamijoko, "Music Education in Nigeria: The Status of Music Learning and Teaching," *The Quarterly* 1, no. 4 (1990): 38; Richard C. Okafor, "Music in Nigerian Education," *Bulletin of the Council for Research in Music Education* 108 (Spring 1991): 63–65.

129. Ramon P. Santos, "Music Education in the Philippines with Reference to the Teaching of Non-Western Music" (unpublished material for the Advisory Panel on World Music #3, ISME, 1996), 1–2.

130. Ibid., 3. On page 14 Dr. Santos comments that "the use of the term "world music" to mean Western classical tradition is clearly indicative of the persisting perception that Western music is '*the* universal musical language.' "

131. Ibid., 5–6.

132. Ramon P. Santos, "Oral and Other Musical Traditions in Literate Institutions of Learning" (unpublished paper presented at the International Festival-Conference, Inter-Universities Department for World Music Cultures Studies, Moscow, February 1–5, 1996), 5.

133. Ramon P. Santos, "Music Education in the Philippines," 10–12.

134. Ibid.

315. Kathy Primos, University of the Witwatersrand, Johannesburg, South Africa, conversation with author, 14 July 1996.

136. Elizabeth Oehrle, "The South African Music Educators Society and Intercultural Music Education," in *Music Education: Facing the Future*, ed. Jack Dobbs (Christchurch, New Zealand: University of Canterbury, 1990), 246–50; and "Music Education in South Africa," *The Quarterly* 1, no. 4 (1990): 6–8.

137. Elizabeth Oehrle, University of Natal, Durban, South Africa, conversation with author, 25 July 1996.

138. Oehrle, "The South African Music Educators Society," 248.
139. Sallyann Goodall, "The So-Called Disadvantaged Student" (paper presented at the Fourth National Music Educators Conference, University of Pretoria, April 10, 1990), cited in Oerhle, "Music Education in South Africa," 8.
140. Oehrle, conversation with author, 25 July 1996..
141. Kathy Primos, conversation with author, 14 July 1996.
142. Jimmy van Tonder, University of Cape Town, Cape Town, South Africa, conversation with author, 24 July 1996.
143. Graça Mota, Escola Superior de Educação, Portugal, conversation with author, 18 July 1996; Huip Schippers, Netherlands Institute for Arts Education, conversation with author, 25 July 1996; Anne Moberg, Norwegian Multicultural Music Centre, letter to author, 28 March 1996; Bengt Olsson, Royal Academy of Music, Stockholm, conversation with author, 19 July 1996; Stefania Luccetti, Mira, Italy, conversation with author, 18 July 1996; Alda de Jesus Oliveira, Loteamento Colina da Fonte-Itapoan, Salvador Bahia, Brazil, conversation with author, 17 July 1996; Tatsuko Takizawa, "Music Beyond Cultural Boundaries— A Teaching Strategy of World Musical Culture from an Asian Viewpoint" (paper presented at the 1996 ISME Conference, Amsterdam, July 1996).

CHAPTER 10

1. Carlesta Henderson, "Preparing Future Music Teachers for Dealing With Minority Students: A Profession at Risk," *Quarterly Journal of Music Teaching and Learning* 4, no. 2 (1993): 36.
2. Allen P. Britton, Dean Emeritus, School of Music, University of Michigan, interview by author, 12 November 1992; Patricia Campbell, Professsor of Music Education, University of Washington, interview by author, 22 October 1992; Charles Gary, Professor of Music, Catholic University, Washington, D.C., interview by author, 13 January 1993; Anthony Palmer, Associate Professor of Music Education, University of Hawaii, Manoa, interview by author, 23 October 1992; Paul Lehman, Senior Associate Dean, School of Music, University of Michigan, interview by author, 22 November 1992; Allen Sapp, Professor of Composition, College Conservatory of Music, University of Cincinnati, interview by author, 20 November 1992; Barbara Smith, Professor Emeritus of Ethnomusicology, University of Hawaii, Manoa, audiotape communication to author, 20 February 1993; James Standifer, Professor of Music Education, University of Michigan, telephone conversation with author, 14 February 1993; Ricardo Trimillos, Professor of Ethnomusicology, University of Hawaii, Manoa, telephone conversation with author, 7 February 1993. Original audiotapes and transcripts in possession of the author.
3. James Standifer, Professor of Music Education, University of Michigan. Telephone conversation with the author, 17 May 1993. In recalling what were probably very typical collegiate preteaching experiences from the late 1930s to the early 1970s, most of the music educators interviewed could remember no specific emphasis on teaching folk songs or dances in their instructional programs. Britton, interview; Campbell, interview; Lehman, interview; Palmer, interview; also William M. Anderson, Associate Dean for Academic Affairs, College and Graduate School of Education, Kent State University, interview by author, 24

February 1993; O. M. Hartsell, Professor Emeritus of Music, University of Arizona, Tuscon, telephone conversation with author, 17 February 1993. Original audiotapes and transcripts in possession of the author.

4. Maria Navarro, "The Relationship Between Culture, Society, and Music Teacher Education" (Ph.D. diss., Kent State University, 1988); Mary Jane Montague, "An Investigation of Teacher Training in Multicultural Music Education in Selected Universities and Colleges" (Ph.D. diss., University of Michigan, 1988).

5. Richard K. Fiese and Nicholas J. DeCarbo, "Urban Music Education: The Teacher's Perspective," *MEJ* 81, no. 6 (1995): 29.

6. Anderson, interview.

7. National Association of State Boards of Education (NASBE), *The American Tapestry: Educating a Nation* (Alexandria, VA: NASBE, 1991); Richard K. Mastain, ed., *Manual on Certification and Preparation of Educational Personnel in the United States* (Dubuque, IA: Kendall/Hunt Publishing Co., for the National Association of State Directors of Teacher Education and Certification, 1991), C–4.

8. Robert L. Erbes, *Certification Practices and Trends in Music Teacher Education*, 4th ed. (Reston, VA: MENC, 1992). Colorado, New Hampshire, Vermont, and Virginia have multicultural music requirements; Michigan, Nebraska, New Hampshire, New Jersey, Pennsylvania, South Dakota, and Oregon have multicultural requirements in professional education for music certification.

9. *National Association of Schools of Music* (NASM) *1995–1996 Handbook* (Reston, VA: NASM, 1995), 72–73, 82–83; Geneva Gay, "Multiethnic Education: Historical Developments and Future Prospects," *Phi Delta Kappan* 64, no. 8 (1983): 562.

10. *NASM Handbook*, 73.

11. *Teacher Education in Music: Final Report* (Washington, D.C.: MENC, 1972), 6–7.

12. Charles Ball, Chair, "Report of the MENC Commission on Graduate Music Teacher Education," *MEJ* 67, no. 2 (1984): 53.

13. William M. Anderson, "Rethinking Teacher Education: The Multicultural Imperative," *MEJ* 78, no. 9 (1992): 52–55; Cornelia Yarbrough Cox, "Multicultural Training: A Missing Link in Graduate Music Education," *MEJ* 67, no. 1 (1980): 38–39+; Marvin Curtis, "Understanding the Black Aesthetic Experience," *MEJ* 77, no. 2 (1988): 26; René Boyer-White, "Reflecting Cultural Diversity in the Music Classroom, *MEJ* 75, no. 4 (1988): 50–54; "David Klocko, "Multicultural Music in the College Curriculum, *MEJ* 75, no. 5 (1989): 38–41.

14. *Music in the Undergraduate Curriculum: A Reassessment* (Boulder, CO: College Music Society, 1989), 8.

15. Rosita Sands, "Multicultural Music Teacher Education," *Journal of Music Teacher Education* 2, no. 2 (1993): 20.

16. William Anderson, "Rethinking Teacher Education," 54; Sands, "Multicultural Music Teacher Education," 21.

17. Anderson, 54; Sands, 21.

18. Such an ear-training program is already in place at West Chester University, West Chester, PA. J. Bryan Burton, West Chester University, e-mail to author, 24 July 1996.

19. Anderson, 55; Sands, 21; Ramona Holmes, e-mail to author, 28 February 1996. This need for a wider range of performance experiences was first identified in 1972 in *Teacher Education in Music: Final Report*, 8.

20. Anderson, 55.

21. Li-Chen Chin, "Multicultural Music in Higher Education: A Description of Course Offerings," *Update* 15 no. 1 (1996): 29.

22. Kwabene Nketia (plenary address, ISME Conference Amsterdam, July 1996).
23. Sands, 22.
24. Sands, 23; see also Bennett Reimer, "Music Education in Our Multimusical Culture," *MEJ* 79, no. 7 (1993): 22.
25. Joan Conlon, "Multicultural Choral Repertoire," *MEJ* 78 no. 9 (1992): 49–51; Terese M. Volk, "Multicultural Selections for Band and Orchestra, *MEJ* 78, no. 9 (1992): 44–45.
26. Terese M. Volk and Jeffrey Spector, "Diverse Musics in Your Country Music Library," *School Music News* 59, no. 4 (1995): 18–20, and "Around the World in the NYSSMA Manual," *School Music News* 59, no. 5 (1996): 34–36; Terese M. Volk, Jeffrey Spector, and William G. Scott, "Recent Compositions With a Multicultural Perspective," *School Music News* 59, no. 6 (1996): 26–27.
27. Anderson, 55; Sands, 22.
28. Anderson, 55.
29. Sands, 24.
30. Barbara Lundquist, "Doctoral Education of Multiethinic-Multicultural Music Teacher Educators," *Design for Arts in Education* 92, no. 5 (1991): 21–38.
31. Carlesta Henderson, "Preparing Future Music Teachers for Dealing with Minority Students: A Profession at Risk," 42.
32. Campbell, interview.
33. Dr. Roy Ernst, Professor of Music Education, Eastman School of Music, conversation with author, 9 April 1996.

CHAPTER 11

1. Mary Hookey, "Culturally Responsive Music Education: Implications for Curriculum Development and Implementation," in *Musical Connections: Tradition and Change*, ed. Heath Lees (Auckland, New Zealand: International Society for Music Education, 1994), 87.
2. Ricardo Trimillos, Professor of Ethnomusicology and Chair, Asian Studies Program, University of Hawaii, telephone interview by author, 7 February 1993. Transcripts and audiotapes in possession of the author.
3. See, for example, *MEJ* special issues of May 1972, October 1983, and May 1992.
4. Patricia Shehan Campbell, ed., *Music in Cultural Context* (Reston, VA: MENC, 1996).
5. Harold E. Griswold, "Multiculturalism, Music, and Information Highways," *MEJ* 81, no. 3 (1994): 42. The reader is encouraged to read this entire article for clarification of Usenet and Bitnet access.
6. Conlon, 49–51.
7. Also see Terese M. Volk, "Multicultural Selections for Band and Orchestra," *MEJ* 78, no. 9 (1992): 44–45.
8. Patricia Shehan Campbell, "Multiculturalism and the Raising of Music Teachers for the Twenty-First Century," *Journal of Music Teacher Education* 3, no. 2 (1994): 27.
9. For a good description of this process, see Patricia Campbell, "Multiculturalism and the Raising of Music Teachers," 28.
10. Judith Cook Tucker, "Circling the Globe: Multicultural Resources," *MEJ* 78, no. 9 (1992): 37–38.

11. Terese M. Volk and Jeffrey Spector, "Achieving Standard #9 With Your Performing Groups: Diverse Music Cultures and the Questions of Authenticity," *School Music News* 59, no. 2 (1995): 29–30. Used with permission.
12. Recent research has indicated that using authentic instruments may be the most effective means of introducing music from another culture. See Randall G. Pembroock, "The effect of mode of instruction and instrument authenticity on children's attitudes, information recall and performance skill for music from Ghana" (paper presented at the ISME Research Commission Seminar, Frascati, Italy, July 1996).
13. Lynn Jessup, *The Mandinka Balafon: An Introduction with Notation for Teaching* (La Mesa, CA: Xylo Publications, 1983), 176.
14. See Patricia Shehan Campbell, *Lessons from the World* (New York: Schirmer Books, 1991), 129, 163, 191.
15. Terese M. Volk, "Chinese Percussion Ensemble for Drum Classes" in *Strategies for Specialized Ensembles*, Robert A. Cutietta, ed. (Reston, VA: MENC, forthcoming). Used with permission.
16. Terese M. Volk, "Chinese Folk Songs for Strings, in *Strategies for Specialized Ensembles*, Robert A. Cutietta, ed. (Reston, VA: MENC, forthcoming). Used with permission.
17. Edwin Schupman, "Lessons on . . . Native American Music," *MEJ* 78, no. 9 (1992): 33. Copyright by Music Educators National Conference, reprinted by permission.

CHAPTER 12

1. Marie McCarthy, "A World Perspective in Music Teaching," *Social Sciences SRIG Newsletter* 11, no. 4 (1994), 2.
2. J. Bryan Burton, e-mail to author, 24 July 1996 .
3. Similar categories have been identified in the development of multicultural music education in other countries. However, their timeline is generally much shorter, for the most part having been compressed into the period following World War II.
4. David J. Elliott, "Key Concepts in Multicultural Music Education," *International Journal of Music Education* No. 13 (1989): 11–18.
5. Marie McCarthy, 2.

CODA

1. Graham Welch, Roehampton Institute, London, conversation with author, 18 July 1996.
2. Richard Colwell, "Will Voluntary National Standards Fix the Potholes of Arts Education?" *Arts Education Policy Review* 96, no. 5 (1995): 7.
3. Kwabene Nketia (plenary speech, ISME Conference, Amsterdam, July 1996).
4. Richard Letts, "Music Education: The Universal Language of All Nations" (plenary speech given at ISME Conference, Amsterdam, July 1996).

GLOSSARY

1. Norris B. Johnson, "On the Relationship of Anthropology to Multicultural Teaching and Learning," *Journal of Teacher Education* 28, no. 3 (1977): 10. This anthro-

pological definition of "culture" is used in Donna M. Gollnick and Philip Chinn, *Multicultural Education in a Pluralistic Society*. It is also the foundation of the work of James A. Banks, "The Nature of Multiethnic Education," in *Education in the 80s: Multiethnic Education*, 15–23. The concept of culture has been a point of contention for anthropologists for many years. Since the 1970s, there have been no significant changes in the field except to extend the argument. As a result, this definition is still viable.

2. Richard Pratte, *Pluralism in Education: Conflict, Clarity, and Commitment* (Springfield, IL: Charles C. Thomas, 1979), 6; and David J. Elliott, "Music as Culture: Toward a Multicultural Concept of Arts Education," *Journal of Aesthetic Education* 24, no. 1 (1990): 151.

3. Arturo Pacheco, "Cultural Pluralism: A Philosophical Analysis," *Journal of Teacher Education* 28, no. 3 (1977): 17–18; also Pratte, 141.

4. James A. Banks, "Multiethnic Education in the United States of America: Practices and Promises," in *Education in Multicultural Societies*, ed. Trevor Corner (New York: St. Martin's Press, 1984), 84; and Brian M. Bullivant, "Culture: Its Nature and Meaning for Educators," in *Multiethnic Education: Issues and Perspectives*, ed. James A. Banks (Boston: Allyn and Bacon, 1989), 39.

5. Philip V. Bohlman,"Old World Cultures in North America," in *Excursions in World Music*, Bruno Nettl et al. (Englewood Cliffs, NJ: Prentice-Hall, 1992), 282–83.

6. Carroll Gonzo, "Multicultural Issues in Music Education," *MEJ* 79, no. 6 (1993): 51.

7. Jerrold Moore, "The Planetary Person: Global Awareness in Arts and Education" (unpublished lecture delivered at the College of the Redwoods, Eureka, CA, Spring 1994).

8. James A. Banks, Introduction, in *Education in the 80s: Multiethnic Education*, ed. James A. Banks (Washington, D.C.: NEA, 1981), 13; Donna Gollnick and Phillip Chinn, *Multicultural Education in a Pluralistic Society*, 2nd. ed. (Columbus, OH: Charles E. Merrill Publishing Co., 1986), 255–56.

9. William M. Anderson and Patricia Shehan Campbell, "Teaching Music from a Multicultural Perspective," in *Multicultural Perspectives in Music*, eds. William M. Anderson and Patricia Shehan Campbell (Reston, VA: MENC, 1996), 1; Patricia Campbell, "Multiculturalism and the Raising of Music Teachers for the Twenty-first Century, *Journal of Music Teacher Education* 3, no. 2 (1994): 23.

10. Alan Merriam, *The Anthropology of Music* (Evanston, IL: Northwestern University Press, 1964): 27.

11. Derived from J. H. Kwabene Nketia, "Music Education in Africa and the West," in *Education and Research in African Music*, ed. Lusaka, 1975. Cited in Barbara Lundquist, "Transmission of Music Culture in Formal Educational Institutions," *The World of Music* 29, no. 1 (1987): 67–68.

12. Campbell, "Multiculturalism," 23, and "Music Instruction," 16.

Index

Accreditation, 104, 133, 160. *See also*
  National Association of Schools of
  Music; National Council for
  Accreditation of Teacher Education
Adamic, Louis, 52, 54
Addams, Jane, 22, 34–36, 89
Aesthetics, 6, 192. *See also* Rationales for
  multicultural music education
African-American musics, 45–46, 49, 70,
  135, 169
Amalgamation, 33–34, 190. *See also*
  209n.54
  in education, 10, 11
  in music education, 12
American Association of Colleges for
  Teacher Education (AACTE), 92
Americanization, 24, 33
  in education, 36, 54
  in music education, 40–42, 189
American Singer, 56, 58
American Songs for American
  Children, 57–58
"American Unity Through Music,"
  57–60
Anglo-American Conference, 55. *See
  also* International conferences
Antiracist education
  in Australia, 8
  in Canada, 8, 141
  in Germany, 146
  in Great Britain, 8, 129
  in United States, 7
Area studies, 69, 90. *See also* Ethnic
  studies
Assimilation
  definition of, 10–11, 209n.54
  in education, 10–11
  in music education, 12, 190
Authenticity, 9, 118, 177–80, 186, 187.
  See also Inauthenticity; Juilliard
  Repertory Project and song
  authenticity

guidelines for, 177–79
  in recordings for school use, 56, 60,
  97–98, 170
  in school music texts, 46, 57, 74–75,
  97–98, 111, 170
Authenticity in learning processes, 120

Band materials. *See* Materials, band
Banks, James, 9, 10, 11
Beattie, John, 58, 64
Bilingual education
  in Germany, 146
  music in, 89–90
  in United States, 88, 89–90, 122
Bilingual Education Act, 87, 89
Bilingualism in Canada, 139, 140, 141,
  143
"Black power"
  in Great Britain, 128
  in United States, 67, 85
Book of Songs, 40, 46
British Nationality Act, 128
Brown v. the Board of Education, 67, 69,
  122
Bruner, Jerome, 69, 101
Burchenal, Elizabeth, 36–37, 43, 168, 170

Calloway, Frank, 73
Canadian Multicultural Act, 140
Capitol records, 75, 152
Carmichael, Stokley, 67, 128
Chicago World's Fair of 1893, 22–23, 30
Chinese Exclusion Act, 21
Choral materials. *See* Materials, choral
Civil Rights Act, 67
Civil rights movement, 53, 66, 67
Clark, Frances Elliot, 42–43, 169
Classroom repertoire, 28, 31, 38
  changes in, 188–89. *See also* Trends in
  multicultural music education
Cold War, 53, 66–67, 69
Coleman, Satis, 46–48, 62, 169